DUMBASS

Outrageous Quotes from the World's Most Powerful Moron

jules carlysle

ISBN 0-9781646-0-1

Cover Photos

(Reuters) Texas Gov. George W. Bush stands on stage during a
light and sound check at the Republican National Convention in
Philadelphia August 2, 2000.
Photo by GARY HERSHORN. 02/08/2000

Acknowledgements

Adam Sheils – Of all the people in the world who look like me and call me Mom…he is definitely my favorite.

Coming Soon by Jules Carlysle

Shitheads Say the Darndest Things

Confessions of a Really, Really, Really
Bad Mother

Contents

To announce that there must be no criticism of the President, or that we are to stand by the President, right or wrong, is not only unpatriotic and servile, but is morally treasonable to the American public.

Theodore Roosevelt

Democracy Is...

Democracy is buying a big house you can't afford with money you don't have to impress people you wish were dead.

And, unlike communism, democracy does not mean having just one ineffective political party; it means having two ineffective political parties. ...

Democracy is welcoming people from other lands, and giving them something to hold onto -- usually a mop or a leaf blower.

It means that with proper timing and scrupulous bookkeeping, anyone can die owing the government a huge amount of money. ...

Democracy means free television, not good television, but free.

And finally, democracy is the eagle on the back of a dollar bill, with 13 arrows in one claw, 13 leaves on a branch, 13 tail feathers, and 13 stars over its head -- this signifies that when the white man came to this country, it was bad luck for the Indians, bad luck for the trees, bad luck for the wildlife, and lights out for the American eagle.

Johnny Carson

WASHINGTON D.C. (B.S.)
Early this morning a devastating fire burned down the personal library of President George W. Bush. Tragically, both books were lost in the blaze. More poignantly, the President, due to his hectic schedule, had not found time to color in the second one.

Preface

Call me crazy, but I think the intellectually deficient should not be allowed to rule the world.

You will notice that I've included in this collection some funny and relevant quotes from comedians, other politicians and historical figures; quotes that by no means fall into the category of "Dumbass".

I could go "highbrow" and say that the added content from comedians brings clarity to the greater impact of having an idiot in the Oval Office. After all, our comedians are our bravest and most astute social commentators. They have a unique ability to break down the most complex and provocative political or social issues to their funniest common denominator. Their jokes strike closer to the truth than any mainstream media dares and reach beyond politics and comedy to actually elevate the public discourse in a most unexpected way. They challenge our perspectives and broaden our intellectual horizons. I think Jon Stewart, Jay Leno, David Letterman and Bill Maher should be pinned with medals and awarded the Nobel Peace Prize.

But, that sentiment notwithstanding, I used their quotes in this book because they make me laugh.

I could tell you the historical quotes provide critical insight into parallels found between past events and current affairs. Among other things, to illustrate that, despite remarkable advances as a civilization, at heart we are simple cave dwellers with TiVo, microwaves and internet porn. To show that despite our phenomenal access to information, we are

still readily seduced by optics and manipulated by fear......
to remind you that history repeats itself.

But ultimately, I used these historical quotes because they made me think.

I could simply describe DUMBASS as a book that chronicles the inexplicable rise and the spectacular (albeit inevitable) demise of a stupid, stupid man in his own words.

Or, I could try telling you that I'm presenting Bush's own words and allowing you to analyze them through the lens of history and popular culture.

But, most of that is swanky bull. This book is what it is. And it's ultimately just a simple quote book.

I highlight some of his blatant lies and contradictions, not all of them. There are literally hundreds of sources you can go to for that. It wasn't my intent, just an interesting byproduct of the process.

Sometimes the connections between W's quotes and the accompanying material will be readily apparent; sometimes it's a little more obscure. I don't spoon-feed. It's more fun when you work for it. But, there is always a reason why I've made my choices.

This is a simple, chronological compilation of stupid comments made by your Commander-In-Chief. They have been gathered from numerous sources, including but not limited to, websites, transcripts, and various articles.

This isn't a historical document.

It's simply entertainment

Introduction

I don't hate George W Bush.

Watching the pre-election coverage back in 2000 was more than a little surreal....

A mentally vacant, slack-jawed yokel with an unusually creepy blinking problem was running for President...WOW, that's rich...The buffoon could barely string together two coherent sentences...surely.....*surely* ...he couldn't win the White House.

After all, they only had to listen to him spout his nonsensical gibberish to know he was in way over his head. This dude from Texas is not presidential. A president is a man of power and prestige, a man of words. A president is a man of greatness who, with those who came before, will loom over history forever. He's not your beer swilling, under achieving, goofy poker buddy. No one would elect a frat boy to the most powerful office on the planet. Of that, I was sure.

Comfortable in my assertion, I allowed myself to be entertained by the spectacle. After all, characters like him seldom escape from their parents' attic. How often does one manage to stagger onto the world stage? We haven't had fun like this since Dan Quayle and Ross Perot.

Sidebar - 5 years later, Quayle is starting to look like a rocket scientist when compared blow-by-blow to President Frat Boy and his Merry Band of Miscreants.

When Bush won the first election I was stunned.

When he won the second election I cried.

How could this happen?

This book may be anti-President Bush, but it is by no means anti-American. I love America as much as I love snowshoes and 6% beer.

Perhaps it's just my generation, we grew up watching American TV & Hollywood movies, reading your magazines and watching your news......When the US sneezes, Canada says, "gesundheit"

So again, let me say...I don't hate George W. Bush. This is an important clarification. If it's easier, consider it a "love the sinner, hate the sin" thing. I don't bear any ill will towards the man personally.

However, here's what I *do* think...

President Bush has revealed himself to be hardly competent enough to manage the drive-thru window at Burger King, much less a military superpower and a global war on terror. (although admittedly, he's a pro at serving up Whoppers) Frankly, if the occasion arose, I'm not sure he could even be judged competent enough to stand trial.

I think he is inept. I think he is a liar and I think he poses a grave danger to America, your civil liberties and by virtue of his military capabilities, the entire world.

He is intoxicated by power and as such, he is incapable of truly advancing the cause of freedom and democracy in the world.

He is blinded by arrogance, devoid of empathy and too immature to acknowledge errors, much less learn from them.

I think he is smug. I think he is evasive and I think he's pathological. He should be medicated appropriately under the supervision of numerous physicians and housed permanently in a secure therapeutic environment...preferably the kind with padded walls and recreational basket weaving......not the White House.

(Has anyone bothered to check his nose lately for jellybeans and pennies?)

I also find him tactless, disingenuous...and I firmly believe he's a hypocrite.

But, I don't hate him.

I think he is a controlling, angry alcoholic who never addressed the underlying insecurities and issues that made him drink in the first place. He's replaced a dependence on booze with an addiction to God and as a power-whore, he is mortally fearful of any threat to his status, real or imagined.

I think years of drinking and drugs have stunted his emotional development and rendered him incapable of accepting responsibility for anything.

I think his inner circle of handlers and yes-men have picked up where his rich daddy left off and shield him from reality and consequences.

That is assuming he is not simply an empty vessel under the direct influence of dark and subversive forces like Satan and/or Karl Rove

George W is a genuine dummy, a puppet that sits idle until someone or something crawls up his butt and forces him into animation. It's a great act. I hardly ever see Dick Cheney's lips moving.

Consider that vacant look in his eyes while he's waiting for his turn at the microphone, staring off to some unseen horizon, completely disconnected and blinking like the clock on my VCR after a blackout. I suspect he slips into some kind of sophisticated power saver mode "they" use to conserve his battery.

Or perhaps, it's like the movie "Being John Malkovich" except, upon entering that tiny door in his cranium, the visitors (lobbyists, Dick Cheney...whatever) find no one is home. So, they are free to advance their corporate interests from their anonymous spot at the helm in his empty little head.

If you're reading this book, it's unlikely that you are unfamiliar with the failures of this administration. The lies, scandals, and dead bodies seem to pile, one upon another, upon another, in greater numbers every day. Oil companies are making record profits. Defense contractors are golden. Halliburton stock, I hear, is way up. The rich are getting richer and the poor are left to starve or drown in their own Louisiana backyards.

It's been reported that Bush believes God has personally called him to bring peace to the Middle East. Frankly, I have a hard time believing that the God I believe in would tell him to use bullets and bombs to do so. There is one subtle distinction between the God-given missions of bin Laden and George W Bush. Judging from the quotes I've read, bin Laden is at war because he believes an Islamic state and killing infidels honors and pleases his God. George W Bush believes that he's under direct and personal orders from the Almighty, "<u>God told me</u> to strike at al Qaida and I struck them, and then He instructed me to strike at Saddam, which I did, ...". It seems to me that when it comes to malinformed religious zealotry, the pot and kettle are both black here.

I don't doubt that Bush, somewhere in the dark recesses of the vacant space left behind after he sold his soul to the devil, probably believes that ultimately, his intentions are good. He'd be wrong of course...but, he must be used to that by now.

It's fair that Saddam Hussein is in jail and standing trial...no doubt about it. But, regardless how the Bush Collective tries to rewrite history, the fact remains that they invoked deceit and manipulated intelligence, not to mention, exploited the fears of a nation in mourning to justify the unjustifiable.....a war under false pretenses. They saw an opportunity and seized it. Bush was presented with his very own Reichstag Fire.

Worse perhaps, the media and political pundits are complicit in the deception. They are so busy spewing venom on each other and making outrageously irresponsible statements

(Coulter, O'Reilly I'm talking about YOU!) that the core issues go unaddressed. Republicans and Democrats alike manipulate their rhetoric by spinning, glossing over or completely ignoring any evidence that hurts their particular hypothesis. They are dishonest, divisive and wholly irresponsible. The rest of us are left ill equipped to draw informed conclusions, which I suppose is the entire point.

We are now so cleverly manipulated and influenced by the media and establishments on both the right and left, that the truth has become hopelessly lost in semantics.

The extreme "Right" is trying to distract our attention away from Iraq, torture, secret CIA prisons and approximately 2000 other fiascos by franticly waving Jesus and the flag. If someone dares question the Administration's leadership or integrity, they drape a flag over the latest mess and cry "treason!". (Ironically, this bears a striking resemblance to the way I clean my house). It's my not-so-humble assertion that this doesn't work on either front.

We are watching a poorly staged rendition of Wag the Dog interpreted for the morbidly stupid and performed by the criminally insane.

We are spectators at a game of Gladiator politics. Blood thirsty and feeding on political carnage. Through mass media, the action spills into the parking lot and we revel in the rioting as political pundits and day-players tear each other to shreds. These guys aren't even part of the game. They are the electoral equivalent of dancing hot dogs singing "Let's all go to the Lobby".

Watch 'em, listen to them, even buy their books. But always remember that they have an agenda.

Brilliant men of substance, integrity, courage and vision founded America. But times were simpler then. Politics has evolved into a sophisticated sport. People devote their lives to the study of political strategy. It's high stakes Capture the Flag and unfortunately for everyone involved, the players have learned to outplay the game.

Bush is a disaster. Everybody knows it. His administration is corrupt and incompetent and America is in immediate peril. The Republicans could earn back some credibility if, instead of supporting this loser right or wrong and trashing anyone who questions the President's actions, if they renounce him and decide that they care about their country more than they care about winning the short game. Lincoln did what was right because it was right not because it was popular

The US House of Representatives Special Investigations Committee produced a report called "Iraq on the Record" (The Waxman Report.) It details 227 lies by Bush, Cheney, Rice, Powell and Rumsfeld about the war and the weapons of mass destruction. It excludes statements that had proven to be false after new information was acquired...it's 227 statements that were known to be false by this administration at the time that they made them.

Think about that...seriously...

Using the Oval Office to cheat on your wife makes you a bad husband and an irresponsible leader.

Using the Oval office to lead your troops into a war born of blatant and continued deception makes you a liar, murderer and a war criminal.

You are playing a game of Three Card Monty and being shafted by a band of shifty street thugs. It's time to wise up.

Let's pretend for a moment that the war was actually declared to overthrow Saddam Hussein and install democracy in Iraq. It was still an inadequate plan executed poorly. At best, President Bush is a hapless rube and an incompetent buffoon......that's at *best.*

Where is that righteous indignation we saw when Clinton was impeached? Remember when you claimed to hold your elected officials to a "higher standard"?

Where are those high standards now?

How much does one administration have to screw up before they get kicked to the curb?

How much collateral damage is America willing to sustain due to pride and vanity?

For Crissakes, this man believes that he was chosen by God! He doesn't care what you think. He is not driven by polls, he's guided by the hand of the Devine and Almighty. It's NOT government by the people for the people. The people are irrelevant. It's government for God by God through his chosen vessel, George W Bush.

I believe that Bush's handlers thought they were installing a puppet government through whom they could rule the world.

But, unfortunately for everyone, Bush thought he was chosen to actually lead.

He ran off the rails.

How do you control a man who thinks God speaks through him?

The puppet needs to know they are a puppet or the whole plan falls apart.

Bush has cruised through life fueled by booze, drugs and bravado. He's proud to be an underachiever and he rests comfortably on the laurels of others. He's failed at every venture he's ever undertaken. And every mess he's created has been cleaned up for him. He is a self-made disaster.

Yet, he was handed the keys to the kingdom...twice...*TWICE!!!*

I honestly don't understand how you could let this happen.

Chapter One

A Pee with Me Guy

Politics:
'Poli' a Latin word meaning 'many'; and 'tics' meaning 'bloodsucking creatures'

Robin Williams

He knew who I was, at that time, because I had a reputation as a writer. I knew he was part of the Bush dynasty. But he was nothing, he offered nothing, and he promised nothing. He had no humor. He was insignificant in every way and consequently I didn't pay much attention to him. But when he passed out in my bathtub, then I noticed him. I'd been in another room, talking to the bright people. I had to have him taken away.

Hunter S Thompson
On meeting George W Bush at
Thompson's Super Bowl party in 1974

Nobody can be rich and stupid for more than one generation.
- Romano Prodi

1. I've got the greatest idea of how to raise money for the campaign. Have your mother send a letter to your family's Christmas-card list. I just did, and I got $350,000!

Republican Party Candidate Training Course
1978

2. There's no such thing as being too closely aligned with the oil industry in West Texas.

Congressional Candidate
1970s

> An honest politician is one who when he is bought will stay bought
>
> - Simon Cameron

3. You fucking son of a bitch I saw what you wrote. We're not going to forget this.

To Wall Street Journal columnist Al Hunt
April 1986

4. I will never apologize for the United States of America - I don't care what the facts are.

Coalition of American Nationalities
Aug 2nd, 1988

5. It's no exaggeration to say the undecideds could go one way or another.

Campaign Rally Troy NY
Oct 21st, 1988

6. I want the folks to see me sitting in the same kind of seat they sit in, eating the same popcorn, peeing in the same urinal.

Time Magazine
Jul. 31st, 1989

Well, not at the same time I hope…

4

7.	You know I could run for governor but I'm basically a media creation. I've never done anything. I've worked for my dad. I worked in the oil business. But that's not the kind of profile you have to have to get elected to public office.

Brief Display of Rational Thought
1989

> Politics will eventually be replaced by imagery. The politician will be only too happy to abdicate in favor of his image, because the image will be much more powerful than he could ever be.
>
> - Marshall McLuhan

8.	Please just don't look at part of the glass, the part that is only less than half full.

Day After Gubernatorial Election
Nov 6th, 1991

9.	I don't want to get, you know, here we are close to the election - sounding a knell of overconfidence that I don't feel.

To David Frost Election Day
Nov 6th, 1988

Knell (verb)
  a) A signal of disaster or destruction
  b) To ring slowly and solemnly, as for a funeral; toll.
  c) To give forth a mournful or ominous sound

10.   Do as I say and not as I did.

*Response to question about whether or not
he engaged in premarital sex after introducing
his $9m abstinence program.
Rolling Stone
Aug. 5th, 1999*

11.   Boy, they were big on crematoriums, weren't they?

*On touring the Auschwitz death camp,
Chicago Sun-Times
Jan 29th, 1992*

12.   All I was doing was appealing for an endorsement, not suggesting you endorse it.

*National Governors Association
Feb 3rd, 1992*

13.   Desert Storm. We sold a lot of tickets.

*Larry King Live CNN
Aug 16th, 1992*

One of the things he said to me, is `One of the keys to being seen as a great leader is to be seen as a commander-in-chief.' And he said, `My father had all this political capital built up when he drove the Iraqis out of (Kuwait) and he wasted it.

*Candidate Bush 1999 to Biographer Mickey Herskowitz
Quoted in The Houston Chronicle 11/01/04*

14.   It was just inebriating what Midland (Texas) was all about
       then.

Interview with Bill Minutaglio
1994

Inebriating (verb)
  a) To make drunk; intoxicate.
  b) To exhilarate or stupefy as if with alcohol

15.   We live in a culture of moral indifference, where movies and
       videos glamorize violence and tolerance is touted as a great
       virtue.

Texas A&M University
College Station Texas
Apr 6th, 1998

16.   There are some great admonitions in the Bible, talking about,
       you know, don't try to take the speck out of your neighbor's
       eye when you've got a log in your own. I'm mindful of that.

New York Times Magazine
Sept 13th, 1998

I'm completely in favor of the separation of Church and
State. My idea is that these two institutions screw us up
enough on their own, so both of them together is
certain death.

                                        - George Carlin

---

17. There is a lot of speculation and I guess there is going to continue to be a lot of speculation until the speculation ends.

.Austin-American Statesman
Oct 18th, 1998

18. You're all going to Hell.

Austin-American Statesman
Dec 1st, 1998

Response when asked what he would say to Israeli Jews upon arriving in the Middle East in 1993

> I care not whether a man is good or evil; all that I care is whether he is a wise man or a fool. Go! Put off holiness, and put on intellect.
>
> - William Blake

19. My faith tells me that acceptance of Jesus Christ as my savior is my salvation, and I believe I made it clear that it is not the Governor's role to decide who goes to heaven. I believe God decides who goes to heaven, not George W. Bush.

Governor Bush
1998

20. America is not ready to overturn Roe v. Wade because America's hearts are not right.

Mar 10th, 1999

21.   Kosovians can move back in.

Inside Politics CNN
April 9th, 1999

22.   There ought to be limits to freedom.

May 21st, 1999

23.   If the East Timorians decide to revolt, I'm sure I'll have a statement.

New York Times
June 16th, 1999

24.   The only thing I know about Slovakia is what I learned first-hand from your foreign minister, who came to Texas.

*Bush's meeting was with the **Prime Minister***
*of **Slovenia** Janez Drnovsek,*
Knight Ridder News Service
June 22nd, 1999.

Nor does he need to know the difference between Slovenia and Slovakia; that the people of Greece and Kosovo are not known as "Grecians" and "Kosovians;" and that the massacres undertaken by the U.S.-backed Indonesia military were not caused because "the East Timorians decide to revolt".........My God, it's Dan Quayle with better parents.

- Bob Harris
Zmag May 2000

25.   I'd probably say foolish things.

The Washington Post
July 25th, 1999

26.   QUESTION:
Name something you're not good at -

BUSH
Sitting down and reading a 500 page book on
public policy or philosophy or something.

Talk Magazine
Sept 1999

LA Times June 5th, 2000

People appreciate somebody who sets a tone, a tone
that values life.

Bush on abortion

27.   Please don't kill me

(Squinting his eyes and pursing his lips)
*Pro-Life advocate GW Bush "sets the tone" as he mocks
Karla Faye Tucker's answer when she was asked before her
execution "What would you say to Governor Bush?"*

*It turned out that this conversation with Tucker never took
place ....Bush was a joking....*

Talk Magazine
Sept 1999

10

28.   In 1994, there were 67 schools in Texas that were rated exemplorary according to our own tests

Manhattan Institute for Policy Research
Oct 5th, 1999

29.   The important question is, How many hands have I shaked?

New York Times
Oct 23rd, 1999

30.   HILLER:
Can you name the President of Chechnya?

BUSH:
No, can you?

HILLER:
Can you name the President of Taiwan?

BUSH:
Yeah, Lee.

HILLER:
Can you name the general who is in
charge of Pakistan?

BUSH:
Wait, wait, is this 50 questions?

HILLER:
No, it's four questions of four leaders in
four hot spots.

BUSH:
The new Pakistani general, he's just been elected, not
elected, this guy took over office. It appears this guy is going
to bring stability to the country and I think that's good news
for the sub-continent.

HILLER:
Can you name him?

BUSH:
General. I can't name the general. General.

HILLER:
And the prime minister of India?

BUSH:
The new prime minister of India is - (pause) No. Can you name the foreign minister of Mexico?

HILLER:
No sir, but I would say to that, I'm not running for President.

Andy Hiller for WHDH-TV
Nov 3rd, 1999

31.　　What I'm suggesting to you is, if you can't name the foreign minister of Mexico, therefore, you know, you're not capable about what you do. But the truth of the matter is you are, whether you can or not.

Andy Hiller for WHDH-TV
Nov 3rd, 1999

Of course with John McCain out of the race, George W. Bush has to pick a running mate. Which is kind of a scary proposition when you think about it. I mean his dad picked Dan Quayle, an he isn't as smart as his dad.

- Jay Leno

> LETTERMAN
> How do you look so youthful and rested?
>
> BUSH
> Fake it.
>
> LETTERMAN
> And that's pretty much how you're going to run the country?
>
> —David Letterman

32.   I think it's important for those of us in a position of responsibility to be firm in sharing our experiences, to understand that the babies out of wedlock is a very difficult chore for mom and baby alike. ... I believe we ought to say there is a different alternative than the culture that is proposed by people like Miss Wolf in society. ... And, you know, hopefully, condoms will work, but it hasn't worked.

Meet the Press
Nov 21st, 1999

33.   I read the newspaper.

Response to question about his reading habits.
New Hampshire Republican Debate
Dec 2nd, 1999

34.   Well, I know it irritates the Jewish people a lot.

Comments regarding Southern Baptist
University's manual instructing Christians in the
conversion of Jewish people.
US News & World Report
Dec 6th, 1999

35. I think the populace needs to make determinations on elections about, is the person honest? Does the person have a good heart? What is the philosophy? So along those lines.

US News & World Report
Dec 6th, 1999

36. But one way is for religion to be introduced - is for me - you know, my heart was changed - one heart at a time, my little old heart.

US News & World Report
Dec 6th, 1999

> George W. Bush has been invoking a lot of Bible imagery. He said Jesus also had 20 missing years and never held a job he couldn't get through his dad.
> - Jay Leno

37. There needs to be debates, like we're going through. There needs to be townhall meetings. There needs to be travel. This is a huge country.

Larry King Live
Dec. 16th, 1999

38. I'm a decisive person.... I'll read. I won't read treatises. I'll read summaries.

National Journal 1999

Sounds decisive to me....oh...wait....
can I change my answer?

14

39.   Mr. Vice President, in all due respect, it is -- I'm not sure 80 percent of the people get the death tax. I know this: 100 percent will get it if I'm the President.

Candidate George W. Bush 1999

Half of being smart is knowing what you're dumb at
- Solomon Short

---

40.   I'm sure there is some kind of heavy doctrinal difference, which I'm not sophisticated enough to explain to you.

*On his switching from Episcopal Church
to a Methodist one.
Candidate George W. Bush 1999*

41.   If the terriers and bariffs are torn down, this economy will grow.

*Rochester New York
Jan 7th, 2000*

42.   I will have a Vice President who can become the President. ...I will have a Vice President that agrees with my policy. I'm going to have a Vice President that likes me.

*GOP Presidential Debate
Michigan Jan 11th, 2000*

Pessimist: One who, when he has the choice of two evils, chooses both
- Oscar Wilde

15

43. Governor Bush will not stand for the subsidation of failure.

Florence South Carolina
Jan 11th, 2000

44. Rarely is the question asked: Is our children learning?

Florence South Carolina
Jan 11th, 2000

NEW RULE: 'Kidiots' Leave the children behind. At least until they learn something. A new study has shown that half of American high schools agree that newspapers should only be able to publish government-approved material. Almost one out of five said people should not be allowed to voice unpopular opinions. This is the first generation after September 11th, who discovered news during a 'watch what you say' administration...George W. Bush once asked, 'is our children learning.' No, they isn't. A better question would be, 'is our teacher's teaching?'

- Bill Maher

---

45. We must all hear the universal call to like your neighbor just like you like to be liked yourself.

Financial Times
Jan 14th, 2000

46. This is still a dangerous world. It's a world of madmen and uncertainty and potential mental losses.

Financial Times
Jan 14th, 2000

16

47.   When I was coming up, it was a dangerous world, and you knew exactly who they were, he said. It was us vs. them, and it was clear who them was. Today, we are not so sure who the they are, but we know they're there.

Iowa Western Community College
Jan 21st, 2000

Just because they really are out to get you doesn't mean you aren't paranoid.

- Steven Brust

---

48.   What I am against is quotas. I am against hard quotas, quotas they basically delineate based upon whatever. However they delineate, quotas, I think vulcanize society. So I don't know how that fits into what everybody else is saying, their relative positions, but that's my position.

San Francisco Chronicle
Jan 21st, 2000

The Bush administration says it will file a brief with the Supreme Court over the University of Michigan's affirmative action policy, saying it's wrong to determine acceptance based on race. Bush said acceptance should be based on fair things like what private school you went to, who's your dad, how much money you gave to the alumni fund

- Jay Leno

---

49.   Some say give it [the Federal Budget Surplus] to the taxpayers who pay the bills. That some is George W. Bush.

Sioux City Iowa
Jan 22nd, 2000

17

50.   I know how hard it is for you to put food on your family.

Greater Nashua New Hampshire
Jan 27th, 2000

Only because they keep squirming

51.   This is Preservation Month. I appreciate preservation. It's what you do when you run for President. You gotta preserve.

Los Angeles Times
Jan. 28th, 2000

52.   Will the highways on the Internet become more few?

Concord New Hampshire
Jan 29th, 2000

The Weakest Link is fascinating program. They ask a bunch of people questions and they keep getting rid of the dumbest person, so just the smartest person is left. It is kind of the opposite way we elect a president.
—Jay Leno

53.   The most important job is not to be governor or First Lady in my case.

San Antonio Express-News
Jan 30th, 2000

54. I think we need not only to eliminate the tollbooth to the middle class, I think we should knock down the tollbooth.

Nashua New. Hampshire.
New York Times
Feb. 1st, 2000

55. It's an old game of switch-and-bait. Say one thing and do another.

Washington Post
Feb 9th, 2000

56. A reformer with results is a conservative who has had compassionate results in the state of Texas.

New York Times
Feb 10th, 2000

> Bush has a new campaign slogan. It's 'Reformer with Results' Which I think is a big improvement on the old one: 'A Dumb Guy with Connections.'
>
> —David Letterman

57. I've changed my style somewhat, as you know. I'm less--I pontificate less, although it may be hard to tell it from this show. And I'm more interacting with people.

Meet the Press
Feb 13th, 2000

58.   I do not agree with this notion that somehow if I go to try to attract votes and to lead people toward a better tomorrow somehow I get subscribed to some—some doctrine gets subscribed to me.

Meet the Press,
Feb. 13th, 2000

59.   I would have said yes to abortion if only it was right. I mean, yeah it's right. Well no it's not right that's why I said no to it.

South Carolina
Feb 14th, 2000

60.   We ought to make the pie higher.

South Carolina Republican Debate
Feb 15th, 2000

It is a very complicated economic point I was making there. Believe me, what this country needs is taller pie.

—George W. Bush

61.   How do you know if you don't measure if you have a system that simply suckles kids through?

On Education
Beaufort South Carolina
Feb 16th, 2000

Thanks for planting that image in my head.

20

62.	If you're sick and tired of the politics of cynicism and polls and principles, come and join this campaign.

Hilton Head South Carolina
Feb 16th, 2000

63.	The Senator has got to understand if he's going to have -- he can't have it both ways. He can't take the high horse and then claim the low road.

Florence South Carolina
Feb 17th, 2000

64.	I understand small business growth. I was one.

New York Daily News
Feb 19th, 2000

65.	I'm very gracious and humbled.

This Week with Cokie Roberts
Feb 20th, 2000

> Maybe it's knocked his syntax straight.
>
> *—ABC's Cokie Roberts*
> *on Bush banging his head on the*
> *door while boarding Marine One*

66.	It is not Reaganesque to support a tax plan that is Clinton in nature.

Los Angeles California
Feb 23rd, 2000

67.   I don't have to accept their tenants. I was trying to convince
        those college students to accept my tenants. And I reject any
        labeling me because I happened to go to the university.

Today Show NBC
Feb 23rd, 2000

68.   I don't make any apologies for what I do on the campaign
        trail.

New York Times
Feb 24th, 2000

69.   I did denounce it. I de- I denounced it. I denounced interracial
        dating. I denounced anti-Catholic bigacy... bigotry.

Virginia Feb 25th, 2000

70.   I'm a patient man, which is hard for me to believe.

San Francisco Chronicle
Feb 25th, 2000

I have opinions of my own -- strong opinions -- but I
don't always agree with them.
                                    - George HW Bush

71.   I thought how proud I am to be standing up beside my dad.
        Never did it occur to me that he would become the gist for
        cartoonists

Newsweek
Feb 28th, 2000

> For rarely are sons similar to their fathers: most are worse, and a few are better than their fathers.
>
> - Homer

The philosopher NOT Simpson!

72.   I don't want to win? If that were the case why the heck am I on the bus 16 hours a day, shaking thousands of hands, giving hundreds of speeches, getting pillared in the press and cartoons and still staying on message to win?

Newsweek
Feb 28th, 2000

Pillar (verb)
To support or decorate with pillars or a pillar.

Is that what the kids are calling it these days?

> Bush is like a stripper with hairy legs. He's got some pretty smooth moves, but even from way back in the bar, you can tell that something is horribly awry.
>
> — Will Durst

73.   We will use our technology to enhance uncertainty abroad.

March 2000

74.   I'm going to be a President who hails success as well as failure.

March 2000

Finally, a candidate not too proud to pursue the seldom-tapped flunky demographic.

75.   It's going to require a President who understands it's in our strategic interests to have a peaceful and economically vile hemisphere.

March 2000

Correction…it's going to take a president who understands the meaning of words like "hemisphere" and "vile".

76.   I will say to countries in the Middle East, don't you dare hold us hostile.

The Economist
Mar 3rd, 2000

Go ahead and say it, but I can't promise not to laugh

The very existence of flame-throwers proves that some time, somewhere, someone said to themselves, You know, I want to set those people over there on fire, but I'm just not close enough to get the job done.

- George Carlin

77.   I'm a uniter not a divider. That means when it comes time to sew up your chest cavity, we use stitches as opposed to opening it up.

Shortly after Letterman's bypass surgery.
The audience booed
Late Night with David Letterman
March 2nd, 2000

Senseless and yet it still manages to offend!

78.   The fact that (Gore) relies on facts - says things that are not factual - are going to undermine his campaign.

New York Times
March 4th, 2000

79.   It's evolutionary, going from governor to president, and this is a significant step, to be able to vote for yourself on the ballot, and I'll be able to do so next fall, I hope.

Associated Press
March 8th, 2000

> Republicans are calling the Bush-Cheney ticket the 'Wizard of Oz' ticket. One needs a heart and the other needs a brain.
>
> —Jay Leno

80.   I don't care what the polls say. I don't. I'm doing what I think what's wrong.

New York Times
March 15th, 2000

81.   People make suggestions on what to say all the time. I'll give you an example; I don't read what's handed to me. People say, 'Here, here's your speech, or here's an idea for a speech.' They're changed. Trust me.

New York Times
March 15ᵗʰ, 2000

Medicated post-nervous breakdown, I guess...

82.   Now let me give you -- and not in anticipation to your questions -- but over the next couple of months, I'm going to lay out a series of -- How are you going to occupy your time?... I'm going to make it clear, which is what I told you, is what I'm going to spend time talking about. I've got a series of policy speeches.

Washington Post
Mar 23ʳᵈ, 2000

83.   I've got a reason for running. I talk about a larger goal, which is to call upon the best of America. It's part of the renewal. It's reform and renewal. Part of the renewal is a set of high standards and to remind people that the greatness of America really does depend on neighbors helping neighbors and children finding mentors. I worry. I'm very worried about, you know, the kid who just wonders whether America is meant for him. I really worry about that. And uh, so, I'm running for a reason. I'm answering this question here and the answer is, you cannot lead America to a positive tomorrow with revenge on one's mind. Revenge is so incredibly negative. And so to answer your question, I'm going to win because people sense my heart, know my sense of optimism and know where I want to lead the country. And I tease people by saying, 'A leader, you can't say, follow me the world is going to be worse.' I'm an optimistic person. I'm an inherently content person. I've got a great sense of where

26

I want to lead and I'm comfortable with why I'm running. And, you know, the call on that speech was, beware. This is going to be a tough campaign.

Washington Post
March 23rd, 2000

Maybe a nation that consumes as much booze and dope as we do and has our kind of divorce statistics should pipe down about "character issues." Either that or just go ahead and determine the presidency with three-legged races and pie-eating contests. It would make better TV.

- PJ O'Rourke

---

84. Other Republican candidates may retort to personal attacks and negative ads.

Fundraising Letter from George W. Bush,
Washington Post
Mar 24th, 2000

At the very least, they may resort to proofreading.

85. We want our teachers to be trained so they can meet the obligations, their obligations as teachers. We want them to know how to teach the science of reading. In order to make sure there's not this kind of federal--federal cufflink.

Fritsche Middle School
Milwaukee WI
Mar 30th, 2000

86. What easy is when you see excellence to herald excellence.

April 2000

87. The benefits of helping somebody is beneficial.

April 2000

> Most political leaders acquire their position by causing large numbers of people to believe that these leaders are actuated by altruistic desires
> - Bertrand Russell

88. I think anybody who doesn't think I'm smart enough to handle the job is underestimating.

U.S. News & World Report
April 3rd, 2000

> In politics stupidity is not a handicap.
> - Napoleon Bonaparte

89. I was raised in the West. The west of Texas. It's pretty close to California. In more ways than Washington, D.C., is close to California.

Los Angeles Times
Apr 8th, 2000

90. FINK:
When you're not talking about politics, what do you and your father talk about?

BUSH:
Pussy.

David Fink Hartford Courant 1988
Republican Convention
Salon April 9th, 2000

91. Laura and I really don't realize how bright our children is sometimes until we get an objective analysis.

Meet the Press NBC
Apr 15th, 2000

92. I hope we get to the bottom of the answer. It's what I'm interested to know.

Associated Press
Apr 26th, 2000

93. I come from a different generation from my Dad.

Apr 27th, 2000

As if there were safety in stupidity alone

- Henry David Thoreau

94. Listen, I'm just as shocked as you are that I'm sitting here talking about the presidency -- it's never been a part of my -- my life's ambition hasn't always been to be the president.

News Hour with Jim Lehrer
Apr. 27th, 2000

95. I'm not going to play like I've been a person who's spent hours involved with foreign policy. I am who I am.

News Hour with Jim Lehrer
Apr 27th, 2000

96. Yesterday I met with the Russian foreign minister and when he left the meeting, he kindly said this is a man who -- I'm going to paraphrase him and you need to check the facts -- but -- sophisticated thinker.

Interview with Jim Lehrer
Apr 27th, 2000

97. BUSH:
I talked to my little brother, Jeb -- I haven't told this to many people. But he's the governor of -- I shouldn't call him my little brother -- my brother, Jeb, the great governor of Texas.

JIM LEHRER:
Florida.

BUSH:
Florida. The state of the Florida.

News Hour With Jim Lehrer
Apr 27th, 2000

98. Oh, I thought you said some *band*.

When asked about the Taliban
Glamour Magazine's David France
May 2000

99. It's clearly a budget. It's got a lot of numbers in it.

Reuters May 5th, 2000

Nice Work Sherlock

100.   My plan is one, by the way, joined by Democrats as well as Republicans, that understands by taking advantage of the compounding rate of interest, younger workers will be able to have some -- have benefits that are -- that we anticipate a promise for the long run.

Fox News
May 18th, 2000

101.   John and I both agree, and strongly agree, that if a shareholder, a stakeholder, a labor union member don't have the right to say where their money is being spending, on a campaign or an idea or on an issue, that shouldn't be spent.

Press Conference with John McCain
May 9th, 2000

102.   I think we agree, the past is over.

Dallas Morning News
May 10th, 2000

103.   Actually, I - this may sound a little West Texan to you, but I like it. When I'm talking about - when I'm talking about myself, and when he's talking about myself, all of us are talking about me.

Hardball MSNBC
May 31st, 2000

One nice thing about egotists: they don't talk about other people

- George Carlin

104.   I'm gonna talk about the ideal world, Chris. I've read--I understand reality. If you're asking me as the President, would I understand reality, I do.

Hardball MSNBC
May 31st, 2000

IMPROBABILITY, n.

His tale he told with a solemn face
And a tender, melancholy grace.
Improbable 'twas, no doubt,
When you came to think it out,
But the fascinated crowd
Their deep surprise avowed
And all with a single voice averred
'Twas the most amazing thing they'd heard --
All save one who spake never a word,
But sat as mum As if deaf and dumb,
Serene, indifferent and unstirred.
Then all the others turned to him
And scrutinized him limb from limb --
Scanned him alive;
But he seemed to thrive
And tranquiller grow each minute,
As if there were nothing in it.
"What! what!" cried one, "are you not amazed At what our friend has told?"
He raised soberly then his eyes and gazed
In a natural way
And proceeded to say,
As he crossed his feet on the mantelshelf:
"O no --not at all; I'm a liar myself.

- Ambrose Bierce

105.   There's not going to be enough people in the system to take advantage of people like me.

Wilton Connecticut
June 9th, 2000

32

> According to the Congressional Budget Office, Social
> Security will be completely depleted by 2052,
> completely broke. Again I don't think President Bush
> understands these issues. He says '2052 -- well, that's all
> right, by then all our old people will be dead.'
>
> -Jay Leno

106.   The only things that I can tell you is that every case I have
        reviewed I have been comfortable with the innocence or guilt
        of the person that I've looked at. I do not believe we've put a
        guilty ... I mean innocent person to death in the state of
        Texas.

                        Nat'l Public Radio
                        June 16th, 2000

107.   This case has had full analyzation and has been looked at a
        lot. I understand the emotionality of death penalty cases.

                        Seattle Post-Intelligencer
                        June 23rd, 2000

                Bush's creative verbalizatiationating skills

**GW Bush Has Executed 131 Inmates
Many With Seriously Flawed Trials**
By Steve Mills, Ken Armstrong & Douglas Holton

AUSTIN,Texas — Under Gov. George W. Bush, Texas
has executed dozens of Death Row inmates whose
cases were compromised by unreliable evidence,
disbarred or suspended defense attorneys, meager
defense efforts during sentencing and dubious
psychiatric testimony, a Chicago Tribune investigation
has found.
                Headline Chicago Tribune
                June 11, 2000

---

108. The fundamental question is, 'Will I be a successful President when it comes to foreign policy?' I will be, but until I'm the President, it's going to be hard for me to verify that I think I'll be more effective.

New York Times
June 28th, 2000

June 28th, 2000

109. States should have the right to enact reasonable laws and restrictions particularly to end the inhumane practice of ending a life that otherwise could live.

Cleveland Ohio
June 29th, 2000

> Earlier this afternoon, George W. Bush resigned as the governor of Texas. This is historic. It's the first job he's left without going bankrupt. It was a nice ceremony. The state of Texas said while he's president, they'll let him stop by every once in a while and execute someone.
>
> —Jay Leno

110. Unfairly but truthfully, our party has been tagged as being against things. Anti-immigrant, for example. And we're not a party of anti-immigrants.

Cleveland Ohio
July 1st, 2000

> [Clip of Bush: America needs to conduct this debate on immigration in a reasoned and respectful tone...We cannot build a unified country by inciting people to anger or playing on anyone's fears]
>
> That's what terrorism and gay people are for.
>
> - Jon Stewart

111. JENNINGS:
Back in October 1998, you told David Broder of The
Washington Post you felt like a cork in a raging river.

BUSH:
Yes. I think that was part of all the speculation
and the swirl around whether I would run or
not. There was kind of a momentum beyond -- beyond being
the governor I guess is the
best way to describe it. And I don't feel like
a cork in a raging river now. I feel like
-- something bigger than a cork.

ABC News with Peter Jennings
July 31st, 2000

112. And if he continues that, I'm going to tell the nation what I
think about him as a human being and a person.

Today Show,
Aug. 1st, 2000

Beware when the great God lets loose a thinker on this
planet.

- Ralph Waldo Emerson

---

113. It's amazing to me that the President of the United States
would spend time trying to be a political <u>pundit.</u> He's so
desperate to keep his legacy intact he'll say anything, just like
Al Gore

Jab at President Clinton
Aug 1st, 2000

Pun-dit (noun)
Expert, scholar, authority, specialist

114. I want you to know that farmers are not going to be secondary thoughts to a Bush administration. They will be in the forethought of our thinking.

Salinas California
Aug. 10th, 2000

115. I think he needs to stand up and say if he thought the president were wrong on policy and issues, he ought to say where.

Associated Press
Aug. 11th, 2000

116. As I understand it, the current [FBI] form asks the question, Did somebody use drugs within the last seven years? and I will be glad to answer that question, and the answer is No.

Time Magazine
Aug 18th, 2000

> It seems a friend of the Bush family, Doug Wead -- I think he's Linda Tripp's first husband if I'm not mistaken -- secretly taped a number of conservations. Bush admitted as a young man he smoked marijuana but he quit when it interfered with his drinking. ... Although he acknowledged trying marijuana, no one has come forward to verify they've actually seen him do marijuana, so it's like the National Guard thing all over again.
>
> - Jay Leno

117.   I have a different vision of leadership. A leadership is someone who brings people together.

Bartlett Tennessee.,
Aug. 18th, 2000

118.   This campaign not only hears the voices of the entrepreneurs and the farmers and the entrepreneurs, we hear the voices of those struggling to get ahead.

Des Moines Iowa
Aug 21st, 2000

You can get medication for that now

119.   I don't know whether I'm going to win or not. I think I am. I do know I'm ready for the job. And, if not, that's just the way it goes.

Des Moines Iowa
Aug. 21st, 2000

120.   We cannot let terrorists and rogue nations hold this nation hostile or hold our allies hostile.

Des Moines IA,
Aug 21st, 2000

In case you thought it was just an accident last time

121.   Well, I think if you say you're going to do something and don't do it, that's trustworthiness.

CNN Online Chat
Aug 30th, 2000

> Politicians are like diapers. They both need changing regularly and for the same reason.
>
> — Anonymous

122. As governor of Texas, I have set high standards for our public schools, and I have met those standards.

CNN Online Chat
Aug 30th, 2000

It was the least he could do really, hold himself to the same high standards that were set for grade-schoolers.

123. When it comes to the overall story, the long-term view of the campaign, it's so important for the campaign to set the long-term view.

Brill's Content Online
Sept 2000

124. After all, religion has been around a lot longer than Darwinism.

September 2000

> I am quite sure now that often, very often, in matters concerning religion and politics a man's reasoning powers are not above the monkeys.
>
> — Mark Twain

125. The people who care more about that land are the hard-working farmers and ranchers of your part of the state of Washington, D.C.

Spokane Washington
Sept 2000

126. The point is, this is a way to help inoculate me about what has come and is coming.

On running anti-Gore Campaign Ads
New York Times
Sept 2nd, 2000

HOT MIKE

The Bush camp wasted little time condemning Kerry's remarks as uncivil. Campaign chairman Marc Racicot called Kerry's off-the-cuff comment, 'unbecoming of a candidate for the presidency.' Bush never had a similar microphone mishap, has he? [Shows tape of Bush saying: 'There's Adam Clymer, major league asshole from the *New York Times.*' Cheney: 'Oh, yeah, he is, big time.'] I gotta tell you, I know there was that one, I was actually thinking more of this one. [Shows tape from Bush's 2003 State of the Union address: 'The British government has learned that Saddam Hussein recently sought significant quantities of uranium from Africa.'] Oh my God, was my mike on? D'oh!

-Jon Stewart

---

127. BUSH:
There's Adam Clymer, major league asshole from the New York Times.

39

DICK CHENEY:
Yeah, big time.

Caught on mike at campaign rally where Bush
pledged to bring a new tone of civility to politics
Naperville Illinois
Sept 4th, 2000

> At least I didn't trade Sammy Sosa,
>
> > - Adam Clymer in response to
> > George W. Bush's vulgarity, referring
> > to Bush's experience as owner of
> > the Texas Rangers.

128.   I regret that a private comment I made to the vice presidential
candidate made it through the public airways.

Allentown Pennsylvania.,
Sept. 5th, 2000.

129.   We'll let our friends be the peacekeepers and the great
country called America will be the pacemakers

Houston Texas
Sept 6th, 2000

> The two candidates were said to have spent the evening
> pouring over the complex and detailed Supreme Court
> ruling. But whereas Gore was pouring over it with his
> eyes and mind, Bush was pouring a glass of juice over it
> because quote, 'I don't want to finish my juice.'
> —Jon Stewart

130. Listen, Al Gore is a very tough opponent. He is the incumbent. He represents the incumbency. And a challenger is somebody who generally comes from the pack and wins, if you're going to win. And that's where I'm coming from.

Detroit Michigan
Sept 7th, 2000

131. That's Washington. That's the place where you find people getting ready to jump out of the foxholes before the first shot is fired.

Westland Michigan
Sept. 8th, 2000

At least they made it into a foxhole to begin with

The White House released documents it claims validates the president's (National Guard) service ... When deciphered the documents showed that in a one-year period, 1972 and 1973, Bush received credit for nine days of active National Guard service. The traditional term of service then and now for the National Guard is one weekend a month and two full weeks a year, meaning that Bush's nine-day stint qualifies him only for the National Guard's National Guard. That's the National Guard's National Guard, an Army of None.

-Jon Stewart

41

132.   I wanna make it clear to people that, you know, the idea of putting <u>subliminable</u> messages into ads is, is ridiculous.

Sept 12th, 2000

> Yes, he said 'subliminable,' but he was probably distracted thinking about executing some criminables.
> -Jon Stewart

133.   Conspiracy theories abound in American politics. I don't even need to be <u>subliminabable</u> about the differences between our views on prescription drugs.

Orlando Florida
Sept 12th, 2000

And again...

> GOP accused of using subliminal advertising; George W. Bush says, 'Why would we advertise underwater?'
> —Jon Stewart

134.   I don't feel like I've got all that much too important to say on the kind of big national issues.

20/20 ABC
Sept 15th, 2000

So President of the United States is the right career choice

135.   The woman who knew that I had dyslexia—I never interviewed her.

Orange California.
Sept. 15th, 2000

Freudian Slip?

136.   A tax cut is really one of the anecdotes to coming out of an economic illness.

The Edge With Paula Zahn
Sept 18th, 2000

Did you hear the one about the Priest the
Tax Cut and the Goat?........

137.   I am a person who recognizes the <u>fallacy</u> of humans.

Oprah Sept 19th, 2000

Put a "ph" on that word and it's a whole new world of jokes

138.   Well, that's going to be up to the pundits and the people to make up their mind. I'll tell you what is a president for him, for example, talking about my record in the state of Texas. I mean, he's willing to say anything in order to convince people that I haven't had a good record in Texas.

MSNBC,
Sept. 20th, 2000

> Courage is going from failure to failure without losing enthusiasm.
>
> - Winston Churchill

139.   I want each and every American to know for certain that I'm responsible for the decisions I make, and each of you are as well.

On Live With Regis
Sept 20th, 2000

> You cannot escape the responsibility of tomorrow by evading it today.
>
> - Abraham Lincoln

140.   It is clear our nation is reliant upon big foreign oil. More and more of our imports come from overseas.

Beaverton Oregon
Sept 25th, 2000

141.   I will have a foreign-handed foreign policy.

Redwood California
Sept 27th, 2000

142.   One of the common denominators I have found is that expectations rise above that which is expected.

Los Angeles California
Sept 27th, 2000

143.   I know the human being and fish can coexist peacefully.

Saginaw Michigan
Sept 29th, 2000

Only until the all fish militia stages a coup.

It has always been my private conviction that any man who pits his intelligence against a fish and loses has it coming.

- John Steinbeck

144.   We don't believe in planners and deciders making the decisions on behalf of Americans.

Scranton Pennsylvania
Sept 6th, 2000

Of course not....that's why he has that
Magic Eight Ball

> Beguiled by George S. Bush's easy smile and casual indifference to the details, we are on the brink of electing him to office. This isn't choosing a president, it's casting the lead in a sitcom about the presidency.
>
> - Roger Ebert

145. Let me make sure the seniors hear me loud and clear. They've had their chance to get something done.

First Presidential Debate
Boston Massachusetts
Oct 3rd, 2000

Take that seniors! You had your chance and you blew it...BLEW IT!....probably just sat around being old and stuff....

146. Drug therapies are replacing a lot of medicines as we used to know it.

National Television
Oct. 3rd, 2000

Chapter Two

A Hopefuller Country?

I hope life isn't a big joke, because I don't get it.

Jack Handy

> Vote: the instrument and symbol of a freeman's power
> to make a fool of himself and a wreck of his country.
> —Ambrose Bierce

147. I've been talking to Vicente Fox, the new President of Mexico... I know him... to have gas and oil sent to U.S.... so we'll not depend on foreign oil.

First Presidential Debate
Boston Massachusetts
Oct 3ʳᵈ, 2000

148. I believe the role of the military is to fight and win war and therefore prevent war from happening in the first place.

First Presidential Debate
Boston Massachusetts
Oct 3ʳᵈ, 2000

Once the military fights and wins war, isn't it too
late to prevent war from happening 'in the first place'?

49

149.   A family in Allentown, Pennsylvania, I campaigned with them
        the other day... Under my plan, they get $1800 of tax relief.
        Under Vice President Gore's plan, they get $145 of tax relief.
        Now you tell me who stands on the side of the fence.

First Presidential Debate
Boston Massachusetts
Oct 3rd, 2000

I will....just as soon as you explain the question.

150.   There's a huge trust. I see it all the time when people come
        up to me and say, 'I don't want you to let me down again.'

First Presidential Debate
Boston Massachusetts
Oct 3rd, 2000

151.   I think if you know what you believe, it makes it a lot easier to
        answer questions. I can't answer your question.

Reynoldsburg Ohio
Oct 4th, 2000

152.   Our priorities is our faith.

Greensboro North Carolina
Oct 10th, 2000

50

153. I mean, there needs to be a wholesale effort against racial profiling, which is illiterate children.

Second Presidential Debate
Winston-Salem North Carolina
Oct 11th, 2000

> Forgive me my nonsense as I also forgive the nonsense of those who think they talk sense
> - Robert Frost

154. And my case to the American people is, if you're happy with inactivity, stay with the horse. The horse is up there now.

Second Presidential Debate
Winston-Salem North Carolina
Oct 11th, 2000

155. Vice President mentioned Nigeria is a fledgling democracy. We have to work with Nigeria. That's an important continent.

Second Presidential Debate
Winston-Salem North Carolina
Oct 11th, 2000

> You can be Vice President in the most prosperous time in America, run against a dumb guy, get more votes and still lose.
> #2 on Top Ten Things We've Learned
> from the Clinton Years
> - David Letterman

156.   I've supported the administration in Colombia. I think it's important for us to be training Colombians in that part of the world. The hemisphere is in our interest to have a peaceful Colombia.

Second Presidential Debate
Winston-Salem North Carolina
Oct 11th, 2000

157.   If you're a Medicare person, on Medicare, you don't get the new procedures. You're stuck in a time warp in many ways. So it will be a modern Medicare system that trusts you to make a variety of options for you.

Third Presidential Debate
St. Louis Missouri
Oct 17th, 2000

> The trouble with this country is that there are too many politicians who believe, with a conviction based on experience, that you can fool all of the people all of the time
>
> - Franklin Pierce Adams

158.   Well, you know, it's hard to make people love one another. I wish I knew the law because I would darn sure sign it. I wish I knew the law that said all of us would be good parents.

Third Presidential Debate
St. Louis Missouri
Oct 17th, 2000

159. The federal government puts about 6% of the money up. They put about, you know, 60% of the strings where you have to fill out the paperwork. I don't know if you have to be a paperwork-filler-outer, but most of it's because of the federal government.

Third Presidential Debate
St. Louis Missouri
Oct 17th, 2000

I hear that paperwork-filling-outing
is very. time -using-upping.

160. Should I be fortunate enough to earn your confidence, the mission of the United States military will be to be prepared and ready to fight and win war. And therefore prevent war from   happening   in   the   first   place.

Third Presidential Debate
St. Louis Missouri
Oct 17th, 2000

You cannot simultaneously prevent and prepare for war
- Albert Einstein

161. Quotas are bad for America. It's not the way America is all about.

Third Presidential Debate
St. Louis Missouri
Oct 17th, 2000

162. It's one thing about insurance, that's a Washington term.

Third Presidential Debate
Oct 17th, 2000

163. Families is where our nation finds hope, where wings take dream.

LaCrosse, Wisconsin.
Oct. 18th, 2000

164. If affirmative action means what I just described, what I'm for, then I'm for it.

St. Louis Missouri
Oct 18th, 2000

165. It's your money. You paid for it.

Lacrosse Wisconsin
Oct 18th, 2000

166. I think we ought to raise the age at which juveniles can have a gun

St Louis Missouri
Oct 18th, 2000

167. This is an impressive crowd, the haves and the have-mores. Some people call you the elite. I call you my base.

Al Smith Memorial Dinner
New York New York
Oct 19th, 2000

> We don't pay taxes. Only the little people pay taxes.
> — Leona Helmsley

168. On principle, there ought to be a limit to how much the federal government can take of anybody's hardworking hard work, of hardworking money.

Financial Times
Oct 21st, 2000

169. We have got people who perform common, common acts of commonplace miracles - commonplace acts of miracle - every day.

Financial Times
Oct 21st, 2000

170. I don't want nations feeling like that they can bully ourselves and our allies. I want to have a ballistic defense system so that we can make the world more peaceful, and at the same time I want to reduce our own nuclear capacities to the level commiserate with keeping the peace.

Des Moines Iowa
Oct 23rd, 2000

Commiserate (verb)
To feel or express sorrow or pity for; sympathize with

171. It's important for us to explain to our nation that life is important. It's not only life of babies, but it's life of children living in, you know, the dark dungeons of the Internet.

Arlington Heights Illinois
Oct 24th, 2000

172.   That's a chapter, the last chapter of the 20th, 20th, the 21st century that most of us would rather forget. The last chapter of the 20th century. This is the first chapter of the 21st century.

Arlington Heights Illinois
Oct 24th, 2000

Deja-Dumbass

[The Holocaust] was an obscene period in our nation's history...this century's history....We all lived in this century. I didn't live in this century
—Dan Quayle

173.   Anyway, after we go out and work our hearts out, after you go out and help us turn out the vote, after we've convinced the good Americans to vote, and while they're at it, pull that old George W. lever, if I'm the one, when I put my hand on the Bible, when I put my hand on the Bible, that day when they swear us in, when I put my hand on the Bible, I will swear to not -- to uphold the laws of the land.

Toledo Ohio
Oct 27th, 2000

When you go in for a job interview, I think a good thing to ask is if they ever press charges.
- Jack Handy SNL

174.   They said, you know, this issue doesn't seem to resignate with the people. And I said, you know something? Whether it resignates or not doesn't matter to me, because I stand for doing what's the right thing, and what the right thing is hearing the voices of people who work.

Portland Oregon
Oct 31st, 2000

56

President Bush has reversed himself and decided to allow Condoleezza Rice to publicly testify before the 9/11 commission under oath. It was a little dicey for awhile because White House lawyers told Bush that they didn't want to set a dangerous precedent. Bush said 'Hey I'm the precedent, I'll decide what's dangerous around here.'

—Jay Leno

175. If you don't stand for anything, you don't stand for anything.

Bellevue Washington
Nov 2nd, 2000

I can't stand that.

176. They want the federal government controlling Social Security like it's some kind of federal program.

Debate in St. Charles Montana
Nov 2nd, 2000

177. We say to seniors, We understand how important prescription drug coverage, so prescription drugs will be an ingrinable part of the Medicare plan.

St. Charles Montana
Nov 2nd, 2000

OK, but when you say that, do the seniors know what you mean?

> If you have a big enough dictionary, just about everything is a word.
>
> - Dave Barry

178.   They misunderestimated me.

Bentonville Arkansas
Nov 6th, 2000

179.   Dick (Cheney) and I felt like we won the first election three times and we're confident that when it's all said and done that he and I will be honored to be the President and Vice President.

Dec 2nd, 2000

> Both candidates are feeling the pressure........Al Gore has been testy with his staff and late today George W. Bush broke down and yelled at his parents, 'You promised!'"
>
> —Bill Maher
> 2000 Florida recount

180.   I knew it might put him in an awkward position that we had a discussion before finality has finally happened in this Presidential race.

Crawford Texas
Dec 2nd, 2000

58

181. Dick Cheney and I do not want this nation to be in a recession. We want anybody who can find work to be able to find work.

60 Minutes II
Dec 5th, 2000

182. The great thing about America is everybody should   vote.

Austin Texas
Dec 8th, 2000

> The best argument against democracy is a five minute conversation with the average voter.
>   - Winston Churchill

183. I am mindful of the difference between the executive branch and the legislative branch. I assured all four of these leaders that I know the difference, and that difference is they pass the laws and I execute them.

Washington DC
Dec 18th, 2000

The laws, not the legislative branch

184. If this were a dictatorship, it'd be a heck of a lot easier, just so long as I'm the dictator.

CNN
Dec 18th, 2000

> The next time they give you all that civic bullshit about voting, keep in mind that Hitler was elected in a full, free democratic election
>
>   - George Carlin

> Experience hath shewn, that even under the best forms (of government) those entrusted with power have, in time, and by slow operations, perverted it into tyranny
>
>   - Thomas Jefferson

185.   Natural gas is hemispheric. I like to call it hemispheric in nature because it is a product that we can find in our neighborhoods.

Austin Texas
Dec 20th, 2000

186.   My friends allege that I showed up in a Nixon mask one year and that another time I dressed as Mahatma Gandhi in a toga that looked like a diaper by the end of the night.

A Charge to Keep
Autobiography p. 135 – 2000

> I went straight from shenanigans to crimes against humanity
>
>   - George Carlin

187. [We're] working hard to convince both the Indians and the Pakis there's a way to deal with their problems without going to war.

Jan 7th, 2001

Let's start with eliminating the use of racial slurs

188. I would have to ask the questioner. I haven't had a chance to ask the questioners the question they've been questioning.

Austin Texas
Jan 8th, 2001

189. As far as I can tell, from what I read, I think she's certainly qualified to be the President -- I mean be a Cabinet Secretary.

On Linda Chavez for Secretary of Labour
Jan 9th, 2001

> The wise understand by themselves; fools follow the reports of others
>
> Tibetan Proverb

190. I believe the results of focusing our attention and energy on teaching children to read and having an education system that's responsive to the child and to the parents, as opposed to mired in a system that refuses to change, will make America what we want it to be, a literate country and a hopefuller country.

Washington DC
Jan 11th, 2001

191. The California crunch really is the result of not enough power-generating plants and then not enough power to power the power of generating plants.

New York Times
Jan 14th, 2001

Powerful statement

192. I would—I would strongly reject that assumption—that John Ashcroft is a open-minded, inclusive person.

NBC Nightly News With Tom Brokaw
Jan. 14th, 2001

Houston, we have your problem.

—Daily Show on Bush's Inauguration

193. Redefining the role of the United States from enablers to keep the peace to enablers to keep the peace from peacekeepers is going to be an assignment.

New York Times
Jan 14th, 2001

194. I'm hopeful. I know there is a lot of ambition in Washington, obviously. But I hope the ambitious realize that they are more likely to succeed with success as opposed to failure.

Associated Press
Jan 18th, 2001

> Due to a small but significant clause in the U.S.
> Constitution, I will be out of the office from January 21,
> 2001 until January 20, 2005.
>
> —Al Gore senior adviser Michael
> Feldman's outgoing message on his
> White House voicemail

195. Then I went for a run with the other dog and just walked. And I started thinking about a lot of things. I was able to-I can't remember what it was. Oh, the inaugural speech, started thinking through that.

U.S. News & World Report
Jan 22nd, 2001

> Bush's inauguration address was interrupted 27 times for applause and three times for vacation.
> - David Letterman

196. I am mindful not only of preserving executive powers for myself, but for predecessors as well.

Washington DC
Jan 29th, 2001

Time travel, another unique policy platform

197. I appreciate that question because I, in the state of Texas, had heard a lot of discussion about a faith-based initiative eroding the important bridge between church and state.

Jan 29th, 2001

> Leave the matter of religion to the family altar, the church, and the private school, supported entirely by private contributions. Keep the church and state forever separate.
>
> - Ulysses S. Grant

198. There's no such thing as legacies. At least, there is a legacy, but I'll never see it.

White House
Jan 31st, 2001

199. The budget caps were busted, mightily so. And we are reviewing... some budgetary reform measures that will reinstate - you know, possibly reinstate budgetary discipline. But the caps no longer - the caps, I guess they're there. But they didn't mean much.

Washington DC
Feb 5th, 2001

200. I confirmed to the prime minister that we appreciate our friendship.

After Meeting with Prime Minister
Jean Chrétien of Canada
Feb 5th, 2001

201. We're concerned about AIDS inside our White House—make no mistake about it.

Washington D.C.
Feb. 7th, 2001

202.   It's good to see so many friends here in the Rose Garden. This is our first event in this beautiful spot, and it's appropriate we talk about policy that will affect people's lives in a positive way in such a beautiful, beautiful part of our national—really, our national park system, my guess is you would want to call it.

Washington D.C.
Feb. 8th, 2001

How about just calling it the Rose Garden?

203.   I assured the Prime Minister of Canada that my vision of the hemisphere goes both north and south.

Aboard Air Force One
Feb 13th, 2001

An aide to the prime minister of Canada called President Bush a moron. Well that's not fair. Here's a guy who never worked a day in his life, got rich off his Dad's money, lost the popular vote and ended up president. That's not a moron, that's genius!

—Jay Leno

204.   You teach a child to read and he or her will be able to pass a literacy test.

Townsend Elementary School
Feb 21st, 2001

…and look what can happen if they don't!

205.   I have said that the sanction regime [against Iraq] is like Swiss cheese. That meant that they weren't very effective.

Press Conference
Feb 22ⁿᵈ, 2001

Swiss cheese is ineffective…let's consider that for a moment. As a tasty sandwich topping…I'd have to say, "effective" But as perhaps, a ship to shore radio or bicycle tire…"ineffective"….The important question is…what does Bush do with his cheese?

206.   As you know, I shy away from hypotheticals, Pancho. I'm going to resist the Christmas tree effect of tax policy. I don't want people putting ornaments on my plan.

Press Conference
Feb 22ⁿᵈ, 2001

I'm hoping the guy's name is actually "Pancho".

207.   INTERVIEWER:
         Well, you're a secular official...

         BUSH:
         I agree. I am a secular official.

         INTERVIEWER:
         And not a missionary.

         BUSH:
         Sir, on the air strikes in Iraq, the Pentagon is now saying that
         most of the bombs used in those strikes missed their targets.

New York Times
Feb 23rd, 2001

When the media ask him [George W. Bush] a question,
he answers, 'Can I use a lifeline?'

                                                    - Robin Williams

---

208.   My pan plays down an unprecedented amount of our national
         debt.

Feb. 27th, 2001

209.   Those of us who spent time in the agricultural sector, and in
         the heartland, we understand how unfair the death penalty is
         ... er ... the death tax is.

Omaha Nebraska
Feb 28th, 2001

210. Most people in Arkansas know where Texas is, and all the people in Texas know where Arkansas is.

*Mar 1*st*, 2001*

You can call some of Arkansas stupid all of the time
You can call all of Arkansas stupid some of the time…
But, you can't….oh forget it….he's a buffoon

211. I think there is some methodology in my travels.

Washington DC
*Mar 5*th*, 2001*

212. It's a sign from above.

Comment made when a studio light caught fire above crowd
Sioux Falls South Dakota
*Mar 9*th*, 2001*

213. Either you got it, or you don't got it. When you come walking in that hall, there's only one person that can get you ready to give the speech, and that's you -- that's the person getting ready to give it. His part of my life is one of just a loving dad.

Washington Post
*Mar 9*th*, 2001*

214.   That's what politics is all about, as far as I'm concerned - it's
the people's will.

Air Force One
Mar 9th, 2001

215.   There are some monuments where the land is so
widespread, they just encompass as much as possible. And
the integral part of the - the precious part, so to speak, I
guess all land is precious - but the part that the people
uniformly would not want to spoil, will not be despoiled. But
there are parts of the monument lands where we can explore
without affecting the overall environment.

Mar 13th, 2001

69

216. The way I like to put it is this: There's no bigger issue for the President to remind the moms and dads of America, if you happen to have a child, be fortunate to have a child.

U.S. Treasury Department
Mar 16th, 2001

217. We need to change that attitude about how prolific_we can be with the people's money.

Mar. 16th, 2001

Prolific (adj.)
Producing in great abundance; abundant works

According to the latest poll in the *Washington Post*, 63 percent of Americans said that so far they approve of President Bush. Not surprisingly, the other 37 percent are English teachers.

—Conan O'Brien

218. The role of government is to create an environment that encourages Hispanic-owned businesses, women-owned businesses, anybody-kind-of-owned businesses.

Mar. 19th, 2001

219. I assured the prime minister, my administration will work hard to lay the foundation of peace in the Middle—to work with our nations in the Middle East, give peace a chance.

Washington DC
Mar 20th, 2001

70

220.   Diseases...such as arthritis and osteoporosis can be less be-
        a, be-a-dilatating.

Mar. 21, 2001

221.   And one of the things I'm not going to forget where it comes
        from, I'm going to remember where it comes from.

Nat'l Newspaper Assoc. Conference
Washington DC
Mar 22nd, 2001

Political experts say President Bush was off his game.
He looked distracted, confused, a little at a loss for
words. Off his game? That is Bush's game.

- Jay Leno

222.   It's in your best interests, by the way, that we have a literate
        tomorrow. You're irrelevant if people can't read. And we need
        to start figuring out whether they can or cannot early in a
        child's career.

Nat'l Newspaper Assoc. Conference
Washington DC
Mar 22nd, 2001

223.   One of the biggest issues is changing the tone in our nation's
        capital. It's not really an issue like we know it.

Nat'l Newspaper Assoc. Conference
Washington DC
Mar 22nd, 2001

224.　I've coined new words, like, misunderstanding and Hispanically.

Radio-Television Correspondents Association
Washington DC
March 29th, 2001

225.　I hope to show Hispanics that Republicans do have a heart, but I also want to send a message to people from around the country as to how to pick up the Hispanic vote.

March 2001

Well, it's honest

226.　It would be helpful if we opened up ANWR. I think it's a mistake not to. And I would urge you all to travel up there and take a look at it and you can make the determination as to how beautiful that country is.

Argument for Oil Exploration in the
Arctic National Wildlife Refuge
Mar 29th, 2001

This morning, prompted by increasing concerns about terrorism, oil prices reached a record high as the cost of a barrel of crude is a whooping $44.34. Wow, it seems shocking that a product of finite supply gets more expensive the more we use it. ... Now the terror alert means higher oil prices, which oddly enough means higher profits for oil companies giving them more money to give to politicians whose policies may favor the oil companies such as raising the terror alert level. As Simba once told us — it's the circle of life.

-Jon Stewart

227.   The Senate needs to leave enough money in the proposed budget to not only reduce all marginal rates, but to eliminate the death tax, so that people who build up assets are able to transfer them from one generation to the next, regardless of a person's race.

Washington D.C.
April 5th, 2001

Race????

228.   This administration is doing everything we can to end the stalemate in an efficient way. We're making the right decisions to bring the solution to an end.

Washington, D.C.
Apr. 10, 2001

229.   It is time to set aside the old partisan bickering and finger-pointing and name-calling that comes from freeing parents to make different choices for their children.

Washington D.C.
April 12th, 2001

> I hope that someday we will be able to put away our fears and prejudices and just laugh at people.
> - Jack Handy

230.   We must have the attitude that every child in America -- regardless of where they're raised or how they're born -- can learn.

New Britain Connecticut
Apr. 18[th]2001

231. It's very important for folks to understand that when there's more trade, there's more commerce.

Quebec City PQ
April 21st, 2001

232. Neither in French nor in English nor in Mexican.

Quebec City Canada,
April 21st, 2001

233. Not all wisdom is in Washington, D.C., as witnessed by what took place up here.

Washington D.C.
Apr. 24th, 2001

> There was a scare in Washington when a man climbed over the White House wall and was arrested. This marks the first time a person has gotten into the White House unlawfully since...President Bush.
> —David Letterman
>
> Today the Secret Service said that at no time was President Bush ever in danger. In fact they said Bush didn't even hear the gunfire because he was sitting in his office popping bubble wrap all day.
> —Jay Leno

234. First, we would not accept a treaty that would not have been ratified, nor a treaty that I thought made sense for the country.

On the Kyoto Accord
Washington Post
Apr. 24th, 2001

74

235. I am a living example of someone who took on an issue and benefited from it.

John King of CNN
Apr. 25th, 2001

I, for one, appreciate his candor

236. There are some times when a president shows up that can make a situation worse... And, you know, I'm adverse to a camera. On the other hand, I think the president can either help or not help a situation, and I'll just have to make a judgment call each time.

John King of CNN,
Apr. 25, 2001

Various anti-Bush groups plan to protest his inauguration by lining the streets and turning their backs to his motorcade. You know it's not going to work though because he's going to get out to see what they're all looking at.

-Amy Poehler SNL

237. John, we're going to get a good bill. I mean, one of the things I've learned is not to try to negotiate with you or me on national TV.

To John King, CNN Interview
Apr. 25, 2001

238. Presidents, whether things are good or bad, get the blame. I understand that.

Washington D.C.,
May 11th, 2001

239.   There's no question that the minute I got elected, the storm
        clouds on the horizon were getting nearly directly overhead.

                            Washington D.C.
                            May 11, 2001

240.   For every fatal shooting, there are roughly three nonfatal
        shootings. Folks, this is unacceptable in America, We're
        going to do something about it.

                        Philadelphia Pennsylvania
                        May 14th, 2001

241.   Thirdly, the explorationists are willing to only move equipment
        during the winter, which means they'll be on ice roads, and
        remove the equipment as the ice begins to melt, so that the
        fragile tundra is protected.

                        Conestoga Pennsylvania.
                        May 18th, 2001

242.   If you're like me, you won't remember everything you did
        here. That can be a good thing.

                            Yale University
                            May 21st, 2001

I don't know a lot about politics, but I can recognize a
good party man when I see one
                                                    Mae West

243. I had no idea we had so many weapons. What do we need them for?

Commenting on America's
Nuclear Weapons System
May, 2001

244. If a person doesn't have the capacity that we all want that person to have, I suspect hope is in the far distant future, if at all.

Hispanic Scholarship Fund Institute,
Washington D.C.
May 22nd, 2001

245. It's important for young men and women who look at the Nebraska champs to understand that quality of life is more than just blocking shots

To the National Women's Volleyball Champs
from University of Nebraska I
Washington D.C.
May 31st, 2001

246. So on behalf of a well-oiled unit of people who came together to serve something greater than themselves, congratulations.

To the National Women's Volleyball Champs
from University of Nebraska I
Washington D.C.
May 31st, 2001

Ironically, this is the same speech Clinton gave to the
departing White House interns

247.   Our nation must come together to unite.

Tampa Florida
June 4th, 2001

Ninety eight percent of the adults in this country are
decent, hardworking, honest Americans. It's the other
lousy two percent that get all the publicity. But then,
we elected them.

- Lily Tomlin

The Washington Post reported that if you add up all the
time Bush has spent in Texas, he's there for a whole
month. Then you add up all the time he spends at Camp
David, and his parent's house in Maine and add up all
the travel time getting to and from these places, and it
adds up to 42 percent of his presidency.
In fact, he'd actually have to win a second term just to
complete his first term.

—Jay Leno

Even if the flag burning amendment does become law,
the larger problem will remain of how to respectfully
dispose of older, tattered flags. Well, fortunately the
U.S. official Flag Code has a suggestion about this.
Quote: 'The flag, when it is in such a condition that it is
no longer a fitting emblem of display, should be
destroyed in a dignified way, preferably by burning.'
Owwwwcchh. In response, the House Republicans are
calling for tattered flags to be kept alive via a feeding
tube.

-Jon Stewart

248. Anyway, I'm so thankful, and so gracious—I'm gracious that my brother Jeb is concerned about the hemisphere as well.

Miami Florida.
June 4th, 2001

The Hemisphere that Broke the Camel's Back

Look, here's the thing...
Bush uses the word hemisphere 5 times in this book and I would say he gives it a different meaning every time but, that's impossible to discern because ...even if we evaluate his sentences and decide "hemisphere" is a wild card that can carry any meaning we want, the fact remains that his statements still don't make any sense

Does Bush think "hemisphere" means something specific that is unfortunately (albeit humorously) incorrect?...

For example... if I suddenly started calling my telephone "pants"....Hey Adam, the pants are ringing can you take a message?.....You've been talking on those pants all night Mister, go do your homework....George called, he'd like you to pants him as soon as you get this message....it's urgent...please pants George immediately..

Or, does Bush use the word "hemisphere" as a generic placeholder....anytime he forgets a word, he just substitutes the word "hemisphere"....like so....

Continued.....

I'm so gracious that my brother Jeb is concerned about the pants as well

I assured the Prime Minister that my vision for the pants goes both north and south.

Lest we forget...

Natural gas is hemispheric. I like to call it hemispheric in nature because it is a product that we can find in our pants.

oh wait...
no....scratch that one...

Although I gotta give the guy credit for his tireless efforts to liberate English from the oppression of grammar and well, SANITY...I don't care who you kill, or who your Dad is... When did the rudimentary understanding of grammar and vocabulary become optional for a president?

P.S. - According to my local library, even if we made an organized and concerted worldwide effort to change the meaning of the word hemisphere, it's unlikely that Webster's Dictionary would automatically fall in line.. So, it will be years before Bush words like 'embetter', 'misunderestimated','suicider', 'ingrinable' and the newly ordained multifunctional 'hemisphere' will find their way into popular vocabulary and ultimately, a dictionary.

However, it was suggested by the librarian, that my picture may be featured under the definition of lunatic at some point in the not-so-distant future...

(I was shooting for crackpot but, it's still an honor just to be nominated).

I was so excited by the prospect that upon returning home, I promptly pantsed all my friends. .

249. I haven't had a chance to talk, but I'm confident we'll get a bill that I can live with if we don't.

McCain-Kennedy Patients' Bill of Rights
Brussels Belgium
June 13th, 2001

250. We spent a lot of time talking about Africa, as we should. Africa is a nation that suffers from incredible disease.

European Union Leaders Meeting,
Gothenburg Sweden,
June 14th, 2001

That gentleman has arrived there, and hopefully he is not as stupid as he seems, nor as mafia-like as his predecessors were.

—Fidel Castro on President Bush

---

251. The power that be, well most of the power that be, sits right here.

To Assembled Senators and House Members
Washington D.C.
June 18th, 2001

I could never be the president. Think about it. I've abused cocaine, I've been arrested, I'm not a very smart guy. It's a big joke to think people would want someone like me just because his dad was president.

—Charlie Sheen, asked on SNL if he'd ever like the job his father has on the West Wing

---

252.   I think [Ambassador Zoellick] deserves a lot of credit. But don't give him any until he describes exactly what he did to you.

Remarks to Agriculture Leaders
June 18th, 2001

> The men and women from the U.S. spy plane in China landed in Hawaii earlier today and George W. Bush, who is still pensive, said, yeah they are in Hawaii, but he is not going to rest until they are on U.S. soil.
> —David Letterman

253.   We cannot start Mitchell, the Mitchell plan, until the cycle of violence   has   been   crushed   and   broken.

Washington D.C.
June 20th, 2001

Proposing a smackdown on violence

254.   Well, there's some things I know today.

Black Music Month
June 29th, 2001

255.   BILL HANGLEY JR (PHILADELPHIA WRITER)
Mr. President, I hope you only serve four years. I'm very disappointed in your work so far.

BUSH
Who cares what you think?

July 4th, 2001

> It has been the political career of this man to begin with hypocrisy, proceed with arrogance, and finish with contempt
>
> - Thomas Paine

256. He knew what he believed, and he really kind of went after it in a way that seemed like a Texan to me.

Receiving a Bust of Winston Churchill
from Tony Blair Washington D.C.
July 16th, 2001

> Some people see things that are and ask, Why? Some people dream of things that never were and ask, Why not? Some people have to go to work and don't have time for all that ...
>
> - George Carlin

257. Sometimes Churchill will talk back, sometimes he won't, depending upon the stress of the moment, but he is a constant reminder of what a great leader is like.

Washington D.C.
July 16th, 2001

Did he happen to mention that telling the press that you have two-sided conversations with the disembodied bronze heads of the long-since-deceased might be something you should keep to yourself?...oh forget it!

258. I happen to believe missile defenses is important to keep the world more peaceful.

London England
July 19th, 2001

> If the human race wishes to have a prolonged and indefinite period of material prosperity, they have only got to behave in a peaceful and helpful way toward one another
>
> - Winston Churchill

259.   And the true threats of the 21st century are the ability for some rogue leader to say to the United States, to Europe, to Russia herself, to Israel, don't you dare move, don't you dare try to express your freedom, otherwise we'll blow you up.

BBC Interview
July 20th, 2001

260.   I look forward to seeing [Tony Blair] at Chequers. And we sat next to each other at my first EU luncheon - NATO luncheon - anyway, at the first luncheon with leaders I sat next to Tony. It was very comforting to sit next to a friend, kind of the new boy in class, you know - sat next to a friend. And he's easy to talk to, which is a high compliment when it comes from a Texan.

BBC Interview
July 20th, 2001

> Some sad news, President Bush's lapdog passed away. Gee, I didn't even know Tony Blair was sick
>
> —Jay Leno

261.   I know what I believe. I will continue to articulate what I believe and what I believe - I believe what I believe is right.

Rome Italy
July 22nd, 2001

> There are two things that are more difficult than making an after-dinner speech: climbing a wall which is leaning toward you and kissing a girl who is leaning away from you.
>
> - Winston Churchill

262. You saw the President yesterday. I thought he was very forward-leaning, as they say in diplomatic nuanced circles.

On Russian President Vladimir Putin,
Rome Italy
July 23rd, 2001

263. I realize that on July 4, you had the Dallas Cowboy Cheerleaders. I recognize I don't look quite as pretty -- but I am from Texas.

To U.S. Troops at Camp Bondsteel,
Kosovo, July 24th, 2001

> Today at the White House President Bush spoke to the astronauts who were orbiting the Earth on the space shuttle Discovery. Yeah, had a chat. Unfortunately the astronauts couldn't hear the president because he was standing on the White House lawn with a megaphone.
>
> -Conan O'Brien

264. A dictatorship would be a heck of a lot easier, there's no question about it.

July 26th, 2001

> The obscure we see eventually. The completely
> obvious, it seems, takes longer.
>
> > - Edward R Murrow

265. There's a lot of people in the Middle East who are desirous to get into the Mitchell process. And -- but first things first. The -- these terrorist acts and, you know, the responses have got to end in order for us to get the framework -- the groundwork -- not framework, the groundwork to discuss a framework for peace, to lay the -- all right.

Crawford Texas
Aug 13th, 2001

266. You can't pass a law that says 'thou shalt love thy neighbor' or 'you will be neighborly'. That's because America is full of just such decent people.

Crawford Texas
Aug 13th, 2001

> NEIGHBOR, n. One whom we are commanded to love as
> ourselves, and who does all he knows how to make us
> disobedient.
>
> > - Ambrose Bierce

267. My administration has been calling upon all the leaders in the - in the Middle East to do everything they can to stop the violence, to tell the different parties involved that peace will never happen.

Crawford Texas
Aug 13th, 2001

86

268. One of the interesting initiatives we've taken in Washington,
D.C., is we've got these vampire-busting devices. A vampire
is a—a cell deal you can plug in the wall to charge your cell
phone.

Denver Colorado
Aug 14th, 2001

269. The suicide bombings have increased. There's too many of
them.

Albuquerque New Mexico
Aug. 15th, 2001

Apparently there is a "right" amount?

270. ... One of the things that impressed me, besides people's
friendliness, is the number of people that said, I pray for you
and your family. For those of you that do that, thanks. It really
is something unique about America -- you don't have to show
me the party registration card.

Harley Davidson Factory
Menomonee Falls Wisconsin
Aug. 21st, 2001

271. You'll hear people say it's racist to test. Folks, it's racist not to test. Because guess who gets shuffled through the system oftentimes? Children whose parents don't speak English as a first language, inner-city kids. It's so much easier to quit on somebody than to remediate

Independence Montana
Aug. 21st, 2001

272. One of the interesting things to do is drink coffee and watch Barney chase armadillos. The armadillos are out, and they love to root in our flower bed. It's good that Barney routs them out of their rooting.

To Judy Keen USA Today
Aug. 22nd, 2001

273. Look up the word. I don't know, maybe I made it up. Anyway, it's an arbo-tree-ist, somebody who knows about trees

USA Today
Aug 22nd, 2001

If trees could scream, would we be so cavalier about cutting them down? We might, if they screamed all the time, for no good reason.

- Jack Handy

274.   In order to go to college or realize your dreams, you have to make right choices in life. As you grow up, you've got to learn to say yes to the good things and no to the bad things, like saying no to drugs. That's going to be important in order to realize your dreams. No to alcohol, excessive alcohol. You've got to learn to make the right choices when you get older.

Crawford Elementary School
Aug. 23rd, 2001

We've got drunk and drunker running here. I say we vote for Bush and Cheney just to get them off the damn highway.

—Jay Leno
On the Bush & Cheney DUI convictions

---

275.   I've seen fox in here, I've seen all kinds of birds. It's a wonderful spot to come up in here and just kind of think about the budget.

Prairie Chapel Ranch
Craword Texas
Aug. 25th, 2001

276.   Thank you from the bottom of my heart for walking across the street when you see somebody in your neighborhood who needs a helping hand.

Pittsburgh Pennsylvania
Aug 26th, 2001

277.   If you've been laid off from work, you're 100 percent unemployed.

Kaukauna Wisconsin
Sept 3rd, 2001

Chapter Three

Misunderestimations

I'm not concerned about all Hell breaking loose, but that a part of Hell will break loose - it'll be much harder to detect

George Carlin

> Bush - I was not elected to serve one party.
> (video overlay)
> Stewart - You were not elected.
> Bush - I have something else to ask you, to ask every
> American. I ask you to pray for this great nation
> Stewart - We're way ahead of you.
>
> - Jon Stewart

278.   My administration has a job to do... We will rid the world of evildoers.

Washington D.C.
Sept. 16th, 2001

Government just took on a dramatic new job...time for long underwear and a stylish cape perhaps?

279.   The American people are going to have to be more patient than ever with the efforts of not just ourselves, but the efforts of our allies, to get them running and to find them and to hunt them down.

Pentagon
Sept 17th, 2001

Hunting down the Allies

93

280.　REPORTER:
Do you want bin Laden dead?

BUSH:
I want justice. There's an old poster out west, as I recall, that said, Wanted: Dead or Alive.

Washington D.C.
Sept. 18th, 2001

> I don't know where bin Laden is. I have no idea and really don't care. It's not that important. It's not our priority.
>
> - President George W

281.　Nobody can threaten this country. Oh, they may be able to bomb a buildings...

Speech to Congress
Washington D.C.
Sept 20th, 2001

> More bad news for the Taliban. Remember how they are promised 72 virgins when they die? Turns out that it's only one 72-year-old virgin.
>
> —Jay Leno

282.　The people who did this act on America and who may be planning further acts are evil people... They're flat evil. All they can think about is evil. And as a nation of good folks, we're going to hunt them down, and we're going to find them, and we will bring them to justice. Ours is a nation that does not seek revenge, but we do seek justice.

To FBI Employees
Sept. 25th, 2001

94

> Let justice be done, though the heavens fall
>
> - Lord Mansfield

283. Oh, isolating the Taliban? Well, I think most people in the world understand that I was very serious, and they're serious, when we say if you harbor a terrorist, you're just as guilty as the terrorist. That's pretty isolated, it seems like to me.

Press Conference
Sept. 25th, 2001

> Know what the Taliban leaders like to do for fun? Just sit around and get bombed.
>
> —Jay Leno

284. And in order to make sure that we're able to conduct a winning victory, we've got to have the best intelligence we can possibly have. And my report to the nation is we've got the best intelligence we can possibly have.

Sept. 26th, 2001

> Earlier this week Congress began investigating these intelligence failures at the FBI and the CIA. They say the hearings will last less than a month and cost $5 million. This is what I love about Congress. Terrorists attack the United States, they investigate it for three weeks, spend $5 million. Have sex with an intern: three years, $40 million.
>
> —Jay Leno

285. And I'm here to thank everybody who loves America in this building.

To CIA Employees
Langley Virginia
Sept 26th, 2001

286. The folks who conducted this act on our country on September 11th made a big mistake. They misunderestimated the fact that we love a neighbor in need. They misunderestimated the compassion of our country. I think they misunderestimated the will and determination of the commander-in-chief, too.

To the CIA
Sept 26th, 2001

287. Some countries may wanna participate in one way, but not in another. All we ask is that you participate. All we ask is that you use the same amounta effort the United States will to win this war against freedom, to win this battle against global terrorism.

Chicago Illinois
Sept. 27th, 2001

Recruiting support for his war on freedom.

288. We are fully committed to working with both sides to bring the level of terror down to an acceptable level for both.

Washington DC
Oct 2nd, 2001

What level of terror is considered acceptable?
rather....what color is it?

289.   And we'll be tough and resolute as we unite, to make sure freedom stands, to rout out evil, to say to our children and grandchildren, we were bold enough to act, without tiring, so that you can live in a great land and in a peaceful world. And there's no doubt in my mind, not one doubt in my mind, that we will fail.

Labor Department
Oct 4th, 2001

Well, as long as there aren't any doubts....

290.   At this Thursday, ticket counters and airplanes will fly outta Ronald Reagan Airport.

Press Conference
Oct 2nd, 2001

291.   If you see somebody who you don't know getting into a crop duster that doesn't belong to you, report them.

Press Conference
October 2001

292.   Our enemies fear a society which is pluralistic and open to worship an Almighty God.

White House
Oct 26th, 2001

The problem with writing about religion is that you run the risk of offending sincerely religious people, and then they come after you with machetes.

- Dave Barry

293.   The culture in our agencies have changed. We are now interested in preventing attack.

Remarks to Business, Trade and
Agriculture Leaders,
Oct. 26th, 2001

A day late and a dollar short perhaps?

294.   And how that -- what that means to the economy, it means that the -- it means that over time, our economy is going to be just as strong as the American spirit. And so I'm very optimistic about the economy. How long it will take to recover to the levels that we hope is just -- is beyond my pay grade.

Homeland Security Council
Oct 29th, 2001

> Al Gore says President Bush's economic plan has zero chance of working. Now, this raises on important question: Bush has an economic plan?
> —David Letterman

295.   We have a renewed appreciation of the character of America. We are a generous people, a thoughtful people who hurt.

Thomas Wootten High School
Rockville Maryland
Oct. 30th, 2001

296.   On one front is the home front.

Thomas Wootten High School
Rockville Maryland
Oct. 30th, 2001

98

297. We're united behind the fact that we must rise to this occasion.

National Association of Manufacturers
Oct 31st, 2001

298. After all, we're at war, and for the first time in our nation's history, part of the battlefront is here at home.

National Association of Manufacturers
Oct. 31, 2001

Somebody buy the President a history book

299. And we are fighting evil, and we will continue to fight evil, and we will not stop until we defeat evil.

White House
Nov. 2nd, 2001

May the forces of evil become confused on the way to your house.
-George Carlin

300. I'm proud to welcome [Nigerian] President Obasanjo back to the White House. We just had a very good visit. We discussed our mutual concern, our mutual desire.

White House
Nov 2nd, 2001

That normally costs $4.99/minute

301.   This is not an instant gratification war.

White House
Nov 2nd, 2001

What war is?

I hate war as only a soldier who has lived it can, only as
one who has seen its brutality, its futility, its stupidity.
                              - Dwight D Eisenhower

---

302.   This is a struggle that's going to take a while.... It's not one of
these Kodak moments. There is no moment to this. This is a
long struggle and a different kind of war.

Press Conference with Tony Blair,
Washington D.C.
Nov 7th, 2001

I don't believe that the big men, the politicians and the
capitalists alone are guilty of the war. Oh, no, the little
man is just as keen, otherwise the people of the world
would have risen in revolt long ago! There is an urge
and rage in people to destroy, to kill, to murder, and
until all mankind, without exception, undergoes a great
change, wars will be waged, everything that has been
built up, cultivated and grown, will be destroyed and
disfigured, after which mankind will have to begin all
over again.

                              - Ann Frank

---

303.   Do you have blacks, too?

Question to Brazilian President
Fernando Henrique Cardoso
Washington D.C.
Nov. 8th, 2001

100

304. You know, a lot of Americans never heard of the CDC. They're wondering what CDC means.

Nov 8th, 2001

"Center for Disease Control" Yep that's a real toughy.

305. You're the kind of guy I like to have in a foxhole with me.

To Russian President Putin
White House
Nov 13th, 2001

[Clip of President Bush addressing national guardsmen in Idaho]: "Nineteen individuals have served both as guardsmen and as president of the United States, and I'm proud to have been one."

Ah, the first rule of public speaking --
always start with a joke.

-Jon Stewart

---

306. I asked them the other day, would it be okay if I cut a 30-minute tape, a piece of propaganda, no questions, just here -- here it is, here's 30 minutes of me talking. Please run it, not only across your airwaves but run it internationally, if you don't mind. I've got something to say about the conflict and our fight against evil. They said, no, they're not going to do that. If I'm going to get on the news, they've got to ask me questions.

Press Conference with Russian
President Vladimir Putin,
Nov 13th, 2001

307. I think it was a -- I don't think it was -- I think it was, as I
understand it -- and again, the Secretary of Defense will be
briefing, the Defense Department will be briefing -- that it was
a facilitated rescue.

Bush's Crawford Ranch
Nov 14th, 2001

308. Secondly, is to make sure that the good hearts of the
American people and the Russian people, and people all over
the world, are affected. By that I mean that we get the aid to
the starving folks in Afghanistan.

Crawford High School
Crawford Texas
Nov 15th, 2001

309. I can assure you, when I was a senior in high school, I never
sat in an audience saying, gosh, if I work hard I'll be
President of the United States.

Crawford High School
Crawford Texas
Nov 15th, 2001

102

310.   And so one of the areas where I think the average Russian will realize that the stereotypes of America have changed is that it's a spirit of cooperation, not one-upmanship. That we now understand one plus one can equal three, as opposed to us and Russia we hope to be zero.

Crawford High School
Crawford Texas
Nov 15th, 2001

His foreign policy is as sound as his math

The White House is giving George W. Bush intelligence briefings. You know, some of these jokes just write themselves.

- David Letterman

---

311.   And terrorism and evil are common threats to both our governments, and will be tomorrow, as well as today, unless we do something about it now. And that's exactly what we're doing.

On Russia at Crawford High School
Crawford Texas
Nov 15th, 2001

312.   I can hear a guy breathing quite heavily. 'Mr President! Mr President! There's an unidentified aircraft heading toward the White House.' So we get out of bed. I'm actually in my running shorts with a T-shirt, old shoes.

Newsweek Interview
Nov 26th, 2001

Shoes in bed? Whatever works for ya

313.   I'm trying to absorb that knowledge. I have nobody to talk to. I'm sitting in the midst of a classroom with little kids, listening to a children's story... and I realize I'm the commander in chief and the country has just come under attack.

Newsweek Interview
Nov 26th, 2001

> The president finally explained why he sat in that classroom on 9/11 for 7 minutes after he was told the country was under attack. He said he was 'collecting his thoughts.' What a time to start a new hobby.
>
> —Bill Maher

314.   There's always a difference of opinion sometimes between the House and the Senate, whether it's at the state or federal level.

Town Hall Meeting Orlando Florida
Dec. 4th, 2001

315.   And we have a role in the government -- in the state government, in the federal government -- to provide immediate help as part of an economic security package, is to provide immediate help.

Town Hall Meeting Orlando Florida
Dec. 4th, 2001

316.   You know, I don't think there's ever going to be an end to evil.

Barbara Walters Interview
Dec. 4th, 2001

317. Jordan, I wasn't sure what to think at first. You know, I grew up in a period of time where the idea of America being under attack never entered my mind -- just like your Daddy's and Mother's mind probably. And I started thinking hard in that very brief period of time about what it meant to be under attack. I knew that when I got all of the facts that we were under attack, there would be hell to pay for attacking America.

Orlando Florida
Dec 4th, 2001

Explaining "Hell to pay" to 8 year olds.

318. We've got to make sure that the education system throughout the world provides people the needs to be able to provide work.

Barbara Walters Interview
Dec. 4th, 2001

319. The point I make is, by putting our troops in alert, obviously I was in a war mentality.

Barbara Walters Interview
Dec. 4th, 2001

The only real diplomacy ever performed by a diplomat is in deceiving their own people after their dumbness has got them into a war.

- Will Rogers

320.   Secondly, you need to pray for the good Lord to protect America, provide a shield over our country, to prevent us from harm.

Town Hall Meeting
Dec. 4th, 2001

> The State of the Union address was tonight. A little fun fact: Historians say that most presidents have begun their State of the Union address by saying 'The state of the union is strong.' ... However President Bush started his speech a little differently. He said 'the State of the Union is strongtastic' and then he wandered away, but they got him back.
>
> Conan O'Brien

321.   I believe that we're making -- taking everything we possibly can to -- I know we're doing everything we can to prevent further attacks.

Orlando Florida
Dec 4th 2001

322.   If we get any whiff, or any sniff that somebody is going to harm an American again, we're acting -- just the way you would want us to.

Town Hall Meeting
Dec. 4th, 2001

323.   I don't believe God picked who was going to be the President.

Barbara Walters Interview
Dec. 4th, 2001

106

In response to a request by the 9/11 commission the White House agreed to declassify the president's daily intelligence briefing from August 6th titled 'Bin Laden Determined to Attack Inside the United States.' The commission also wants to see the August 20th briefing, 'No Seriously Bin Laden Determined to Attack Inside the United States' and also from August 26th, 'Mr. President, Please Put Down the Game Boy, Bin Laden Determined to Attack Inside the United States.'

—Tina Fey SNL

324.   And I was sitting outside the classroom waiting to go in, and I saw an airplane hit the tower -- the TV was obviously on, and I use to fly myself, and I said, There's one terrible pilot.

Orlando Florida
Dec. 4th, 2001

Ignoring the fact that this attempt at humor is in decidedly poor taste and I find it unlikely that a TV equipped with cable was on in a school hallway...let's focus on the fact that there was no live footage available of the first plane hitting the tower until day 2...and we already have footage of him receiving the news of #2 while seated in the classroom.

325.   Far be it from me to try to put words in God's mouth.

Barbara Walters Interview
Dec. 4th, 2001

326.   He's a good man.

About the First Dog, Barney
Barbara Walters Interview
Dec. 4th, 2001

327.   The problem with the kind of federal approach and only
        federal approach is, is that we may encourage you to become
        trained in a job that doesn't exist. And so the real thing is, is
        there money available for job training? Is there money
        available from the federal government to say to Governor
        Bush of Florida, here is some dough. Set up a system that
        will actually match people with skills and jobs that exist.

Orlando Florida
Dec. 4th, 2001

> President Bush said that American workers will need
> new skills to get the new jobs in the 21st century. Some
> of the skills they're going to need are Spanish, Chinese,
> Korean, because that's where the jobs went. Who
> better than Bush as an example of what can happen
> when you take a job without any training.
>
> —Jay Leno

328.   I see women of cover here, and I want to thank you for
        coming from the Muslim community here in America.

Town Hall Meeting
Dec. 4th, 2001

329.   I'll never forget the story of people in a Midwestern city, when
        they heard me on TV talk about how distressed I was that
        women of cover would not leave their homes, for fear of some
        other American treating them harshly, and then Jewish
        citizens and Christians alike, getting on the phone, and
        saying, we want to help you. We want to take you to the
        neighborhood store. This isn't the America we know.

Town Hall Meeting
Dec. 4th, 2001

330.   They wear boots in other places.

Barbara Walters Interview
Dec. 4th, 2001

Oh God, I'm afraid to ask...also kinda curious
...but, definitely afraid to ask

331.   And, finally, next Tuesday our nation will play the National Anthem at 8:34 a.m. eastern standard time. We will do so, and we're encouraging other nations to play their anthems and/or appropriate tunes at about the same time or an appropriate time, to send this clear signal to the terrorists.

With Norwegian Prime Minister
Dec. 5th, 2001

332.   The Anthem will be played at 8:46 a.m. I wanted to correct the time, so that as we prepare this reminder about the evil, and as we stand fast against terror, that we've got the correct time that we're going to do so.

With Norwegian Prime Minister
Dec. 5th, 2001

> Not only do I not know what's going on, I wouldn't know what to do about it if I did
>
> - George Carlin

333.   I couldn't imagine somebody like Osama bin Laden understanding the joy of Hanukkah.

White House
Dec. 10th, 2001

109

334. The American people must understand that I have no timetable in mind. There's no - I don't have a calendar that says, 'Gosh, if he's not gotten by this certain moment, then I'll be disappointed.'

Meeting with Thai Prime Minister
Dec. 13th, 2001

> Politicians are people who, when they see light at the end of the tunnel, go out and buy some more tunnel.
>
> - John Quinton

335. Dr. Rice is not only a -- brilliant person, she is a -- experienced person.

Dec. 17th, 2001

> Condoleezza Rice brings an impressive resume to her new job. The granddaughter of a cotton farmer, the former provost of Stanford University, she is fluent in four languages, an accomplished classical pianist, and even an expert figure skater. Wow, it seems like the only thing she can't do is make peace with other nations.
>
> —Jon Stewart

336. REPORTER:
Mr. President, can you tell us where you are, sir, on your deliberations over John Walker, and have you ruled out a charge of treason?

BUSH:
I'm heading into the Oval Office.

White House
Dec. 20th, 2001

110

337.   It must be hard to describe how to cause people to love one another.

Washington D.C.
Dec. 20th, 2001

The Pentagon Reveals Rejected Chemical Weapons

New Scientist Print Edition.
January 15. 2005

THE Pentagon considered developing a host of non-lethal chemical weapons that would disrupt discipline and morale among enemy troops, newly declassified documents reveal.

Most bizarre among the plans was one for the development of an "aphrodisiac" chemical weapon that would make enemy soldiers sexually irresistible to each other. Provoking widespread homosexual behaviour among troops would cause a "distasteful but completely non-lethal" blow to morale, the proposal says.

Other ideas included chemical weapons that attract swarms of enraged wasps or angry rats to troop positions, making them uninhabitable. Another was to develop a chemical that caused "severe and lasting halitosis", making it easy to identify guerrillas trying to blend in with civilians. There was also the idea of making troops' skin unbearably sensitive to sunlight.

The proposals, from the US Air Force Wright Laboratory in Dayton, Ohio, date from 1994. The lab sought Pentagon funding for research into what it called "harassing, annoying and 'bad guy'-identifying chemicals". The plans have been posted online by the Sunshine Project, an organisation that exposes research into chemical and biological weapons.

338. But Tommy said, this war -- the phase of this war is kind of like a baseball game. Of course, my ears perked up.

Washington D.C.
Dec. 21ˢᵗ, 2001

We are all born ignorant, but one must work hard to remain stupid.

- Benjamin Franklin

---

339. The border here has got a little Texan in it.

Describing New Carpet in the Oval Office
Dec. 21ˢᵗ, 2001

Does your little Texan have a name?

340. I'm real proud of how the administration and our government has responded to the attacks on America. Got a good strategy in the first phase of the war, to rout terror.

Dec. 21ˢᵗ, 2001

341. Every morning I come into the desk, and I would read the threat assessments to America.

Dec. 21ˢᵗ, 2001

Is Paris burning?

- Adolf Hitler

---

342.   We're looking at border policies, both with Canada and with Mexico. And we'll continue doing what we're doing now, which is any time we get a lead, we're going to disrupt -- we're going to bring them in and give them a chance to protect Americans.

Crawford Texas
Dec. 31st, 2001

343.   Over 50 percent of our energy comes from overseas. Fortunately, a lot of it comes from Canada

Jan. 5th, 2002

I get to go to lots of overseas places, like Canada
                                            - Britney Spears

---

344.   Not over my dead body will they raise your taxes.

Jan. 5th, 2002

345.   I've been to war. I've raised twins. If I had a choice, I'd rather go to war.

Jan. 27th, 2002

By profession I am a Soldier and take pride in that fact, but I am prouder to be a father

                                            - Douglas MacArthur

---

346.   I'm so honored that people came down from Tallahassee to say hello to Jeb's little -- big brother.

Daytona Beach Florida
Jan. 30^{tht}, 2002

347.   The enemy hit us. As I like to kind of tease the enemy, they must have been watching too much daytime TV. They thought we were soft. They thought we were materialistic. They thought we wouldn't fight for what we believed. They thought we would cower in the face of terror. And my, my, are they wrong.

Daytona Beach Florida
Jan. 30^{tht}, 2002

348.   And if you don't have a place, we've started what's called the USA Freedom Corps. It's a chance for retired police officers or fired off -- firemen to help out the local law enforcement authorities to be on alert. That's why we're going to hold people account.

Daytona Beach Florida
Jan. 30^{tht}, 2002

Huh?

I would not say that the future is necessarily less predictable than the past. I think the past was not predictable when it started
- Donald Rumsfeld

Huh?

114

349.   I'm a baseball fan, I want a scorecard.... And I actually got a
chart. There's an 'X' right there.

Feb. 3rd, 2002

*Bush pointing out the 'X' placed on al-Qaeda military chief
Muhammad Atef's picture, who had just died in U.S. bombing*

President George W. Bush will appear tonight on Bob
Costas' show talking about baseball. Finally, a subject
he knows something about. Bush is a huge baseball fan
— well, duh. A sport where millionaires work two hours
a day? That's the story of his life.

—Jay Leno

350.   Part of having a secure homeland is to have a good airport
system, that's safe for people to travel, an airport system that
is inspecting bags by inspectors who are qualified to inspect
bags.

Pittsburgh Pennsylvania
Feb. 5th, 2002

351.   You know, the enemy hit us, and they said, oh, this great
country is going to wilt. They're not great, they're weak. I like
to needle them by saying, they must have been watching too
much daytime TV.

University of Pittsburgh
Feb. 5th, 2002

> Yesterday was Groundhog Day and the State of the Union Address. It is an ironic juxtaposition: one involves a meaningless ritual in which we look to a creature of little intelligence for prognostication and the other involves a rodent.
>
> - Air America Radio

352.   This nation is in the process, I believe, of ushering in a period where we said each of us are responsible for the decisions we make in life.

New York City
Feb. 6th, 2002

Ironic statement, considering the source.

353.   By being active citizens in your church or your synagogue, or for those Muslims, in your mosque, and adhering to the admission to love a neighbor just like you'd like to be loved yourself, that's how we can stand up.

Cattle Industry Annual Convention
Denver Colorado
Feb. 8th, 2002

354.   As a result of hardening the homeland against a bioterrorist attack with first-time responders, our neighborhoods will be ultimately safer for crime.

Denver Colorado
Feb. 8th, 2002

116

355.   I understand how risky agriculture can be. It wouldn't be so risky if we could control the weather. That's one of the things we haven't figured out how to do yet. It wouldn't be so risky if we could make it rain all the time. There would be hay to feed the cows. Somehow, that doesn't happen all the time. I know.

Cattle Industry Annual Convention
Denver Colorado
Feb. 8th, 2002

> Scientists tell us that the fastest animal on earth, with a top speed of 120 feet per second, is a cow that has been dropped out of a helicopter.
>
> - Dave Barry

356.   We expect there to be transparency. People who have something to hide make us nervous.

Anchorage Alaska
Feb. 16th, 2002

> The issue of Kerry's military service has spawned a number of recent news-like events which have led to Republican charges the decorated war hero has something to hide. Because if there is one thing the Bush administration will not tolerate, it is ... other people's secrecy.
>
> -Jon Stewart

117

357.   My trip to Asia begins here in Japan for an important reason. It begins here because for a century and a half now, America and Japan have formed one of the great and enduring alliances of modern times. From that alliance has come an era of peace in the Pacific.

Tokyo Japan
Feb. 18th, 2002

150 years of peace? What about WWII?

358.   Imagine how less dependent America will be on foreign sources of energy, and how more easy it'll be to clean up our air.

Washington D.C.
Feb. 25th, 2002

Cheney's Energy Plan
March 2001

Documents released under America's Freedom of Information Act reveal that an energy task force led by Vice President Dick Cheney was examining Iraq's oil assets two years before the latest war began...The 16 pages, dated March 2001, show maps of Iraq oil fields, pipelines, refineries and terminals. A document titled Foreign Suitors for Iraqi Oilfield Contracts is also included, listing which countries were keen to do business with Saddam's regime.

English, Simon,Telegraph (London, 7/23/2003)

---

359.   You know, I was campaigning in Chicago and somebody
        asked me, is there ever any time where the budget might
        have to go into deficit? I said only if we were at war or had a
        national emergency or were in recession. Little did I realize
        we'd get the trifecta.

Charlotte North Carolina
Feb. 27th, 2002

Washington Post - July 2, 2002

**A Sound Bite So Good, the President Wishes He Had
Said It - by Dana Milbank**

In this space last week, it was noted that President
Bush often tells audiences that he promised during the
2000 presidential campaign that he would allow the
federal budget to go into deficit in times of war,
recession or national emergency, but he never imagined
he would "have a trifecta." Nobody inside or outside the
White House, however, had been able to produce
evidence that Bush actually said this during the
campaign.

Now comes information that the three caveats were
uttered before the 2000 campaign -- by Bush's
Democratic opponent, Vice President Al Gore. The
Post's Glenn Kessler found in the archives this promise
from Gore: "Barring an economic reversal, a national
emergency, or a foreign crisis, we should balance the
budget this year, next year, and every year." Gore said
that to the Economic Club of Detroit in May 1998, then
repeated it at least twice more, in speeches in June
and November of that year.

360. You're going to hear the statisticians, the number crunchers, the bean counters -- as we call them in Texas -- say this might have been a recession, this might not have been a recession, this, that and the other. Well, when they do that, they get crossways with the Bush boys.

St. Pete Beach Florida
Mar. 8th, 2002

361. Look, I don't care about the numbers. I know the facts.

St. Petersburg Florida
Mar. 8th, 2002

> Democrats were quick to point out that President Bush's budget creates a 1 trillion dollar deficit. The White House quickly responded with 'Hey, look over there, it's Saddam Hussein.'
>
> —Craig Kilborn

362. I know they understand the proper role of government. And that is that government can't make people love one another.

Philadelphia Pennsylvania
Mar. 12th, 2002

363. We understand that Pennsylvania, like the other states in our Union, are full of compassionate people. And the job of government is to serve as a catalyst to capture that compassion.

Philadelphia Pennsylvania
Mar. 12th, 2002

I suggest bear traps

364.   You know, the enemy, when they hit America, didn't
        understand us. They didn't think we were a nation that could
        conceivably sacrifice for something greater than ourself, that
        we were soft, that we were so self-absorbed and so
        materialistic that we wouldn't defend anything we believed in.
        My, were they wrong. They missed -- they just were reading
        the wrong magazine, or watching the wrong Springer show.

White House
Mar. 12th, 2002

365.   We're a peaceful nation and moving along just right and just
        kind of having a time, and all of a sudden, we get attacked
        and now we're at war, but we're at war to keep the peace.

White House
Mar. 13th, 2002

366.   So I don't know where he is. You know, I just don't spend that much time on him... We haven't heard much from him. And I wouldn't necessarily say he's at the center of any command structure. And, again, I don't know where he is. I- I'll repeat what I said. I truly am not that concerned about him.

White House
Mar. 13th, 2002

On bin Laden

367.   There's nothing more deep than recognizing Israel's right to exist. That's the most deep thought of all. ... I can't think of anything more deep than that right.

Washington D.C.
Mar. 13th, 2002

122

368.   At the beginning of this war, I made it very clear -- as clear as a fellow from Texas could make it -- either you're with us or you're against us.

Fayetteville North Carolina
Mar. 15th, 2002

> New Rule: If everybody was wrong about the weapons of mass destruction, then somebody has to say, 'My bad.' ... For some reason, the two words this president just can't seem to say are 'sorry' and 'nuclear.'
> Something is terribly wrong when the only person who has been fired over terrorism is me.
>
> —Bill Maher

369.   Now I'm going to eat my lasagna. If it gets cold you have to eat the lasagna.

Fort. Bragg North Carolina
Mar. 15th, 2002

370.   Well, first of all, I knew our troops were good because I've been reading reports about how good they are.

Fort. Bragg North Carolina
Mar. 15th, 2002

371.   I talked about making the death tax permanent, so that Rolf can pass his assets to a family member, if he so chooses.

O'Fallon Missouri
Mar. 18th, 2002

Or if that doesn't work, try repealing the death tax

123

372. Listen, we caught a bunch of them bunched up the other day. And they're not bunched up any more.

O'Fallon Missouri
Mar. 18ᵗʰ, 2002

The Commander-in-Chief describes
complicated military maneuvers.

This Iraqi intelligence scandal is growing. Americans are asking, 'What did President Bush not know?' and 'When did he mispronounce it?'

—Craig Kilborn

373. High taxes is a road block.

O'Fallon Missouri
Mar. 18ᵗʰ, 2002

President Bush released his new $2.4 trillion federal budget. It has two parts: smoke and mirrors.

—Jay Leno

374. Let me see if I can put this into English, or Texan.

O'Fallon Missouri
Mar. 18ᵗʰ, 2002

Bush joked last week during his meeting with Schwarzenegger that they are both sometimes accused of misspeaking the language. Mr. President, he's from a foreign country.

—Jon Stewart

124

375. We've got pockets of persistent poverty in our society, which I refuse to declare defeat—I mean, I refuse to allow them to continue on. And so one of the things that we're trying to do is to encourage a faith-based initiative to spread its wings all across America, to be able to capture this great compassionate spirit.

O'Fallon, Missouri.
Mar. 18, 2002

Wanna catch the spirit? Who you gonna call? Ghostbusters!

376. The enemy must have thought they were hitting a society that was so soft, so self-absorbed, so materialistic that we would sue them.

Missouri Republican Party Dinner,
St. Louis Missouri
Mar. 19th, 2002

377. There is no cave deep enough for the justice of the United States of America.

Missouri Republican Party Dinner,
St. Louis Missouri
Mar. 19th, 2002

A lot of controversy over this possible invasion of Iraq. In fact, Nelson Mandela was so upset, he called Bush's dad. How embarrassing, when world leaders start calling your father.

—Jay Leno

125

378.   There's no doubt in my mind, Harold, that the American people will respond. And when they do, Laura and I will thank them from the bottom of my heart.

Samuel W. Tucker Elementary School
Alexandria Virginia
Mar. 20th, 2002

379.   You can help by helping build one of these school chests. It doesn't matter how you do it, how you raise the money. Just get it done.

Samuel W. Tucker Elementary School
Alexandria Virginia
Mar. 20th, 2002

Putting grade schoolers in their place…

380.   I don't want to hold two press conferences in one week.

Mar. 20th, 2002

> You can always count on Americans to do the right thing
> - after they've tried everything else.
>   - Winston Churchill

381.   And we will not relent to any terrorist who think they can take our freedom or the freedom from anybody else in the world away from us.

El Paso Texas
Mar. 21st, 2002

Read it twice if you have to…

126

382.   We don't take a bunch of polls and focus groups to tell us
        what -- to how to, to how to -- to what we ought to do in the
        world.

White House
Mar. 21st, 2002

383.   We're in for a long struggle, and I think Texans understand
        that. And so do Americans.

El Paso Texas
Mar. 21st, 2002

384.   Colin Powell has cobbled together one of the great coalitions
        ever, a coalition determined to fight terror wherever we find it.

El Paso Texas
Mar. 21st, 2002

Cobbled verb -
To put together clumsily; bungle

385.   And there will be -- I take it back. It will be a signature -- I
        won't hesitate. It will probably take about -- you know, about
        three seconds to get to the W, I may hesitate on the period,
        and then rip through the Bush.

On signing his name
Washington D.C.
Mar. 24th, 2002

386.   It is awfully hard to realize there can be peace in a place like the Middle East.

Georgia Institute of Technology
Atlanta Georgia
Mar. 27th, 2002

387.   I mean, after all, you might remember that some of the initial discussions after September the 11th about potential threat was about crop dusters. Now, they don't have a lot of crop dusters, you know, in Manhattan. They've got a lot of crop dusters in South Carolina or Texas. In other words, some of the intelligence we were getting was that not only were the enemy willing to use airplanes, obviously, as weapons, but what we were concerned about was that they would use other methods -- like using a crop duster to spray a weapons of mass destruction, if possible. It's an indication that we had to be on alert to defend all sites and all locations in our country.

Greenville South Carolina
Mar. 27th, 2002

> I don't know what the facts are but somebody's certainly going to sit down with him and find out what he knows that they may not know, and make sure he knows what they know that he may not know.
>
> - Donald Rumsfeld

388.   While we have held the doctrine in Afghanistan -- the doctrine of thou shall not harbor a terrorist -- there still are killers running loose. There just are.

Greenville South Carolina
Mar. 27th, 200

389.   I appreciate so very much Tom Ridge's service. You know, he was a governor there in Pennsylvania, just kind of cruising along.

Greenville South Carolina
Mar. 27th, 200

> Homeland Security Chief Tom Ridge made that critical leap from 'be afraid' to 'be very afraid,' raising the terrorist threat level to orange for financial sectors in New York, Washington, D.C., and northern New Jersey. ... Ridge's announcement comes amidst reports he will step down as head of homeland security after the election. Ridge himself has refused to comment on the story, though colleagues say he has often expressed a desire to spend more time at home, scaring his family.
>
> -Jon Stewart

390.   I see a peaceful world, I do. The rest of the world watches us very carefully. I like to say, If the United States blinks, they'll go to sleep. We're not going to blink.

Republican Party Luncheon
Dallas Texas
Mar. 29th, 2002

Why do you like to say that?

391.   Everybody in Crawford says hello, starting with Laura. She is doing a fabulous day. I tell people it's because she's from Midland, Texas.

Dallas Texas
Mar. 29th, 2002

Why do you do that?

129

> I believe what I said yesterday. I don't know what I said, but I know what I think, and, well, I assume it's what I said
>
> - Donald Rumsfeld

392. But there needs to be a focused, coalition effort in the region against peace -- I mean, against terror for peace.

Crawford Texas
Mar. 30th, 2002

393. BUSH:
The people of New York are discerning voters. Well, most of the time they're discerning voters. If you know what I mean.

REPORTER:
No, what do you mean?

BUSH:
Well, you're a smart guy. Read between the lines.

Event honoring New York Governor George Pataki and New
York City Mayor Michael Bloomberg -
White House, Apr. 1st, 2002

394. Sometimes when I sleep at night I think of Hop on Pop.

Pennsylvania State University
Apr. 2nd, 2002

If you don't know, Hop on Pop is a Dr. Seuss book suitable
for children ages 2-5 yrs (5 is pushing it somewhat). My son
had me read it every night for 2 months when he was around
18 months old. But, then he became more sophisticated and
the childish pursuits no longer appealed, he moved on to One
Fish Two Fish and learned to use the potty. Way to 'go', Mr
President!

130

395.   In order for all Americans to realize the American Dream, you've got to make sure every child has the necessary foundation to be good readers, good writers, good comprehenders.

Pennsylvania State University
Apr. 2nd, 2002

> As you know President Bush gave his State of the Union Address, interrupted 70 times by applause and 45 times by really big words.
>
> —Jay Leno

396.   My mom often used to say, The trouble with W -- although she didn't put that to words.

White House
Apr. 3rd, 2002

397.   The invisible part of everything that you thought you could see, you can't see.

Interview with ITN
Crawford Texas
Apr. 5th, 2002

> You know what really makes this embarrassing? The other day the president said the leaders in Iraq are 'ready to take off the training wheels.' That's what he said, 'take off the training wheels.' Then he goes out and falls off his bicycle. And they wonder why the rest of the world doesn't take us seriously.
>
> —Jay Leno

398.   Far be it from the American President to get to decide who
        leads what country... I made up my mind that Saddam needs
        to go.

                        Interview with ITN
                        Crawford Texas
                        Apr. 5th, 2002

Since the general civilization of mankind, I believe
there are more instances of the abridgment of the
freedom of the people by gradual and silent
encroachments of those in power than by violent and
sudden usurpation

                                        - James Madison

---

399.   We share a vision of two states, Israel and Palestine, living
        side by side in peace and insecurity.

                        New York Times
                        Apr. 6th, 2002

400.   BUSH:
        Maybe I should be a little less direct and be a little more
        nuanced, and say we support regime change.

        REPORTER:
        That's a change though, isn't it, a change in policy?

        BUSH:
        No, it's really not. Regime change was the policy of my
        predecessor, as well.

        REPORTER:
        And your father?

        BUSH:
        You know, I can't remember that far back. It's certainly the
        policy of my administration. I think regime change sounds a

lot more civil, doesn't it? The world would be better off without him. Let me put it that way, though. And so will the future.

Press conference with Tony Blair
Crawford Texas
Apr. 6th, 2002

What the Bush administration is primarily interested in is regime change in the United States, not regime change in Iraq or South East Asia or the Balkans. A foreign war is a wonderful lollipop to stuff in the mouth of a possibly quarrelsome press.

- Lewis H Lapham

---

401. The best way to fight evil is to do some good. Let me qualify that -- the best way to fight evil at home is to do some good. The best way to fight them abroad is to unleash the military. It is so important for citizens in this country to put a face on America for the world to see, the true face.

Knoxville Tennessee
Apr. 8th, 2002

I am not only a pacifist, but a militant pacifist. I am willing to fight for peace. Nothing will end war unless the people themselves refuse to go to war.

- Albert Einstein

---

402. This doesn't have nothing to do with reputation.

New York Times
Apr. 8th, 2002

403.   And so, in my State of the -- my State of the Union -- or state
        -- my speech to the -- nation, whatever you wanna call it,
        speech to the nation -- I asked Americans to give 4,000 years
        -- 4,000 hours over the next -- of the rest of your life -- of
        service to America. That's what I asked. I said 2 -- 4,000
        hours.

Bridgeport Connecticut
Apr. 9th 2002

Politics is a pendulum whose swings between anarchy
and tyranny are fueled by perpetually rejuvenated
illusions.

- Albert Einstein

404.   I'm a patient man, and so is the American people, much to
        the chagrin -- much to the chagrin of the enemy that still
        wants to take us on.

Bridgeport Connecticut
Apr. 9th 2002

405.   It would be a mistake for the United States Senate to allow
        any kind of human cloning to come out of that chamber.

Washington D.C.
Apr. 10th, 2002

Boy, he ain't kidding…

Today President Bush said he wants a ban on cloning.
Meanwhile, Attorney General Ashcroft said he wants a
ban on making humans the old-fashioned way.

—Conan O'Brien

134

Chapter Four

The Problem with the French

If this is a blessing, it is certainly very well disguised.

Winston Churchill

> The meaning of words had no longer the same relation to things, but was changed by them as they thought proper. Reckless daring was held to be loyal courage; prudent delay was the excuse of a coward; moderation was the disguise of unmanly weakness; to know everything was to do nothing. Frantic energy was the true quality of a man.
>
> - Thucydides
> History of the Peloponnesian War

Truer words are seldom spoken. As accurate today as it was in Ancient Greece

406.   I want to talk about three issues facing America. The first are homeland security.

Cedar Rapids Iowa
Apr. 15th, 2002

407.   The people who care more about the Iowa children when it comes to education, are Iowans, not people in Washington, D.C.

Cedar Rapids Iowa
Apr. 15th, 2002

Breaking it gently to Iowa. It's over! We don't like you anymore....so stop calling!..

408.   First, any time we commit a troop into action, that person must have the best equipment, the best training, the best possible -- the best pay possible.

Cedar Rapids Iowa
Apr. 15th, 2002

TROOPS IN IRAQ FACE PAY CUT
Pentagon says tough duty bonuses are budget buster
San Francisco Chronicle
Thursday August 14, 2003

Washington – The Pentagon wants to cut the pay of its 148,000 US troops in Iraq, who are already contending with guerrilla-style attacks, homesickness and 120 degree plus heat.

By the numbers
U.S. troops in Iraq: 148,000
U.S. troops in Afghanistan: 9,000
Imminent danger pay: $225/mo scheduled to drop to $150/mo Family separation allowances: $250/mo, scheduled to drop to $100/mo

---

409.   And that thing greater than ourselves is freedom. And that thing greater than ourselves is a country based upon fabulous values.

Cedar Rapids Iowa
Apr. 15th, 2002

Nothing wrong about this per se...it's just a queer
choice of adjective

138

410. I believe that one of these days we're going to have brand new types of cars that are going to make us less dependent on foreign sources of crude oil, and we'll be more better at cleaning our air.

Cedar Rapids Iowa
Apr. 15th, 2002

I'm feeling more better already

> The president was supposed to spend Earth Day at a national park in Tennessee, but it had to be canceled because there was a freak hail storm. So, instead, they had a photo op at the airport because nothing says conservation like an oil man standing in front of a 747.
> -Bill Maher

411. When the enemy hit, they not only killed a lot of innocent people, but they affected our economy. And it's one of the reasons I'm so proud we cut the taxes on the people who work.... I want to remind the people about what took place before September the 11th. Tax rebate checks started coming in the mail.

Cedar Rapids Iowa
Apr. 15th, 2002

412. I don't know what got in their mind on that day, when they attacked us. They must have thought this country of ours was so weak, and so materialistic, so self-absorbed, that all we would do would be to file a lawsuit.

Cedar Rapids Iowa
Apr. 15th, 2002

> The sound shivers through the walls, through the table, through the window frame, and into my finger. These distraction-oholics. These focus-ophobics. Old George Orwell got it backward. Big Brother isn't watching. He's singing and dancing. He's pulling rabbits out of a hat. Big Brother's holding your attention every moment you're awake. He's making sure you're always distracted. He's making sure you're fully absorbed... and this being fed, it's worse than being watched. With the world always filling you, no one has to worry about what's in your mind. With everyone's imagination atrophied, no one will ever be a threat to the world.
>
> - Chris Palahniuk

413. I don't have a calendar on my desk that says by a certain date, all this business has got to end. That's not how it works. That's what the enemy wants. They want us to quit, because we're impatient. But it's not going to happen. It can't happen. History has called us into action. We must never look back and say, how come we didn't act when there's called into action. We must be steadfast in that which we believe, and steady in our resolve. And I can assure you it doesn't matter whether you're a Republican or whether you're a Democrat, or whether you don't even give a darn about political parties.

Cedar Rapids Iowa
Apr. 15th, 2002

> The more you observe politics, the more you've got to admit that each party is worse than the other
>
> - Will Rogers

414.　And I've told world leaders: either you're with us or you're not
with us. And I mean every word of it. And they now know our
country means every word of it, as well.

Cedar Rapids Iowa
Apr. 15th, 2002

415.　One victim put it this way: They explained the defendant's
constitutional right to the Nth degree. They couldn't do this
and they couldn't do that because of his constitutional rights.
And I wondered what mine were. And they told me, I hadn't
got any. The guy sounded like he came from Texas.

Washington D.C.
Apr. 16th, 2002

416.　We've got money in our budget for first-time responders --
those are your police and your fire and your emergency
medical teams -- so that they can have a capacity to respond
to any emergency that may occur, if one does.

Washington D.C.
Apr. 16th, 2002

First Responders – highly trained emergency crews first on
site at major disasters/crises
First Time Responders – something decidedly less comforting

141

417.   And when they end up helping somebody who's been on welfare, they realize they're more help than the person they're trying to help.

Speech on Welfare Reform
White House
Apr. 18th, 2002

418.   I said, does she make a pretty good hand? -- that's Texan for Is she a good worker?

White House
Apr. 18th, 2002

419.   You know, people oftentimes ask me what can they do to help fight in the war against terror. Fire fighters answer that call every day.

White House
Apr. 18th, 2002

Ring Ring!

(answering) Fire Station!

Uhhh....hi, I was wondering what I can do to help fight in the war against terror?

You can start by not calling here anymore.
We are very busy!
It's not just fires you know, it's caring for the hoses ....

Wow you got Canadians over there?

...and Sparky the Dalmatian and all those beefcake calendars. What? Canadians?...what are you....(muttering) Jesus Christ...No, that's "hosers"...I said hoses. I don't know what you can do to help in the war on terror. But, I know I will feel more peaceful if you leave me alone. I've been answering these calls stupid calls everyday........

142

420.   I like to tell people, Laura and I are proud to be Texas -- own a Texas ranch, and for us, every day is Earth Day.

Wilmington New York
Apr. 22nd, 200

421.   This foreign policy stuff is a little frustrating.

New York Daily News,
April 23rd, 2002

Friends say that each day President Bush spends two hours playing video games. Now let's think about this -- there's a war in Iraq, gas prices have never been higher and what is he working on? Getting Spiderman to the third level. ...Yeah George loves video games. His favorite? Grand Theft Election.

- David Letterman

---

422.   The farm bill needs to get done quickly so that the farmers who are out there fixing to plant know what the rules of the game is.

Sioux Falls South Dakota
Apr. 24th, 2002

423.   And as to how to achieve that vision is something we must consult with our friends.

Meeting with Crown Prince of Saudi Arabia
Crawford Texas Apr. 25th, 2002

424.   BUSH:
Now I've got to go over to a friend-raiser.

REPORTER:
A friend-raiser?

BUSH:
Well, that's opposed to a fundraiser.

REPORTER:
What's a friend-raiser?

BUSH:
A friend-raiser? Well, it's a -- well, it's just kind of a cute way of saying I'm going to go over and see people and thank them for being a part of my campaign. And they actually get to do this for free. And I'm glad. But these will be people, evidently, from all around the country. I haven't seen the list, but I'm told that they are. And I look forward to thanking them-- it's really a way of thanking people, many of whom I -- I suspect I haven't seen since I've been the President. It's a nice, casual setting to say hello to people. And I'm looking forward to it.

Crawford Texas
Apr. 26th, 2002

425.   There are some Palestinians -- a lot of Palestinians who wonder whether or not life is worth living. And we've got, as a world, have got to help them understand there is a positive life ahead for they and their children.

Crawford Texas
Apr. 28th, 2002

Bush urges the entire world to band together and talk Palestine in off the ledge. I didn't even know they were depressed.

144

426. You know, in Washington there's a lot of -- there can be a lot of noise, a lot of shrill voices, people who are -- people up there sometimes are the ones who like to divide people into camps and call names and point fingers.

Albuquerque New Mexico
Apr. 29th 2002,

It's like gym class all over again...

427. To put it in Midland, Texas terms, any time we get a hint, we're following up on it.

Albuquerque New Mexico
Apr. 29th 2002,

> They claim now that President Bush spends two hours a day playing video games. ... Here's the good news -- that's two hours less that he spends being president.
> -David Letterman

428. I don't have a calendar on my desk, that beautiful desk, that says, by such-and-such a date, you will be finished. That's not how I think.

Los Angeles California
Apr. 29th, 2002

> President Bush said the other day the war is not about timetables. It's about winning. Hey, it worked in Florida.
> —Jay Leno

429.   I do not have a calendar on my desk that says, at such and such a time you will stop. You, President Bush, on such and such a date will have run out the string and it's time for you to quit -- that calendar doesn't exist. Because my mind-frame is this -- when it comes to defending our freedoms, no matter how long it takes, that's exactly what this country is going to do.

Albuquerque New Mexico
Apr. 29th, 2002

Flashback:

George W Bush comments on President Clinton's military action in Kosovo

I think it's also important for the president to lay out a timetable as to how long [U.S. troops] will be involved and when they will be withdrawn.

George W Bush
Seattle Post-Intelligencer
Jun. 5, 1999

Victory means exit strategy, and it's important for the president to explain to us what the exit strategy is.

- George W Bush
Houston Chronicle
Apr. 9, 1999

Ironic in hindsight...

---

430.   You see, the President is -- can still learn.

Los Angeles California
Apr. 29th, 2002

431.   The public education system in America is one of the most important foundations of our democracy. After all, it is where children from all over America learn to be responsible citizens, and learn to have the skills necessary to take advantage of our fantastic opportunistic society..

Santa Clara California
May 1st, 2002

Op·por·tun·is·tic (adj.)
Taking immediate advantage, often unethically, of any circumstance of possible benefit.

> Ambition is like a frog sitting on a Venus Flytrap. The flytrap can bite and bite, but it won't bother the frog because it only has little tiny plant teeth. But some other stuff could happen and it could be like ambition.
> - Jack Handy SNL

432.   And I sit there at this fantastic desk, called the H.M.S. Resolute.

The desk was crafted from the timbers of the H.M.S. Resolute and presented by Queen Victoria to the president in 1880. It is referred to as the Resolute Desk.
Santa Clara California
May 1st, 2002

433.   I'm grateful to all of you, who remind us that a great people must spend time on bended knee, in humility, searching for wisdom in the presence of the Almighty.

White House
May 2nd, 2002

Constitution – Shmonstitution...Separation of what now?
Church & State...woops

434.   Listen, I deeply hurt when there is a lack of hope for moms and dads of anybody.

Meeting with Prime Minister Sharon
Washington D.C.
May 7th, 2002

435.   And one of the things we've got to make sure that we do is anything.

Meeting with Prime Minister Sharon
Washington D.C.
May 7th, 2002

436.   Now, it's going to take a while -- it's going to take a while. But much to the chagrin -- I guess to the chagrin -- I haven't spent a lot of time talking with the enemy, but I got the feeling they're going to be disappointed to hear that we're going to remain united as a country.

Milwaukee Wisconsin
May 8th, 2002

> I guess I kinda lost control, because in the middle of the play I ran up and lit the evil puppet villain on fire. No, I didn't. Just kidding. I just said that to help illustrate one of the human emotions, which is freaking out. Another emotion is greed, as when you kill someone for money, or something like that. Another emotion is generosity, as when you pay someone double what he paid for his stupid puppet.
>
> - Jack Handy

148

437.   This isn't the kind of war that you're used to studying in the textbooks. This is the kind of war we've never seen before. We face a group of international killers -- and that's what they are -- who are a kind of -- hide in caves and they're not necessarily an organized government.

Milwaukee Wisconsin
May 8th, 2002

Every day we learn more and more about this wacky Osama bin Laden. He lives in a cave and at one time he was a womanizer. But now he has settled down with his five wives and 26 kids, so that's now all over. ... He also had a drinking problem at one time. I believe he went through 'Jihab'

—David Letterman

438.   We've got to trust the local people. We've got to trust the Andys, the teachers here. We've got to trust the Keiths, the principals all across the parents.

Milwaukee Wisconsin
May 8th, 2002

439.   As a matter of fact, the people who love the children in Wisconsin are the people of Wisconsin.

LaCrosse Wisconsin
May 8th, 2002

440.   With all due respect to the cameras, I hope you read more than you watch TV.

Clarke Street Elementary School
Milwaukee Wisconsin
May 8th, 2002

441. And, finally, in order to go to college, to meet the goal you've set, make sure you make right choices. Tell them, no, when somebody tries to say drugs are cool, or alcohol is good. Make the right choices. You'll be in college, and that's what we want.

Clarke Street Elementary School
Milwaukee Wisconsin
May 8th, 2002

> The true hypocrite is the one who ceases to perceive his deception, the one who lies with sincerity
> - Andre Gide

442. I'm here to talk about welfare reform, but I'm also here to make sure that the good people of Ohio send this good man back to the Governor's Mansion. There was a lot of reasons to send him back, but none greater than the fact that he married well.

Hyatt Regency Hotel
Columbus Ohio
May 10th, 2002

443. When it comes to our freedoms -- defending our freedoms -- and securing our homeland, and protecting our innocent Americans, and never forgetting what happened on September the 11th, we are some kind of tough.

Washington D.C.
May 14th, 2002

> Dictatorships start wars because they need external enemies to exert internal control over their own people.
> - Richard Perle

150

444.   You know, sometimes in Washington we actually are able to put our political parties aside and focus on what's best for the country. And we're able to say, let's make sure America comes -- is the first priority of all of us.

Washington D.C.
May 14th, 2002

I predict future happiness for Americans if they can prevent the government from wasting the labors of the people under the pretense of taking care of them.

- Thomas Jefferson

445.   We've got a vast coalition of nations that are still with us. They heard the message, either you're with us, or you're not with us. They're still with us.

Washington D.C.
May 14th, 2002

The coalition of the willing continues to grow. It is now an impressive group of 49 countries. Here's the thing, only four of those countries are actually supplying military forces in Iraq. The other 45 countries were like, willing yes, but about the able.

—Jon Stewart

446.   I want to tell you it's an honor to be here amongst people who dedicate their lives to the embetterment of our fellow human beings.

Washington D.C.
May 16th, 2002

151

447. We welcome all religions in America, all religions. We honor diversity in this country. We respect people's deep convictions. ...Since America's founding, prayer has reassured us that the hand of God is guiding the affairs of this nation. We have never asserted a special claim on His favor, yet we've always believed in God's presence in our lives. This has always been true.

Washington D.C.
May 16th, 2002

> When politics and religion are intermingled, a people is suffused with a sense of invulnerability, and gathering speed in their forward charge, they fail to see the cliff ahead of them
>
> - Frank Herbert

448. The last eight months have showed the world the American character is incredibly strong and confident. Yet prayer reminds us that a great people must be humble before God, searching for wisdom -- constantly searching for wisdom -- from the almighty Dios.

Washington D.C.
May 16th, 2002

449. Prayer is a vital part of our national life. ...Prayer and faith are an especially vital part of the life of Hispanos in este pais. ...The power of faith is found among the young, and that's good news, really good news. Ministers say that a revolucion espiritual is taking place amongst los jovenes Hispanos aqui.

Washington D.C.
May 16th, 2002

152

450. And there's nothing more powerful in helping change the country than the faith -- faith in Dios.

Washington D.C.
May 16th, 2002

451. This is a nation that loves our freedom, loves our country.

Washington D.C
May 17th, 2002

452. We're working with Chancellor Schröder on what's called 10-plus-10-over-10: $10 billion from the U.S.,$10 billion from other members of the G7 over a 10-year period, to help Russia securitize the dismantling—the dismantled nuclear warheads.

Berlin Germany
May 23rd, 2002

453. Sometimes things aren't exactly black and white when it comes to accounting procedures.

Commenting on SEC investigation into his
oil firm's accounting practices
Washington D.C.
July 8th, 2002

153

> Men occasionally stumble over the truth, but most of them pick themselves up and hurry off as if nothing had happened.
>
> - Winston Churchill

454.   REPORTER:
On Iraq, can the American people expect that by the end of your first term you will have affected a regime change in Iraq, one way or another? And by the same token --

BUSH:
That's hypothetical.

REPORTER:
But can the American people expect that? Should they expect that?

BUSH:
That's a hypothetical question. They can expect me not to answer hypothetical questions.

REPORTER:
On Osama bin Laden does your promise still --

BUSH:
On sensitive subjects. (Laughter.)

REPORTER:
Sir, on Osama bin Laden, does your promise still hold that he will be caught, dead or alive, at some point?

BUSH:
What? Say that again?

REPORTER:
Does your promise on -- or your goal of catching Osama bin Laden dead or alive, does that still stand?

BUSH:
I don't know if he is dead or alive, for starters -- so I'm going to answer your question with a hypothetical. Osama bin Laden, he may be alive. If he is, we'll get him. If he's not alive, we got him.

White House
July 8th, 2002

455. Secretary Powell has won the Presidential Medal of Freedom twice -- once with distinction. I'm not sure what happened the other time.

Washington D.C.
July 9th, 2002

456. REPORTER:
The NAACP is meeting this week in Houston, as you probably know. And there's been some criticism that you've not attended their convention since the 2000 campaign. How would you respond to that, and respond generally to suggestions from some critics that your civil rights record in the administration is not a stellar one?

BUSH:
Let's see. There I was, sitting around the leader with -- the table with foreign leaders, looking at Colin Powell and Condi Rice.

White House
July 9th, 2002

Ahhh yes, the "but some of my best friends are_____"
argument...a timeless classic

*I don't actually know, at this point, whether this is a literal
or figurative statement. Was their actual dog poop on the floor of
the Oval Office? Did the esteemed and decorated Secretary of
State actually have to pick it up? Either way, it's
an extraordinarily apt representation of the regard Bush
has for the office of the presidency.*

457. REPORTER:
The accounting procedures at Harken and Aloha have been
compared to what went on at Enron. Would you agree with
that?

BUSH:
No.

REPORTER:
Why not, sir?

BUSH:
Well, again, this is -- uhh -- there was no malfeance involved.
This was a honest disagreement about -- uhh -- accounting
procedures. And the SEC took a good look at it, and decided
that the procedures used by the auditors, and the accounting
firm -- needed to -- were not the right procedure in this
particular case, or the right -- ruling, and, therefore, asked
Harken to restate earnings, which it did. I mean, that's the
way the SEC works. That's the proper role of an oversight
group. There was no malfeance, no attempt to hide anything.

156

458.   It was just a accounting firm making a decision, along with the
        -- corporate officers, as to how to account for a complex
        transaction.

White House
July 9th, 2002

Dog Ate His Homework....Errr...
SEC Filing

Bush sold $848,560 worth of Harken stock one week
before the company posted poor quarterly earnings and
Harken stock plunged sharply. When Bush sold his
shares, he was a member of the company's audit
committee and engaged in company restructuring to
appease anxious creditors. This position gave Bush
detailed knowledge of the company's deteriorating
financial condition. The SEC received word of Bush's
trade eight months late. An internal memo showed that
company directors had been warned not to sell their
shares based upon inside information. Bush has said he
filed the notice but that it was lost.

The Washington Post later revealed Bush's former
personal attorney was the SEC general counsel at the
time the commission cleared him of wrongdoing.

---

459.   I also understand how tender the free enterprise system can
        be.

White House
July 9th, 2002

460.   Yet when a company uses deception -- deception accounting
        to hide reality, executives should lose all their compensation -
        - all their compensation -- gained by the deceit.

Wall Street
July 9th, 2002

461.   The problem with the French is that they don't have a word for 'entrepreneur.

Washington Post
July 10th, 2002

Entrepreneur – derived from the FRENCH word entreprendre, meaning to undertake

462.   You know, the threats we face are real. I mean, it is real. I like to remind people that I'm an early morning guy. I get to the Oval Office about -- oh, generally about 6:50 a.m. or so. It's not a very long commute (laughter). And I sit at the great desk that other Presidents have used -- Teddy and Frank, and -- I can call them that, since (laughter) -- and Spot the dog comes in with me, and I read a threat assessment.

Washington D.C.
July 10th, 2002

463.   I believe people have taken a step back and asked, What's important in life? You know, the bottom line and this corporate America stuff, is that important? Or is serving your neighbor, loving your neighbor like you'd like to be loved yourself?

Minneapolis Minnesota
July 11th, 2002

I'm sure Bush's buddy Ken Lay of Enron loves to love his neighbors just like he likes to be loved himself...but what will that mean when he goes to prison?

> First Enron, then Tyco and now WorldCom. How come all these companies are off billions in their accounting and nothing ever happens to them? If you bounce a $15 check at the Quickmart, the feds are at your door!
> —Jay Leno

464.   I'm sorry the room is so small. I suspect we could have accommodated a lot more people if we had a bigger room.

Washington D.C.
July 12th, 2002

> Yesterday at the White House, in the middle of an interview, President Bush jumped up out of his chair and started swatting at a housefly. When asked about it, the White House spokesperson said, 'Hey, that's nothing. You should see him chase a tennis ball.'
> —Conan O'Brien

465.	But the truth of the matter is, we can't pass a law that says you'll love your neighbor like yourself. And we can't pass a law that says you will be honest. We can pass laws that say, if you're not honest, we'll get you.

Birmingham Alabama
July 15th, 2002

How is that different from passing a law that says you will be honest? They can't pass a law that says you won't steal Frisbees. However, if you do steal Frisbees …they can "get you"….makes tons of sense.

466.	Of course, I like to remind people that Washington is full of all kinds of numbers crunchers. They talk about this number here, and that number there.

Birmingham Alabama
July 15th, 2002

> President Bush has chosen scientist Michael Griffin to be the new NASA administrator and he has ordered him to save the Hubble telescope and build a new manned space vehicle. It's kind of ironic isn't it? George Bush telling a rocket scientist what to do.
>
> - Jay Leno

467.	As well, in order for us to have the security we all want, America must get rid of the hangover that we now have as a result of the binge, the economic binge we just went through. We were in a land of -- there was endless profit, there was no tomorrow when it came to, you know, the stock markets and corporate profits. And now we're suffering a hangover for that binge.

Birmingham Alabama
July 15th, 2002

Finally! He's using his expertise

160

468.   So they started quoting these textbooks that said, when times
        are slow, raise taxes. When times are slow, don't let the
        people keep their money. The textbook I read says that if we
        let you have your own money, you'll decide to spend it on a
        good and service. And if you decide to spend it on the good
        and service, somebody will produce the good and service.
        And when somebody produces the good and service, it
        means somebody is going to find work.

Birmingham Alabama
July 15th, 2002

President Bush unveiled his new economic stimulus plan
this week. It was reported that if the plan passes the
president himself would save $44,000 in taxes, Dick
Cheney would save $327,000, and you could afford to
take the whole family down to Burger King to pick up
job applications.

—Tina Fey SNL

469.   The wars of the past had known battlefields and it was clear
        that such-and-such had to happen. There had to be an
        invasion in order to achieve this or that. This is a hunt for
        individuals. We're chasing down one person at a time. They
        were foolishly collected up at one point in time in the Sha-i-
        kot Mountains, and it was a tough chore. But our brave
        soldiers, along with coalition soldiers, were able to go in and
        score great success at bringing them to justice, as I like to put
        it.

Interview with Polish Journalists
Washington D.C.
July 15th, 2002

As he likes to put it....

470. And I think that's an important nuance, as we say, in foreign policy. I think that's the word, isn't it? Nuance?

White House
July 17th, 2002

471. [Responding to reporter] It's interesting you said the next phase of the war against terror. Almost every day is a new phase, in some ways, because we're reminding different countries which may be susceptible to al Qaeda, that you're either with us or against us. And so we're constantly working on bolstering confidence amongst some nations which may sometimes forget that either you're with us or you're with the terrorists. That's kind of a -- that's a phase, I guess you could say. Phase one was Afghanistan, phase two is to make sure that other countries don't become places for training or places where the al Qaeda think they can hide.

Press conference with President of Poland
White House
July 17th, 2002

It is not truth that matters, but victory

\- Adolf Hitler

472. Mr. President, the people of America are deeply grateful for your support and the support of the people of Poland. See, a lot of people in our country, and perhaps yours, wonder why would, why would an enemy -- by the way, nothing bunch of -- nothing but a bunch of cold-blooded killers -- strike America.

Directed to the President of Poland,
Rochester Michigan
July 18th, 2002

162

473.   When we landed our chopper out there on the playing fields --
        or some kinds of field -- I know it was a field -- we were met
        by two really fine Americans, Helen Suchara and Erin Chekal.
        Now they're here, and I want them to stand up here in a
        minute. But I want to describe to you their hearts.

                          Oakland University
                          Rochester Michigan
                          July 18th, 2002

474.   There are no calendars on our desks in Washington that say,
        by such and such a moment we've got to quit. That's not how
        we think, Mr. President, and you know that.

                    Directed to the President of Poland,
                          Oakland University
                          Rochester Michigan
                          July 18th, 2002

President Bush and Vice President Cheney have
officially conceded that Saddam Hussein did not have
weapons of mass destruction. And today the soldiers in
Iraq said, uh, can we come home now?

                                              - Jay Leno

---

475.   There's a lot of war talk these days, as there should be, but
        it's all aimed at making sure the world is peaceful.

                    Directed to the President of Poland,
                          Oakland University
                          Rochester Michigan
                          July 18th, 2002

476. I want to thank Tom Ridge for coming. He's a man -- I asked him, I said, you know, you need to serve your country. He was serving as the Governor of Pennsylvania. I said, you've got a nice mansion over there.

Argonne National Laboratory
Illinois July 22nd, 2002

Tom Ridge has set up a five-stage, color-coded system to warn Americans against threats. The colors are green, blue, yellow, orange and red. This is what the Republicans meant when they said they are trying to get more color in the party...This thing is so confusing. Yesterday the alert went from blue to pink; now half the country thinks we're pregnant.

—Jay Leno

477. It's important for people to understand, particularly in Washington, this Department of Homeland Security is not a good Republican idea, it's not a good Democrat idea, it's simply an American idea, and they need to get their work done.

Argonne National Laboratory
Illinois July 22nd, 2002

Yes, simply an American idea
....a bad idea, poorly executed

The Department of Homeland Security recommends a three-day supply of water consisting of one bottle per day for each person in your home. Plus one extra bottle to give you all something to kill each other over on day four.

—Jon Stewart

164

478. Anybody who goes into court and wins their case ought to get full economic damages. At the same time, we must prevent excessive awards that drive up costs, encourage frivolous lawsuits, and promote drawn-out legal proceedings. And that is why we need a reasonable federal limit on non-economic damages awarded in medical liability lawsuits, and the reasonable limit in my judgment ought to be $250,000.

Greensboro North Carolina
July 25th, 2002

Insurance-reform.org

April 7, 2003 - New Study Shows Insurance Industry, Not Lawsuits, Causing Insurance Rates to Rise.

I'm going to boil this down. They have known since 2003 that the problem lies with the insurance company's behavior and not high jury awards in malpractice suits. In fact, in "constant dollars" payouts for lawsuits have been decreasing for the last decade.

"Insurers, whose own investment actions have made insurance unaffordable and unavailable, are blaming others for their own mismanagement by manufacturing a crisis for surgeons and other doctors that simply should not exist. By increasing rates, insurers are forcing hospitals, doctors, and ultimately patients, to suffer for their poor business and investment decisions." - J. Robert Hunter, former Texas Insurance Commissioner and AIR co-founder.

The reason this issue comes up in the Senate repeatedly is that it gives Republicans the opportunity to put the bill's opponents into a position that looks as if they don't care about accessibility or quality of healthcare for regular people. It's an election year. This is about playing semantic games to win votes. This is politics. Don't be fooled!

479.   But the best way to protect the homeland is to hunt the killers down one by one and bring them to justice, and that's what this government is going to do

Greensboro North Carolina
July 25th, 2002

My only hope is when those terrorists get to heaven, they meet up with the kind of virgins we had in Catholic school: Sister Mike Ditka from Our Mother of Eternal Retribution.

—Robin Williams

Chapter Five
Jill Mahaffey Gets Lucky

Fighting for peace is like screwing for virginity

George Carlin

Start a small war. Pick a country where there is justification you can jump on, go ahead and invade.

- Dick Cheney, Chairman of the House
Republican Policy Committee
During Reagan Administration

BUSH WANTED TO INVADE IRAQ IF ELECTED IN 2000

GNN TV - Russ Baker
Oct 27, 2004

"Bush's circle of pre-election advisers had a fixation on the political capital that British Prime Minister Margaret Thatcher collected from the Falklands War. They were just absolutely blown away, just enthralled by the scenes of the troops coming back, of the boats, people throwing flowers at [Thatcher] and her getting these standing ovations in Parliament and making these magnificent speeches."

"According to Herskowitz, ...Bush and his advisers were sold on the idea that it was difficult for a president to accomplish an electoral agenda without the record-high approval numbers that accompany successful if modest wars."

In aggressive military action, he saw the opportunity to emerge from his father's shadow. The moment, Herskowitz said, came in the wake of the September 11 attacks. "Suddenly, he's at 91 percent in the polls, and he'd barely crawled out of the bunker."

Continued...

"He was thinking about invading Iraq in 1999," ..."It was on his mind. He said to me: 'One of the keys to being seen as a great leader is to be seen as a commander-in-chief.' And he said, 'My father had all this political capital built up when he drove the Iraqis out of Kuwait and he wasted it.' He said, 'If I have a chance to invade....if I had that much capital, I'm not going to waste it.'"

480.　People in America understand that we're into a different era, we're heading to a different culture. ...It means that you of course make a living for your family. But it also means that when you find a neighbor in need, you love that person.

West Ashley High School
Charleston South Carolina
July 29th, 2002

Do I advise you to love the neighbor? I suggest rather to escape from the neighbor and to love those who are the farthest away from you. Higher than the love for the neighbor is the love for the man who is distant and has still to come.

- Friedrich Nietzsche

Please don't let "love your neighbor" be limited by geography or polluted by fear or tainted by ignorance. Love your neighbors even when you don't understand them.

481.　Inherent in the 70 percent number means that we've got to help people at the same time.

West Ashley High School
Charleston South Carolina
July 29th, 2002

170

482.   And I just -- I cannot speak strongly enough about how we must collectively get after those who kill in the name of -- in the name of some kind of false religion.

Press Conference with
King Abdullah of Jordan
Aug. 1ˢᵗ, 2002

The tools of conquest do not necessarily come with bombs, and explosions, and fallout. There are weapons that are simply thoughts, ideas, prejudices, to be found only in the minds of men. For the record, prejudices can kill and suspicion can destroy. A thoughtless, frightened search for a scapegoat has a fallout all it's own for the children yet unborn. And the pity of it is, is that these things cannot be confined to the Twighlight Zone

- Rod Serling

483.   We must understand that the consequences we take to make the area more secure also, uh, must be in -- these decisions to make the area more secure must be made in the context of peace for the long run.

Press Conference with
King Abdullah of Jordan
Aug. 1ˢᵗ, 2002

484.   Today, through sonograms and other technology, we can clearly -- see clearly that unborn children are members of the human family, as well. They reflect our image, and they are created in God's own image.

Pittsburgh Pennsylvania
Aug. 5ᵗʰ, 2002

> They always throw around this term 'the liberal elite.'
> And I kept thinking to myself about the Christian right.
> What's more elite than believing that only you will go to
> heaven?
>
> - Jon Stewart

485. And that's another part of the spirit of America I want to herald, and that is the prayers that were said by thousands of your citizens -- I mean, people from all walks of life. They didn't say, I'm a Republican, therefore, I get to pray, or I'm a Democrat, I pray. I don't care about either of them, I pray. Everybody prayed. A lot of people -- if I say everybody, I don't know if everybody prayed. I can tell you, a lot prayed. A lot prayed for your safety, a lot prayed for your families. A lot pled to an Almighty God that you were rescued. And thank God the prayers were answered.

Green Tree Pennsylvania
Aug. 5th, 2002

> Tough times in Israel. The settlers didn't want to leave
> because they feel that the land was given to them by
> God. It's the same way that Republicans feel about the
> White House.
>
> - Jay Leno

486. He's a star today. He's going to be a bigger star tomorrow, because he's a man of principle. See, he doesn't get up there and kind of try to wag his finger to figure out which way the wind is blowing.

Pickering for Congress Luncheon
Jackson Mississippi
Aug. 7th, 2002

172

487.   I love to speculate about what was going through the enemy's mind -- what were they thinking when they hit America. They must have thought that we were so materialistic, or self-absorbed, or shallow, or so worried about our own prosperity, our own individual wealth that we were unwilling to serve something greater than ourself in life, that when the enemy hit we would just kind of make noise and do nothing about it.

Jackson Mississippi
Aug. 7th, 2002

488.   Believe this or not, fortunately, she was getting toxic and the doc induced labor before he quit his practice.

Madison Central High School
Madison Mississippi
Aug. 7th, 2002

489.   No, I know all the war rhetoric, but it's all aimed at achieving peace.

Madison Central High School
Madison Mississippi
Aug. 7th, 2002

Political language. . . is designed to make lies sound truthful and murder respectable, and to give an appearance of solidity to pure wind.

- George Orwell

490.   Jill Mahaffey, says she got lucky. She and her husband are
        here, they live in the Delta, too. She got lucky.

Madison Central High School
Madison Mississippi Aug. 7th, 2002

491.   If you believe every child can learn, therefore we ought to
        know whether that's the case.

Pickering for Congress Luncheon
Jackson Mississippi
Aug. 7th, 2002

Bush's overall approval ratings have hit an all-time low
... If Bush's numbers don't improve, he could become
the first president held back and forced to repeat his
presidency.

-Tina Fey

---

492.   We've got to be able to put the right people in the right job at
        the right time, without a thick book of rules that have little to
        do with protecting the American people.

Madison Central High School
Madison Mississippi
Aug. 7th, 2002

President Bush is trying to put a positive spin on the
latest bad economic numbers. Today he declared
victory in the 'War on Jobs.'

- Craig Kilborn

---

493. Listen, thank you all for coming. I promise you I will listen to what has been said here, even though I wasn't here.

President's Economic Forum
Baylor University Waco Texas
Aug. 13th, 2002

As long as you only give him the tops and not the stalks, and especially if it has a great cheese sauce.

— First Lady Laura Bush, on how to get her husband to eat his broccoli

494. I think one of the things you'll hear is that even though times are kind of tough right now, that we're America.

President's Economic Forum
Baylor University Waco Texas
Aug. 13th, 2002

The Senate has passed a resolution to make English the official language of the United States. Today President Bush said this is the 'goodest news' he's heard in a long time.

-Jay Leno

495. The thing about the death tax, the death tax is punitive on small business owners. It is very tough on farmers and ranchers. it's hard to be able to keep your farm and your family if you've got a big appraisal value when a loved one dies. I firmly believe the death tax is good for people from all walks of life all throughout our society.

President's Economic Forum
Baylor University Waco Texas
Aug. 13th, 2002

496.   Tommy is a good listener, and he's a pretty good actor, too. He can get things done. Action man, we call him.

President's Economic Forum
Baylor University Waco Texas
Aug. 13th, 2002

497.   We've got a fabulous military, a lot of young men and women who are taking a risk on behalf of freedom.

Des Moines, Iowa,
Aug. 14th, 2002

> I hope our wisdom will grow with our power, and teach
> us that the less we use our power the greater it will be.
> - Thomas Jefferson

498.   I appreciate so very much your governor, Bill Janklow, for being here. Bill has been a friend of mine for a long period of time. He might have invented the word piece of work. But he's a good piece of work.

Mt. Rushmore South Dakota
Aug. 15th, 2002

499.   I had the honor of meeting a fellow named Jerome Harvey. He's a professional fire fighter who volunteers his time to help people in need. He grew up in a volunteer fire department, in the sense of taking on this important job as -- for his lifetime. I bring him up because he's helping others learn how to fight fire. He's a part of what I call a soldier in the army of compassion.

Mt. Rushmore South Dakota
Aug. 15th, 2002

176

500.   Listen, out of the evil done to this great land is going to come incredible good, because we're the greatest nation on the face of the earth, full of the most fine and compassioned and decent citizens.

Mt. Rushmore South Dakota
Aug. 15th, 2002

501.   Nothing he has done has convinced me -- I'm confident the Secretary of Defense -- that he is the kind of fellow that is willing to forgo weapons of mass destruction, is willing to be a peaceful neighbor, that is -- will honor the people -- the Iraqi people of all stripes, will -- values human life. He hasn't convinced me, nor has he convinced my administration.

Crawford Texas
Aug. 16th, 2002

502.   Listen, it's a healthy debate for people to express their opinion. People should be allowed to express their opinion. But America needs to know, I'll be making up my mind based upon the latest intelligence and how best to protect our own country plus our friends and allies.

Crawford Texas
Aug. 16th, 2002

> There must be no majority decisions, but only responsible persons, and the word 'council' must be restored to its original meaning. Surely every man will have advisers by his side, but the decision will be made by one man.
>
> – Adolf Hitler

503. I came away from that summit that the small business person feels constrained by tax policy and regulatory policy and I was really appreciated the people coming.

Crawford Texas
Aug. 16th, 2002

504. There was certainly a very strong sentiment that we're on the right track when it comes to holding people to account who lie, steat or cheal -- lie, cheat or steal, who defraud people by cooking the books. There was some strong sentiment from CEO and non-CEO alike.

Crawford Texas
Aug. 16th, 2002

505. I try to go for longer runs, but it's tough around here at the White House on the outdoor track. It's sad that I can't run longer. It's one of the saddest things about the presidency.

Washington Post
Aug. 21st, 2002

I'm glad he's got his priorities straight

506.   President Musharraf, he's still tight with us on the war against
        terror, and that's what I appreciate. He's a—he understands
        that we've got to keep al-Qaeda on the run, and that by
        keeping him on the run, it's more likely we will bring him to
        justice.

Ruch Oregon.
Aug. 22nd, 2002

They say now that Mullah Omar is living out of his car.
You know things are not going well for the jihad when
your Supreme Leader is living in his Toyota.
—David Letterman

507.   I appreciate Congressman Greg Walden being here, as well. I
        don't know if --All I can see is a hand and shining head. But
        Walden is a good man; he's doing a fabulous job as a
        congressman.

Portland Oregon
Aug. 22nd, 2002

A hypocrite is the kind of politician who would cut down
a redwood tree, then mount the stump and make a
speech for conservation.
- Adlei Stevenson

508.   We need to thin. We need to make our forests healthy by
        using some common sense ... We need to understand, if you
        let kindling build up and there's a lightning strike, you're going
        to get yourself a big fire.

Central Point Oregon
Aug. 22nd, 2002

Brilliant strategy for preventing forest fires…
cut down all the trees!

179

509.   People are beginning to get the message. I mean, Americans who have no idea what good forest policy means are beginning to see the fires on TV. It's a sad way for people to learn, but it's happening, and we're beginning to make some progress.

Central Point Oregon
Aug. 22nd, 2002

Good forest policy may actually be in the eye
of the beholder

> Always watch where you are going. Otherwise, you may step on a piece of the Forest that was left out by mistake.
>
> - Winnie-the-Pooh

510.   I remember telling people that where I came from, at least the economic book that I believe in say, if you've got tough times in your economy, you got to let people keep more of their own money.

Central Point Oregon
Aug. 22nd, 2002

511.   People ask me how can they help in the war against terror. My answer is, love a neighbor like you'd like to be loved yourself.

Central Point Oregon
Aug. 22nd, 2002

But my neighbor keeps running away from me

180

512. I'm thrilled to be here in the bread basket of America because it gives me a chance to remind our fellow citizens that we have an advantage here in America—we can feed ourselves.

Stockton California
Aug. 23rd, 2002

513. My call to people in this country is that if you want to join on the war on terror, if you want to fight evil, love your neighbor like you'd like to be loved yourself.

Santa Ana California
Aug. 23rd, 2002

Love thy neighbor--and if he happens to be tall, debonair and devastating, it will be that much easier.
                                                        - Mae West

514. [The enemy] can't stand the thought of Republican and Democrat actually getting along.

Santa Ana California
Aug. 23rd, 2002

Well keep giving the enemy exactly what they want...wait...is the enemy Fox News? What am I saying....Of course, the enemy is Fox News

Marta was watching the football game with me when she said, "You know, most of these sports are based on the idea of one group protecting its territory from invasion by another group." "Yeah," I said, trying not to laugh. Girls are funny.
                                                        - Jack Handy

181

515. I believe the enemy has wakened a spirit in this country that understands in order to fight evil, in order to fight evil -- that in order to fight evil, you can do so by loving your neighbor just like you'd like to be loved yourself.

Stockton California
Aug. 23rd, 2002

Fighting Evil, One Neighbor at a Time

....two if you're lucky

It may be difficult to determine exactly how our neighbors like to be loved themselves if we don't hide in their closet and watch occasionally.. If they find you and ask, "what you are doing?"....tell them you are "fighting evil" for the president....then run!
On your way past the bed, grab a sheet and tie it around your neck...This is your evil-fighting, super-neighbor-lover cape.
As you bound, gazelle-like from their window, shout, "I am Super Neighbor!"
Try not to scream like a girl (even if you are one) as you plummet to the pavement.
You - my evil-busting/closet peeping friend, are a patriotic American, answering your President's call to action. Never have the words "serving at the pleasure of the president" meant more. God Bless you, Super Neighbor....God Bless you Mr President....PS remember to post those photos of neighbor-love on the Internet.

---

516. I'm so proud to be here to embrace his candidacy. Bill Simon is a proven businessman

Yes, proven by a court of defrauding a partner
out of $78 million dollars.? The verdict was
overturned under questionable circumstances.
Stockton California
Aug. 23rd, 2002

182

517.   Because of a quirk in the Senate law, all the work that we did reverts back to normal in 10 years, normal being what it was prior to the tax relief. In other words it's kind of hard to explain. But you get tax relief and you don't get tax relief, see. It stays in place for 10 years and then it goes away.

Stockton California
Aug. 23rd, 2002

Don't be so sure, I thought Bush would go away after four

518.   The evildoers can't stand the thought of a nation which recognizes that people can worship an Almighty God in different ways.

Stockton California
Aug. 23rd, 2002

Just not grasping the principles behind freedom of religion…nor
those related to the separation of
church and state for that matter

It seems to me that Islam and Christianity and Judaism all have the same god, and he's telling them all different things.
- Billy Connolly

The worst government is the most moral. One composed of cynics is often very tolerant and humane. But when fanatics are on top there is no limit to oppression.
- Henry Louis Mencken

519.   That's what America is about. ...We proudly call you an
        American. We don't say, show us your birth certificate, how
        you're born, where you're born.

Santa Ana California
Aug. 23rd, 2002

Immigration is the big issue right now. Earlier today,
the Senate voted to build a 370-mile fence along the
Mexican border. ... Experts say a 370-mile fence is the
perfect way to protect a border that is 1,900 miles
long.

-Conan O'Brien

---

520.   The federal government and the state government must not
        fear programs who change lives, but must welcome those
        faith-based programs for the embetterment of mankind.

Stockton California
Aug. 23rd, 2002

521.   The stakes are these -- whether or not our children can grow
        up in a free and peaceful world. Those are the stakes. And
        that's why I talk about making sure that the world's worst
        leaders aren't able to develop and harbor the world's worst
        weapons. Now, listen, I've got a lot of tools at my disposal,
        and I'm a patient, patient man. But I understand freedom. And
        I understand history has put the spotlight on this country. And
        so long as I'm the President, this country isn't going to blink,
        we're going to lead.

Las Cruces New Mexico
Aug. 25th, 2002

> We have just enough religion to make us hate, but not enough to make us love one another.
>
> — Jonathon Swift

522.   See, we love, we love freedom. That's what they didn't understand. They hate things; we love things. They act out of hatred; we don't seek revenge, we seek justice out of love.

Oklahoma City
Aug. 29th, 2002

523.   I want the students to understand here why someone would want to hurt America in the first place. And it's because your country loves freedom. That's why. We love freedom.

Little Rock Arkansas
Aug. 29th, 2002

> The entire Islamic world condemned Iran. Nowadays, because of the unwarranted invasion of Iraq by Bush and Blair, which was a completely unjust adventure based on misleading statements, and the lack of any effort to resolve the Palestinian issue, there is massive Islamic condemnation of the United States.
>
> — Jimmy Carter

524.   They act out of hatred. We don't seek revenge. We seek justice out of love.

Oklahoma City Oklahoma
Aug. 29th, 2002

Invasion of love compliments of GW Bush

War is an instrument entirely inefficient toward
redressing wrong; and multiplies, instead of
indemnifying losses.

- Thomas Jefferson

525.   You all have got to understand the best way to protect the
homeland security is to chase these killers, these people
down, one by one, and bring them to justice... I say justice
because we don't seek revenge. We seek justice. We seek
justice. And you need to know that when we go into a country
to enforce a doctrine -- see, there was a doctrine that said, if
you harbor a terrorist, if you feed a terrorist, if you hide a
terrorist, you're just as guilty as the terrorist.

Little Rock Arkansas
Aug. 29th, 2002

526.   Every life matters, whether it be an American life or the life of
an Afghan girl.

Little Rock Arkansas
Aug. 29th, 2002

An interim government has been set up in Afghanistan
which includes two women, one of whom will be
Minister of Women's Affairs. Man, who'd she have to
show her ankles to to get that job?

—Tina Fey SNL

186

527.   I had the privilege of saying good-bye for a brief period of time to our First Lady who's down there in Crawford. She is -- she was born and raised in West Texas. That's kind of like western Oklahoma, not a lot of native trees and not a lot of water.

Oklahoma City Oklahoma
Aug. 29th, 2002

528.   I figured if [Rod Paige] could handle the Houston Independent School District, the Department of Education was nothing.

Little Rock Arkansas
Aug. 29th, 2002

> Sometimes life seems like a dream, especially when I look down and see that I forgot to put on my pants
> - Jack Handy SNL

529.   But today I want to talk about what we're creating in Arkansas, called the Center for State Scholars... and the catalyst will be what they call the Business Roundtable. ... They start interviewing children in 8th grade about their ambitions, and explaining reality. If you don't have any ambitions, the minimum wage job isn't going to get you to where you want to get.

Little Rock Arkansas
Aug. 29th, 2002

Actually if you don't have any ambition a
minimum wage job will take you exactly
where you want to go...or "get" in this case.

530. He's got his priorities straight. He has faith foremost in his life, and his family are his two priorities. ...And his first priority -- his first priority is to make sure every child in this state gets educated.

Oklahoma City Oklahoma
Aug. 29th, 2002

531. It's clear when you get to know Steve [Largent] that he's got his principles indelibly etched on his heart.

Oklahoma City Oklahoma
Aug. 29th, 2002

Ouch

532. See, we value the idea of being able to -- people being able to worship freely an Almighty God. That's what we value in America. And we're not going to change.

Little Rock Arkansas
Aug. 29th, 2002

People who want to share their religious views with you almost never want you to share yours with them.
- Dave Barry

---

533.   They hate things. We love things.

Oklahoma City Oklahoma
Aug. 29th, 2002

I use emotion for the many and reserve reason for the few.
- Adolf Hitler

Lovers of Liberty Love Loving Freedom --
Someone Please Get Real About Terrorism?

"They hate us because we love freedom."

"As long as we love freedom, they will try to come and get us".

"We love. They hate"

Could it really be that straightforward?
If it's that simple, why haven't they come after Canada?
We certainly love freedom here too.

In fact, Canada also loves lots of controversial things like homosexuals, lap dancing, religious freedom, killing unborn babies and cannabis in small quantities. You'd think we'd be infidels too.

This over-simplification should be considered an insult to our intelligence and wholly insufficient to explain why the US is subject to such hate and derision from certain parts of the world.

I'm no expert and good, honest information is hard to come-by but from what I can tell, al Qaeda's beef with America is not about freedom in the US, neither religious nor democratic. They don't care that you are "free to worship an Almighty God any way you want." and they are not seeking to install an Islamic Fundamentalist Government in the United States.

al-Qaeda claims that both the U.S. and U.K. are oppressive toward Muslims, citing the invasion and occupation of Iraq, presence of military bases in several Islamic countries and U.S. support for Israel in the Arab-Israeli conflict.

The US , as al Qaeda sees it, represents the exact oposite of everything their particular brand of Islamic faith stands for. The Americans have set up their bases and establishments on what they consider to be their most sacred lands. They brought with them alcohol, women who run around half dressed (by their standards) and Western values that are deeply offensive to their beliefs.

From BBC's Quick Guide to al Qaeda:

"Al-Qaeda claims to be avenging wrongs committed by Christians and Jews against Muslims over the ages.

It wants to re-shape the Muslim world, replacing secular states with a single Islamic political leadership.

It also wants to drive Americans and other non-Muslims from Saudi Arabia, the home of Islam's holiest sites.

Al-Qaeda draws support from people who see the US's military action in Iraq and Afghanistan, and its support for Israel, as a war against Islam itself"

Nowhere did I see the words, "we hate them because they love freedom"

It's a culture clash to be sure. Bin Laden wants to purge his society of the influece of the infidels.

Operative word..."his" society...not American society. If the US stopped trying to remake the Middle East in it's own image...maybe they wouldn't have such a problem. Bin Laden is an extremeist kook and is recognized as such by most of the Muslim world. But, as the US continues to occupy their lands and kill their people, the growing frustrations are breeding an entirely new batch of terrorists. The War on Terror isn't eliminating terrorism it's propagating it.

Jimmy Carter summed it up like this, "The entire Islamic world condemned Iran. Nowadays, because of the unwarranted invasion of Iraq by Bush and Blair, which was a completely unjust adventure based on misleading statements, and the lack of any effort to resolve the Palestinian issue, there is massive Islamic condemnation of the United States."

He also said, "We sent Marines into Lebanon and you only have to go to Lebanon, to Syria or to Jordan to witness first-hand the intense hatred among many people for the United States because we bombed and shelled and unmercifully killed totally innocent villagers -- women and children and farmers and housewives -- in those villages around Beirut. ... As a result of that ... we became kind of a Satan in the minds of those who are deeply resentful."

I'm not supporting terrorism and I'm not condoning al Qaeda....But it's irresponsible to not investigate why this has happened and attempt to enhance our understanding of the enemy and their motives in a honest and substantive way.
To walk into a school, or stand before a crowd populated by folks still reeling from the attacks of 9/11 and say, 'they attacked us because we love freedom', doesn't seem to further any cause beyond keeping the populace ignorant. Are they afraid we are too stupid to comprehend their actual motives?

Terrorists belong to a cult of blood-lusting lunatics who believe that non-Muslims are enemies of Allah and that killing them/us is necessary...even obligatory. Their doctrine is so twisted it is impossible to debate with. Yes, they need to be dealt with and no, I wouldn't know how. But I am positive it doesn't involve launching a massive attack against an entire nation. Invading Iraq was a horrific act of terrorism. And yet we are not supposed to question it and we are ridiculed for any attempt to understand terrorism.

What happened to "know thine enemy".

It's strange to me that when , for example, a serial killer emerges in society, there is active inquiry into the root causes and conditions that generated this particular breed of killer. Psychiatrists and law enforcement look at everything from organic anomalies and IQ, to childhood issues and external influences. This is how they attempt to understand the problem and enact measures that will enable them to detect potential problems early or prevent others from emerging in the future. They do it to protect society. No one accuses them of condoning serial murder, being a murderer or hating America.

That's what happens if you try to look at terrorism beyond the "They hate us because we love freedom" explanation. When did reason and free inquiry become enemies of the state?

As long as the only reason remains "they hate us because we love", what potential is there for any real or lasting peace?

The only way to eliminate that kind of broad threat would be extermination on a massive scale of anyone who "hates freedom"... what does that mean..."hates freedom"? Is it just the terrorists? OK, let's settle on just terrorists. Only terrorists hate freedom... This is a global war on terrorism, so does that mean all terrorists everywhere hate freedom? If they believe they are fighting to protect their land and their religion and you want their land and disregard their religion and summarily execute them,. more terrorists are created to fight the extermination. Is this liberation or genocide?

Terrorism was not born in a vacuum. It's a complex problem that is not even remotely addressed with "They hate us because we love freedom."

The arrogant refusal to acknowledge the other side or look more deeply at the problem dooms us all and there can be no peace.

> A fanatic is one who can't change his mind and won't change the subject.
>
> - Winston Churchill

534.   So long as we love freedom, which we'll do forever, and so long as this enemy is -- still stand, they're going to come and try to get us.

Pittsburgh Pennsylvania
Sept. 2ⁿᵈ, 2002

535.   They've hijacked a great religion and they're willing to kill innocent people in the name of their sordid attitude about the future.

Pittsburgh Pennsylvania
Sept. 2ⁿᵈ, 2002

I'm ok with everything till "sordid attitude about the future"
He had to take a good sentence and give it the W twist.

536.   In the old days, you could count tanks and figure out how strong the enemy was. This is an enemy that hides in caves. They try to find the darkest cave, the deepest cave, and then they send youngsters to their suicidal deaths. It's a different kind of hater than we're used to.

Pittsburgh Pennsylvania
Sept. 2ⁿᵈ, 2002

Comparing old "haters" to the new "haters"

537. I'm sure your kids, they're wondering, why would you hate America? We didn't do anything to anybody. Well, they hate America because we love freedom.

Pittsburgh Pennsylvania
Sept. 2nd, 2002

He who knows nothing is closer to the truth than he whose mind is filled with falsehoods and errors
- Thomas Jefferson

538. I don't need to tell that to the people in this room, but there is some in our country believe in the -- what I call the soft bigotry of low expectations. They don't believe in the bigotry, but because there's low expectations, there is a soft bigotry.

White House
Sept. 4th, 2002

539. [Arkansas and Alabama] don't need fancy theories, or what may sound good. Science is not an art -- I mean, reading is not an art. It's a science. We know what works.

White House
Sept. 4th, 2002

They just seem to be wrapped in bubbles, surrounded by sycophants. Bush was in Tampa today in front of one of those invited audiences he speaks to. The first question, this is not a joke, said the nation was blessed to have Bush as president. That was a question. The second one referred to Jeb as 'your great brother.' You know, at least when Clinton got blown it was in private.
-Bill Maher

194

540.   I will first remind the United Nations that for 11 long years, Saddam Hussein has side-stepped, crawfished, wheedled out of any agreement he had made not to harbor -- not to develop weapons of mass destruction, agreements he's made to treat the people within his country with respect. And so I'm going to call upon the world to recognize that he is stiffing the world.

White House
Sept. 4th, 2002

President Bush said it's now time for a change in Iraq and he wants them to have a Western-style democracy like ours. So right now in Iraq, the economy is collapsing, businessmen are corrupt, and Hussein wants his son to take over as president. Sounds like mission accomplished.

—Jay Leno

541.   I'm proud to come back to my alma mater -- well, that is, my honorary alma mater. I'm proud to come back to support Chris Cacho -- Chocola.

South Bend Indiana
Sept. 5th, 2002

Did you know former President Garfield could write Latin with one hand and Greek with the other at the same time? That was Garfield. When President Bush heard about it, he said, 'We had a talking cat for president?'

-Jay Leno

> We need to decide that we will not go to war, whatever
> reason is conjured up by the politicians or the media,
> because war in our time is always indiscriminate, a war
> against innocents, a war against children
>
> - Howard Zinn

542.   I want you to tell your children that when they hear all the talk
and all the speculation and all the thousands of hours of so-
called experts babbling away about this, that or the other, that
the true policy of this government is to achieve peace for
generations to come.

South Bend Indiana
Sept. 5th, 2002

543.   You need to tell your loved ones, the little ones in particular,
that when they hear the President talking about al Qaeda,
Iraq and other places, I do so because I long for peace.

Louisville Kentucky
Sept. 5th, 2002

> If we are to teach real peace in this world, and if we
> are to carry on a real war against war, we shall have to
> begin with the children.
>
> - Mahatma Gandhi

544.   But here's the problem, here's the problem -- because of the Senate rules, all the tax relief that we passed, which both Republicans and Democrats voted for, goes away after 10 years. Now, that's a hard one to explain at the coffee shop there in Crawford.

South Bend Indiana
Sept. 5th, 2002

545.   There's no doubt in my mind that we should allow the world worst leaders to hold America hostage, to threaten our peace, to threaten our friends and allies with the world's worst weapons.

South Bend Indiana
Sept. 5th, 2002

Like the former days of the witch-hunt, they are convinced that they exist, and if you see a black cat, well, that's evidence of a witch

- Hans Blix UN Weapons Inspector

546.   See, they've hijacked a great religion, and they don't care about life. They've got their desires, their dark, dark ambitions. And if people get in the way from them, that's just too bad, as far as they're concerned.

South Bend Indiana
Sept. 5th, 2002

547.   As a society we must demand something better, because there is no second-rate children in America.

South Bend Indiana
Sept. 5th, 2002

548.   It's -- this fundraiser is going to be history in about 30 minutes
        -- or if I keep it shorter than that, about 20 minutes.

                        Anne Northup for Congress Luncheon
                             Louisville Kentucky
                             Sept. 5th, 2002

549.   Our antenna, by the way, are much more sensitive now than
        they were prior to September the 11th, obviously.

                             South Bend Indiana
                             Sept. 5th, 2002

550.   More than one person, Chris, said they wished Laura were
        here. ...Now she's the First Lady of the United States, and
        she's doing a fabulous job.

                             South Bend Indiana
                             Sept. 5th, 2002

198

551. One of my jobs is to think ahead and to think -- is to cause debate, and I started that yesterday, to encourage the American people to listen to and have a dialogue about Iraq.

Louisville Kentucky
Sept. 5th, 2002

552. I want to send the signal to our enemy that you have aroused a compassionate and decent and mighty nation, and we're going to hunt you down.

Louisville Kentucky
Sept. 5th, 2002

> If you're in a war, instead of throwing a hand grenade at the enemy, throw one of those small pumpkins. Maybe it'll make everyone think how stupid war is, and while they are thinking, you can throw a real grenade at them.
>
> - Jack Handy

553. We value a free press. We value freedom. And the more we value freedom, the more they hate us. That's why. That's why the enemy still exists.

Louisville Kentucky
Sept. 5th, 2002

> The only foes that threaten America are the enemies at home, and these are ignorance, superstition and incompetence.
>
> - Elbert Hubbard

554. This is one of these kind of wars where things happen and you just don't know about it. But I bet we have hauled in over a couple of thousand of these people.

South Bend Indiana
Sept. 5th, 2002

> Bush the younger has two things going for him that his father never had. One: an easy charm with regular people and two: the power to make them disappear without a trial.
>
> —Bill Maher

555. They hide in caves. See, this is a different kind of war. And part of my responsibilities as your President is to remind people about the realities that we face in America. One of the realities is, is that these people hide in caves.

South Bend Indiana
Sept. 5th, 2002

556. We're going to talk about our shared values of -- recognizes the worth of every individual.

With British PM Tony Blair
Camp David Maryland
Sept. 7th, 2002

557. I appreciate so very much the Prime Minister, Jean Chretien, for joining us here. He has been a steadfast friend. I really enjoy dealing with him on a personal basis. He's a plain-spoken fellow, with a good sense of humor. Probably won't go too good up here in Canada, but he'd be a great Texan.

Detroit Michigan
Sept. 9th, 2002

NEWSFLASH

Detroit is not "up here in Canada"

Mr. Chretien was elected Prime Minister 3 times... so, I'd have to say it "goes good up here" for the plain-spoken fellows.. For the record, I'm not saying Chretien wasn't a dickhead at times, just that we don't have to tie everything on the planet back to Texas.

---

558. Tom is my advisor for Homeland Security, former governor of Pennsylvania. I want to thank Tom for working hard. With the Deputy Prime Minister John Manley from Canada, who both these two men work hard to.

Detroit Michigan
Sept. 9th, 2002

559. I want to appreciate very much Congressman John Conyers as well, and Sander Levin and Nick Smith from the both Republicans and Democrats.

Detroit Michigan
Sept. 9th, 2002

This is the grammatical equivalent of
"borrow me some sugar"

560.　Let me get to the U.N. and give what is an important speech for me.

White House
Sept. 10ᵗʰ, 2002

> More than 150 heads of state attended the UN Summit, giving New Yorkers a chance to get in touch with prejudices they didn't even know they had.
> - Jon Stewart

561.　One year ago, the people of Afghanistan lived under oppression. Their country was a haven for terror. Today, they're an emergency democracy -- an emerging democracy, and building a better future.

White House
Sept. 10ᵗʰ, 2002

> One in four returning Iraqi veterans have been diagnosed with a mental disorder. I know that sounds high, but it does include everybody who says, 'Am I crazy, or were we sent there under false pretenses?'
> - Bill Maher

562.　Yet we do know that God has placed us together in this moment, to grieve together, to stand together, to serve each other and our country.

Ellis Island New York
Sept. 11ᵗʰ, 2002

> Humans feel deeply the suffering of their friends and allies, and easily discount / dismiss the comparable experience of their enemies.
> - Ray Kurzweil

563.   The United States helped found the United Nations. We want the United Nations to be effective, and respectful, and successful.

United Nations General Assembly
Sept. 12th, 2002

President Bush has said that he does not need approval from the UN to wage war, and I'm thinking, well, hell, he didn't need the approval of the American voters to become president, either.

- David Letterman

564.   I especially want to say a word of phrase to Kofi Annan, who is the Secretary General of the United Nations, for his -- for his strong leadership and his good heart and his decency. I enjoy working with him a lot. He's a class act, as we say in the State of Texas.

New York New York
Sept. 12th, 2002

We are able to keep his arms from him. His military forces have not been rebuilt

- Condoleeza Rice NSA

565.   And in 1995, after four years of deception, Iraq finally admitted it had a crash nuclear weapons program prior to the Gulf War. We know now, were it not for that war, the regime in Iraq would likely have possessed a nuclear weapon no later than 1993. Today, Iraq continues to withhold important information about its nuclear program -- weapons design, procurement logs, experiment data, an accounting of nuclear materials and documentation of foreign assistance. Iraq employs capable nuclear scientists and technicians. It retains physical infrastructure needed to build a nuclear weapon. Iraq

203

has made several attempts to buy high-strength aluminum tubes used to enrich uranium for a nuclear weapon. Should Iraq acquire fissile material, it would be able to build a nuclear weapon within a year. And Iraq's state-controlled media has reported numerous meetings between Saddam Hussein and his nuclear scientists, leaving little doubt about his continued appetite for these weapons.

United Nations General Assembly
Sept. 12th, 2002

It ain't what you don't know that gets you into trouble. It's what you know for sure that just ain't so.

- Mark Twain

---

566.   The first time we may be completely certain he has a -- nuclear weapons is when, God forbids, he uses one.

United Nations General Assembly
Sept. 12th, 2002

567.   I should have clarified it by my statement. I just clarified it by my -- not should have, I just.

Camp David Maryland
Sept. 14th, 2002

President Bush gave his speech outlining the case against Iraq, and the Fox network was the only major network to televise the president's address. Not surprisingly, Fox insisted on calling the speech 'When Presidents Attack.'

—Conan O'Brien

---

568. Secondly, I had a chance to speak to the United Nations to talk about another threat face -- that we face -- that we face, all of us face, in the civilized world -- and that is a threat of weapons of mass destructions in the hands of leaders who disregard human liberty, that do not believe in freedom. A leader, in this case, who's poisoned his own people, poisoned his neighbors, attacked in his neighborhood, and refuses -- refuses -- to comply with United Nations' regulations, as a matter of fact, defies the United Nations.

Press Conference with
Prime Minister Berlusconi of Italy
Camp David Maryland
Sept. 14th, 2002

(Saddam Hussein) 'has not developed any significant capability with respect to weapons of mass destruction. He is unable to project conventional power against his neighbors.
- Colin Powell Secretary of State
Speech to UN February 1991

Today, the United Nations approved a resolution to lift the sanctions against Iraq. ... Yeah, the move will allow Iraqis to buy things they don't have, such as medicine and weapons of mass destruction.
—Conan O'Brien

569. My, we have got a fabulous United States military.

Davenport Iowa
Sept. 16th, 2002

There's that adjective again. I thought it was supposed to be "Don't ask – Don't tell"

205

570. They're nothing but a bunch of cold-blooded killers. You've just got to understand that about the nature of the enemy. They hate us because we love. They hate, we love freedom, is why they hate us, and we're not going to quit loving freedom.

Davenport Iowa
Sept. 16th, 2002

571. I gave a speech to the United Nations talking about Iraq, and making it crystal-clear to the United Nations that Saddam poses an international problem. ...He basically told the United Nations, your deal don't mean anything to me.

Davenport Iowa
Sept. 16th, 2002

Why We Didn't Remove Saddam
by George Bush [Sr.] and Brent Scowcroft,

Extending the war into Iraq would have incurred incalculable human and political costs. We would have been forced to occupy Baghdad and, in effect, rule Iraq. The coalition would instantly have collapsed, the Arabs deserting in anger and other allies pulling out as well. Exceeding the U.N.'s mandate would have destroyed the precedent of international response to aggression we hoped to establish. Had we gone the invasion route, the U.S. could still be an occupying power in a bitterly hostile land.

Time Magazine
1998

572.   You see, when you love a neighbor, you fight evil, but you
        also leave behind a legacy of compassion and decency. It's
        what I call the gathering momentum of millions of acts of
        kindness and decency, which take place in spite of
        government.

Davenport Iowa
Sept. 16th, 2002

Bush is certainly gathering momentum but, it won't leave him
with a legacy of decency.

573.   We're going to have a White House forum there in
        Washington, D.C., obviously—that's where the White House
        is.

Nashville Tennessee
Sept. 17th, 2002

574.   Speaking about barbaric regimes, we must deal with probably
        one of the most -- not probably -- one of the most real threats
        we face, and that is the idea of a barbaric regime teaming up
        with a terrorist network and providing weapons of mass
        destruction, to hold the United States and our allies and our
        friends blackmail.

Nashville Tennessee
Sept. 17th, 2002

In California, 50 women protested the impending war
with Iraq by lying on the ground naked and spelling out
the word peace. Right idea, wrong president.
                                            —Jay Leno

575.   I want you to remind your children, with all -- in the midst of all
this war talk, the midst of the -- on the television screens
seeing our troops, and all the stuff going on -- remind them
that this mighty nation went into a country as we upheld that
doctrine.

Lamar Alexander for Senate Luncheon
Nashville Tennessee
Sept. 17th, 2002

576.   And all our history says we believe in liberty and justice for
all, that when we see oppression, we cry.

East Literature Magnet School
Nashville Tennessee
Sept. 17th, 2002

Among those who dislike oppression are many who like
to oppress.

- Napoleon Bonaparte

208

Chapter Six

Hey, American Dream!

Political extremism involves two prime ingredients:
an excessively simple diagnosis of the world's ills,
and a conviction that there are identifiable villains
back of it all.

John W Gardner

> We cannot defend freedom abroad by deserting it at home.
>
> - Edward R Murrow

577. There's an old saying in Tennessee -- I know it's in Texas, probably in Tennessee -- that says, fool me once -- shame on -- shame on you. You fool me, you can't get fooled again.

East Literature Magnet School
Nashville Tennessee
Sept. 17th, 2002

Elect Me Once, Shame On Me
Elect Me Twice, Shame On You

578. When we were kids, a lot of us were kids growing up, oceans septarated us from danger.

East Literature Magnet School
Nashville Tennessee
Sept. 17th, 2002

579.   American children are not born knowing what they should cherish -- are not born knowing why they should cherish American values. A love of democratic principles must be taught.

White House
Sept. 17ᵗʰ, 2002

> It is the State which educates its citizens in civic virtue, gives them a consciousness of their mission and welds them into unity
>
> - Benito Mussolini

580.   We didn't need any more theory in Washington. We needed people that actually done.

East Literature Magnet School
Nashville Tennessee
Sept. 17ᵗʰ, 2002

> When the search for truth is confused with political advocacy, the pursuit of knowledge is reduced to the quest for power
>
> - Alston Chase

581.   Especially important in a time of war that our children understand the context of why we fight.

East Literature Magnet School
Nashville Tennessee
Sept. 17ᵗʰ, 2002

212

582.   The United States will remain strong in our conviction that we must not, and will not, allow the world's worst leaders to hold the United States and our friends and allies blackmail, or threaten us with the world's worst weapons.

Nashville Tennessee
Sept. 17th, 2002

"Hold us hostile", "hold us blackmail"…just in case you want to dismiss these as one-timers.

583.   You see, the Senate wants to take away some of the powers of the administrative branch

There is no "administrative" branch. Bush means to say Executive Branch. I'm a dumb Canadian and even I know that
White House
Sept. 19th, 2002

584.   If you want to keep the peace, you've got to have the authorization to use force.

White House
Sept. 19th, 2002

We cannot be both the world's leading champion of peace and the world's leading supplier of the weapons of war

- Jimmy Carter

213

585. People say, how can I help on this war against terror? How can I fight evil? You can do so by mentoring a child; by going into a shut-in's house and say I love you.

Washington D.C.
Sept. 19th, 2002

Here's your Meals on Wheels...and now I'd like to whisper some sweet nothings so, turn up that hearing aid!

586. And so, they -- the burden of proof is -- must be place squarely on their shoulders. But there's no negotiations about whether or not they've been telling the truth or not.

White House
Sept. 19th, 2002

> I look forward to a great future for America - a future in which our country will match its military strength with our moral restraint, its wealth with our wisdom, its power with our purpose.
>
> - John F Kennedy

587. I want you to remind your kids that when it came to enforcing the doctrine that said either -- the doctrine said, if you harbor one of those killers, you're just as guilty as the killers, that we went into Afghanistan -- the first theater we went into, as a great country -- with friends, but we went in not to conquer anybody, not to conquer anybody.

Trenton New Jersey
Sept. 23rd, 2002

> Cruelty must be whitewashed by a moral excuse, and a pretense of reluctance.
>
> - George Bernard Shaw

214

588.   And we're making progress. It's hard to tell whether we're making progress or not, but we are.

Trenton New Jersey
Sept. 23rd, 2002

If you're keeping score at home, so far our war in Iraq has created a police state in that country and socialism in Spain. So, no democracies yet, but we're really getting close.

                                                    - Jon Stewart

589.   The other day, as you noticed, there was a fellow hiding in the dark caves -- or dark corners, not caves, it was in the city, dark -- dark corners of a city in Pakistan. He was going to be the 20th hijacker, bin al-Shibh. He wanted to come here to kill. He didn't make it, because we fortunately did not give him access.

Trenton New Jersey
Sept. 23rd, 2002

Unfortunately. The did give access to the other 19
...congrats on the 5% success rate.

The Taliban is on the run and don't know where to go. Pakistan doesn't want them. Iran doesn't want them. Of course, they'll have no problem getting into this country.

                                                    —David Letterman

590.   I say priorities. I say priorities. The most important priority we have today and tomorrow is to protect the homeland. That's the most priority in America.

Trenton New Jersey
Sept. 23rd, 2002

591.   We've got to understand, in America there are pockets of despair and hopelessness, places where people hurt because they're not sure if America is meant for them, places where people are addicted. And government can help eradicate these pockets by handing out money.

Trenton New Jersey
Sept. 23rd, 2002

Hell YES! Now this is a strategy I can get behind
Wait…if you eradicate the pockets, where will we
keep the money?

When stupidity is a sufficient explanation, there is no need to have recourse to any other

- Mitchell Ulman

---

592.   I'm talking about Iraq. That country has got a leader which has attacked two nations in the neighborhood, a leader who has killed thousands of people, a leader who is brutal -- see, remember, we believe every life matters and every life is precious -- a leader, if there is dissent, will kill the dissenter, a leader who told the United Nations and the world he would not develop weapons of mass destruction, and for 11 long years has stiffed the world.

Trenton New Jersey
Sept. 23rd, 2002

It's common for Men to give 6 pretended reasons instead of one real one.

- Benjamin Franklin

---

593. It's very important for the school children here to listen to what I'm about to say. You're probably wondering why America is under attack. And you need to know why. We're under attack because we love freedom, is why we're under attack. And our enemy hates freedom. They hate and we love. They hate the thought that this country is a country in which people from all walks of life can worship an almighty God any way he or she fits.

Trenton New Jersey
Sept. 23rd, 2002

If there were no God, it would have been necessary to invent him

- Voltaire

594. You'll hear, we're going to spend -- the government is going to spend the government money here, and the government is going to spend the government here.

Trenton New Jersey
Sept. 23rd, 2002

Both President Bush and Vice President Dick Cheney released their income tax figures for last year. President Bush made $894,000. Dick Cheney made $36 million. The vice president made 40 times more than the president. That doesn't seem right. It's not like Dick Cheney is 40 times smarter than — ooohhh.

—Jay Leno

595. It changes when you walk into a shut-in's house, and say, Can I love you? or Can I help you?

Trenton New Jersey
Sept. 23rd, 2002

Restraining orders change a lot of things

217

596.   We need an energy bill that encourages consumption.

Trenton New Jersey
Sept. 23rd, 2002

597.   But as we fight terror -- ah -- particularly in the Middle East, they've gotta build the institution necessary for a Palestinian state to emerge. That we've gotta promote the leadership that is willing to condemn terror and, at the same time, work toward the embetterment of the lives of the Palestinian people.

Washington D.C.
Sept. 24th, 2002

Tomorrow President Bush is expected to announce that the war in Iraq is over. As a result, Bush will be able to resume his war on the English language.
—Conan O'Brien

598.   Got one the other day, one of the ones kind of bragging about he thought he was going to be the 20th -- 20th killer on September the 11th. He poked his head up, and we found him.

Washington D.C.
Sept. 25th, 2002

Caddyshack meets the war on terror.

599.   Saddam Hussein is a man who invaded two countries twice -- two countries, once each time.

Washington D.C.
Sept. 25th, 2002

218

600.   It's not a very glamorous war from the sense that the cables
        and all the air time can cover, but it's happening.

                        Houston Texas
                        Sept. 26th, 2002

                Thank God, I was afraid the war wasn't
                glamorous enough

601.   This is an American issue, a uniquely American issue. And
        it's -- as I reminded the members, that -- I say uniquely
        American issue because I truly believe that now that the war
        has changed, now that we're a battlefield, this man poses a
        much graver threat than anybody could have possibly
        imagined. Other countries, of course, bear the same risk.

                        Houston Texas
                        Sept. 26th, 2002

> He who permits himself to tell a lie once, finds it much
> easier to do it a second and a third time till at length it
> becomes habitual.
>   - Thomas Jefferson

602.   We're going to stay in Afghanistan to hunt down the killers --
        they still lurk around. They occasionally come in, and we'll
        find them. They kind of bunch up somewhere and they're just
        -- they think they're allusive and they think they're clever, but
        they've got the mighty United States on them.

                        Houston Texas
                        Sept. 26th, 2002

Allusive adj.
Characterized by or containing indirect references

219

603.   So long as we love freedom, they hate us, and they want to hurt us. That's just the facts of life, as we head into the 21st century.

Houston Texas
Sept. 26th, 2002

> Voice or no voice, the people can always be brought to do the bidding of the leaders. All you have to do is tell them they are being attacked and denounce the pacifists for lack of patriotism and exposing the country to danger. It works the same way in any country
> - Hermann Göring 1946.

604.   After all, this is a guy that tried to kill my dad at one time.

Houston Texas
Sept. 26th, 2002

> To me, clowns aren't funny. In fact, they're kind of scary. I've wondered where this started and I think it goes back to the time I went to the circus, and a clown killed my dad.
> - Jack Handy SNL

605.   We need people up there who understand that if Congress overspends it will serve as an anchor to economic vitality and growth.

Houston Texas
Sept. 26th, 2002

220

606. We're allowing our forests to grow up like giant piles of kindling, and just hoping that something doesn't happen. We're -- backwards policy.

Denver Colorado
Sept. 27th, 2002

President Bush was clearing brush at his ranch when he was scratched by a tree. That's a switch, a tree harming a Republican, when does that ever happen? I guess Bush has cut down so many trees they're starting to fight back now

-Jay Leno

607. I don't need a giant -- and when I say I, it's not only me, it's other Presidents -- don't need a thick book of regulations trying to micromanage the department of homeland security.

Denver Colorado
Sept. 27th, 2002

Uhhhh....not so fast...

608. These are folks that have hijacked a great religion and then take innocent life. And that's a huge difference between America.

Denver Colorado
Sept. 27th, 2002

Before God we are all equally wise - and equally foolish.

-Albert Einstein

221

609. We don't measure success based upon our capacity to destroy the terrorists' ability to fight war.

Denver Colorado
Sept. 27th, 2002

During his trip, Wolfowitz took a positive view of the peril he put the troops in, noting 'The more successful we are, the more we can expect them to go after those things that represent success.' Does this guy know how to motivate the troops or what? Apparently the best way to measure our accomplishments is to witness the destruction of our accomplishments.

- Jon Stewart

---

610. There's no second-rate children in Arizona. There is no second-rate children in America.

Phoenix Arizona
Sept. 28th, 2002

Amusingly ironic grammar in a speech touting
the importance of education

611. This is a man who continues to murder his own people, a man who has gassed -- used gas on his own citizens, a man who has used chemical weapons on his neighbors, a man who has invaded two countries, a man which hates -- who hates America, a man who loves to link up with al Qaeda, a man who is a true threat to America, to Israel, to anybody in the neighborhood.

Phoenix Arizona
Sept. 28th, 2002

There's overwhelming evidence there was a connection between al-Qaeda and the Iraqi government. I am very confident there was an established relationship there.

- Dick Cheney Jan 22nd, 2004

Iraqi officials deny accusations of ties with al-Qaeda. These denials are simply not credible.

- Colin Powell Feb 5th, 2003

There clearly are contacts between al-Qaeda and Saddam Hussein that can be documented.

- Condoleeza Rice Sept 25th, 2002

Saddam Hussein -- no one has said that there is evidence that Saddam Hussein directed or controlled 9/11, but let's be very clear, he had ties to al-Qaeda, he had al-Qaeda operatives who had operated out of Baghdad.
Condoleeza Rice Sept 28, 2003

Rep. Henry Waxman's Report "Iraq On the Record" identifies 61 incidents where Bush Administration officials lied about links between Iraq and al Qaeda despite all credible reports disproving the relationship.

MSNBC June 16th, 2004

WASHINGTON - The commission investigating the Sept. 11 attacks reported Wednesday that Osama bin Laden met with a top Iraqi official in 1994 but found "no credible evidence" of a link between Iraq and al-Qaeda in attacks against the United States

> It is always better to have no ideas than false ones; to believe nothing, than to believe what is wrong.
>
> > - Thomas Jefferson

612. America must remember that tragic story, because it speaks volumes about the great spirit of the country. People flying across the plane, 40 passengers and I think four crew members, I believe it was.

Phoenix Arizona
Sept. 28th, 2002

613. This is a—this is a—any strike's a tough—tough situation, but this one happens to come at a—or a lockout is a tough situation, or no work is a tough situation—is to come at bad time.

Washington D.C.
Oct. 1st, 2002

> If life deals you lemons, why not go kill someone with the lemons (maybe by shoving them down his throat).
>
> > - Jack Handy

614. You need to listen carefully to the debates that goes on in our nation's capital. You see, some of them are -- goes on with people trying to get to the nation's capital. Some of them, they talk about the government's money.

Manchester New Hampshire
Oct. 5th, 2002

> I think it's both good ethics and good economics to scrap this notion that we can fight a war on terror and give rich folks like me a tax cut. It amounts to class warfare.
> - Bill Clinton

615.   The problem we have, and the reason we have to continue to talking about this issue is because of a quirk in the Senate rules. And I'm going to let old Judd after I leave back to go see my mother, tell you what -- how this happened. Let me just put it to you this way, in plain language. The Senate has got the kind of rule where you pass the tax cut and then ten years it goes back to where we were. The way I like to put it, if I can -- in plain English is, on the one hand, they taketh away, on the other hand, they giveth. On the one hand they give tax relief, on the other hand, you don't get tax relief. It's hard to explain in Manchester, New Hampshire, and it's darn sure hard to explain in Crawford, Texas.

Manchester New Hampshire
Oct. 5th, 2002

Well, you can hardly blame Crawford,

616.   Some communities you say, hey, American Dream -- and they go, what does that mean?

Manchester New Hampshire
Oct. 5th, 2002

617.   I was proud the other day when both Republicans and Democrats stood with me in the Rose Garden to announce their support for a clear statement of purpose: You disarm, or we will.

Manchester New Hampshire
Oct. 5th, 2002

That's very clear…wrong…but clear.

225

> The majority of Americans, the ones who never elected you, are not fooled by your weapons of mass distraction.
>
> - Michael Moore

618.   It's also important for people to know we never seek to impose our culture or our form of government. We just want to live under those universal values, God-given values.

Washington, D.C.
Oct. 11th, 2002

> Much of Central America is in the coalition mostly because we already liberated them repeatedly, vigorously and covertly, and believe me, they don't want to go through one of those liberations again.
>
> —Jon Stewart

619.   Well, I think that the free world is -- must recognize that no one is safe, that if you embrace freedom you're not safe from terrorism.

Washington D.C.
Oct. 14th, 2002

> When the tyrant has disposed of foreign enemies by conquest or treaty and there is nothing to fear from them, then he is always stirring up some war or other, in order that the people may require a leader.
>
> - Plato

620. Those of us who love freedom must work together to do everything we can to disrupt, deny and bring to justice these people who have no soul, no conscience, people that hate freedom.

Washington D.C.
Oct. 14th, 2002

621. All of us here in America should believe, and I think we do, that we should be, as I mentioned, a nation of owners. Owning something is freedom, as far as I'm concerned. It's part of a free society... It's a part of -- it's of being a -- it's a part of -- an important part of America.

Washington D.C.
Oct. 15th, 2002

See what happens when good sentences go bad?

622. This is -- an ownership society is a compassionate society.

Washington D.C.
Oct. 15th, 2002

> What is it that makes a complete stranger dive into an icy river to save a solid gold baby? Maybe we'll never know
>
> - Jack Handy

623. If you put your mind to it, the first-time home buyer, the low-income home buyer can have just as nice a house as anybody else.

Washington D.C.
Oct. 15th, 2002

Delusions of grandeur?

624.   There's three different agencies down there -- three agencies
        full of really fine people. You've got your Customs, your INF
        and your Border Patrol. Sometimes they have different
        strategies per sector along the border. They're wearing
        different uniforms.

Downingtown Pennsylvania
Oct. 22nd, 2002

President Bush is proposing sending six thousands
National Guard troops to bolster patrols along the U.S.-
Mexican border. Or as he's calling it, "No Juan Left
Behind.

                                        -Jay Leno

625.   There's a lot of good folks at the federal level and the state
        level and the local level working hard -- listen, any time -- we
        understand the stakes now, and any time somebody is
        thinking about doing something to America, and somehow
        we're reading their thoughts, or reading their mail, we're
        moving on them.

South Bend Indiana
Oct. 31st, 2002

First our emails, then our phone calls, now they
are engaging in warrantless mind-reading

I am mortified to be told that, in the United States of
America, the sale of a book can become a subject of
inquiry, and of criminal inquiry too.

                                        - Thomas Jefferson

228

626.   We say in our country, everybody matters, everybody is precious in the sight of an Almighty.

Aberdeen South Dakota
Oct. 31st, 2002

Iraq Body Count.com

These disasters are the outcome of what George W Bush characterized in his London speech of November 20th as a "noble mission" to rid the world of terrorists. Of such terrorists he said "We see their contempt, their utter contempt, for innocent life."

So far, in the "war on terror" initiated since 9-11, the USA and its allies have been responsible for over 13,000 civilian deaths, not only the 10,000+ in Iraq, but also 3,000+ civilian deaths in Afghanistan

---

Well, we do not keep records for the simple reason that there is no really accurate way. ...It would be irresponsible to give firm estimates given the wide range of variables. For example we've had cases where during a conflict, we believed civilians had been wounded and perhaps killed, but by the time our forces have a chance to fully assess the outcomes of a contact, the wounded or the dead civilians have been removed from the scene. Factors such as this make it impossible for us to maintain an accurate account.

US military spokesman Col Guy Shields
August 4th 2003,

"We say in our country, everybody matters, everybody is precious in the sight of an Almighty"...too bad the citizens of other countries aren't as precious.

627.   I want to thank all my citizens for coming.

Aberdeen South Dakota
Oct. 31st, 2002

This is one of the most intellectually gifted presidents
we've had.

Karl Rove
Hardball MSNBC
Jan. 19th, 2005

628.   I need somebody in Congress who is a cold-eyed realist.

South Bend Indiana
Oct. 31st, 2002

Great, more creepy-looking people in Congress

629.   I need to be able to move the right people to the right place at
the right time to protect you, and I'm not going to accept a
lousy bill out of the United Nations Senate.

South Bend Indiana
Oct. 31st, 2002

We should change our attitude toward the United
Nations. There has to be some power in the world
superior to our own. We should not have attacked Iraq
without the okay of the United Nations. Now we have to
live with that mistake. We're living with it, and too
many of our guys are dying with it.

- Andy Rooney

230

630.   Millions of -- thousands of people -- millions of dollars and thousands of people -- millions of dollars aren't being invested and thousands of people aren't working.

Portsmouth New Hampshire.
Nov. 1st, 2002

631.   I don't know what was going through the mind of the enemy. They must have thought the national religion of America was materialism, therefore we're selfish and self-absorbed, we'd take a couple of steps back after September the 11th, 2000. They probably said, oh, they'd file a lawsuit or two

St. Paul Minnesota
Nov. 3rd, 2002

What a difference a year makes
...September 11, 2001

632.   No child should be left behind in the state of South Dakota.

Sioux Falls South Dakota
Nov. 3rd, 2002

So, please abandon your children across
state lines...I can see the signs now...
Adopt this stretch of highway and the
Johnson kids

633.   I one time in this state described him as a piece of work. But he's your piece of work.

Sioux Falls South Dakota
Nov. 3rd, 2002

634.   And here at home, we can be a better tomorrow -- better
        America, too.

                    Bentonville Arkansas
                    Nov. 4th*, 2002*

635.   And don't be afraid to -- talking to Democrats. There's some
        discerning Democrats who know the difference between
        lousy government and good government.

                    Cedar Rapids Iowa
                    Nov. 4th*, 2002*

636.   I know something about being a government. And you've got
        a good one.

                    Bentonville Arkansas
                    Nov. 4th* 2002*

We have become a Nazi monster in the eyes of the
whole world -- a nation of bullies and bastards who
would rather kill than live peacefully. We are not just
Whores for power and oil, but killer whores with hate
and fear in our hearts. We are human scum, and that is
how history will judge us. No redeeming social value.
Just whores. Get out of our way, or we'll kill you.
Well, shit on that dumbness, George W. Bush does not
speak for me or my son or my mother or my friends or
the people I respect in this world. We didn't vote for
these cheap, greedy little killers who speak for America
today -- and we will not vote for them again in 2002. Or
2004. Or ever.
Who does vote for these dishonest shitheads? Who
among us can be happy and proud of having all this
innocent blood on our hands? Who are these swine?
These flag-sucking half-wits who get fleeced and fooled
by stupid rich kids like George Bush? They are the same
ones who wanted to have Muhammad Ali locked up for
refusing to kill gooks. They speak for all that is cruel
and stupid and vicious in the American character. They
are the racists and hate mongers among us -- they are
the Ku Klux Klan. I piss down the throats of these Nazis.
And I am too old to worry about whether they like it or
not. Fuck them.

- Hunter S Thompson

637.   Not only do I want you to remember September the 11th, but
I want you to think about Indonesia, and the attack on our
Marines in Kuwait, the attack on a French freighter. I mean,
they're out there. And the only way to deal with them -- and
by the way, I've come to the conclusion, and I hope you have,
that therapy is not going to work.

Cedar Rapids Iowa
Nov. 4th, 2002

Sadly yes, I too have drawn that conclusion

233

> So who turns out for the screening of this movie Fahrenheit 9/11 last night? You ready? Now, here are the celebrities that turn out. Here are the people who would turn out to see Josef Goebbels convince you that Poland invaded the Third Reich. It's the same thing, by the way. Propaganda is propaganda.
>
> - Bill O'Reilly

Is O'Reilly advocating censorship? Can we not, in a free society, draw our own informed conclusions? Don't we need to access information on both sides of an issue to make our judgments? Perhaps someone in the government or media should be put in charge of deciding what movies and books we, the people have access to. He invokes the name of Goebbels an awful lot to describe others. Bill O'Reilly is the single biggest, smelliest terd in the press pool.....I don't know how he sleeps at night.

638.   One of the problems we have is that enough people can't find work in America.

Bentonville Arkansas
Nov. 4th, 2002

639.   Of course, we've got a -- our economy is kind of bumping along. It's not as strong as it should be. It's bumping and bumping.

Cedar Rapids Iowa
Nov. 4th, 2002

I'm sure this term was gleaned from that economics textbook he keeps mentioning

234

640.   I want the youngsters here to remember the story of Flight 93, one of most profound parts of this entire history of the recent history we've been through.

St. Louis Missouri
Nov. 4th, 2002

Here's a weird irony...Bush wants youngsters to remember the story of flight 93 but, he likes to think about the Dr Seuss book Hop on Pop..(#394)

641.   The solid truth of the matter is, when you find -- if you want to help heal the hurt -- if you want to hurt people and help people in pain, the best way to do so is to call upon the great strength of the country, which is the compassion of our fellow Americans.

Bentonville Arkansas
Nov. 4th, 2002

Yes, by all means hurt people...???

If you think a weakness can be turned into a strength, I hate to tell you this, but that's another weakness
- Jack Handy

---

642.   I'm using this as an opportunity to make a point on judicial reform. And that is that if a judge thinks he's going to retire, give us a year's notice, if possible. And then we will act -- we, the administrative branch -- will nominate somebody and clear them within 180 days

White House
Nov. 7th, 2002

Once again, Mr. President, You work for the executive branch of government there is no "administrative" branch.

643.   A lame duck session -- for people who don't know what that means -- it means the Senate is coming and the House is coming back between now and Christmas and they've got a few days to get some big things done.

White House
Nov. 7th, 2002

Lame Duck (noun)
a) An elected officeholder or group continuing in office during the period between failure to win an election and the inauguration of a successor.
b) An officeholder who has chosen not to run for reelection or is ineligible for reelection.
c) An ineffective person; a weakling.

644.   BUSH:
How's your child, April?

REPORTER:
She's wonderful.

BUSH:
Georgia W?

REPORTER:
My husband is watching, and the name is Ryan Tyler James.

BUSH:
You might as well turn to the camera when you say that.

White House
Nov. 7th, 2002

It's just weird, ok…. weird…

645.   And job creation and economic security -- job creation and economic security, as well as homeland security, are the two most important priorities we face.

White House
Nov. 7th, 2002

1+2=2 ...Maybe rudimentary math should be
on the list of priorities

646.   See, every morning I go into that great Oval Office and read threats to our country -- every morning. As a matter of fact, there hadn't a morning that hadn't gone by that I haven't saw -- seen or read threats.

Washington D.C.
Nov. 12th, 2002

Triple negative...Two wrongs don't make a right...
.but, three is a whole other story.

647.   I am the commander, see? I do not need to explain why I say things. — That's the interesting thing about being the President. Maybe somebody needs to explain to me why they say something, but I don't feel like I owe anybody an explanation.

As reported by Bob Woodward to CBS
Nov 17th, 2002

And herein lies the problem.

Nearly all men can stand adversity, but if you want to test a man's character, give him power.
                                              - Abraham Lincoln

648. Well, I think what has to happen is there first be a strategy that recognizes that the Czech Republic can provide a certain contribution, or the French, or the British -- not the French -- but the Germans or the British can provide certain kind of capabilities, and that we dovetail each capability to an overall strategy.

Washington D.C.
Nov. 19th, 2002

649. BUSH:
I'll answer some questions.

REPORTER:
I have one question for President Bush, and a second question for President Havel. President Bush, you have said some lofty words here. The Czech Republic...

BUSH:
I said some what?

REPORTER: Lofty words.

BUSH:
No one has ever accused me of being a poet before, but thank you

Prague Czech Republic
Nov. 20th, 2002

And that record still holds...

Lofty adj
a) Affecting grandness; pompous.
b) Arrogant; haughty.

238

650.   I had a cordial meeting at that meeting last night. We greeted each other, cordially.

Prague Czech Republic
Nov. 21ˢᵗ, 2002

"And he apparently ate his tasty breakfast at the breakfast, and it was tasty when he tasted it."

This quip belongs to the hardworking Justin Thorn and his very funny website *www.dubyaspeak.com*.

651.   Sure, of course. I press any leader that doesn't believe 100 percent in freedom. And of course I do -- I'm freedom of the press, or Chechnya, or issues that indicate that there might not be a whole-hearted commitment to freedom of the people. I do it in a way that's a friendly way.

Lithuania
Nov. 21ˢᵗ, 2002

Bringing new meaning to the phrase "friendly fire"

652.   BUSH:
         I don't want you to get used to asking too many questions. I've been answering them all the whole time I've been here, question after question after question. If you were to ask a question, Stretch, what would it have

been, so I can think about it for tomorrow? I won't answer it now.

REPORTER:
What's your reaction to the confirmation of bin Laden being alive on the tape?

BUSH:
Thank you. I've got a formulated answer.
[PRESS CONFERENCE ENDS]

Prague Czech Republic
Nov. 21st, 2002

653.   Great evil is stirring in the world. We've faced perils we've never thought about, perils we've never seen before, but they're dangerous, they're just as dangerous as those perils that your fathers and mothers and grandfathers and grandmothers faced.

Pushkin Russia
Nov. 22nd, 2002

This Just In...Perils are dangerous...I repeat...
PERILS ARE DANGEROUS

654.   Well, first of all, you got to understand some of my view on freedom, it's not American's gift to the world. See, freedom is God -- is God given.

Interview with TVR Romania
Nov. 23rd, 2002

> Those who say religion has nothing to do with politics do not know what religion is.
>
> - Mahatma Gandhi

240

655.   I had -- I was there on September 11th, 2001, at Offutt. I
        remember their motto. It says, 'The Sun Never Sets on the
        Fighting 55th.' And that's good for the defense of the country,
        by the way.

Washington D.C.
Nov. 25th, 2002

Uhhhh...how?

656.   I want to thank all the local and state officials who are here
        with us today. I see governors and county judges, mayors for
        coming. My own mayor -- the Mayor of Washington, D.C., I
        appreciate you coming, Mr. Mayor. I want to thank the local
        and state law enforcement officials who are here, the chiefs
        of police and fire chiefs who are with us today. I see the chief
        of my city now is here as well. Thank you, Mr. Chief, for
        coming.

Washington D.C.
Nov. 25th, 2002

I'm willing to bet he forgot everybody's names

657.   The law I sign today directs new funds and new focus to the
        task of collecting vital intelligence on terrorist threats and on
        weapons of mass production.

September 11th Commission Bill Signing
Washington DC
Nov 27th, 2002

Instead of building newer and larger weapons of mass
destruction, I think mankind should try to get more use
out of the ones we have

- Jack Handy SNL

241

658.   I regret that the first team of our family isn't here today. She's helping decorate the White House.

Shreveport Louisiana
Dec. 3rd, 2002

It really is hard to believe he doesn't drink anymore

> President Bush's approval ratings have taken somewhat of a dive. A senior slump, if you will. Leading President Bush to one conclusion: He is the only one who realizes what a great job he's being doing.
>
> -Jon Stewart

659.   Sometimes, Washington is one of these towns where the person -- people who think they've got the sharp elbow is the most effective person.

Shreveport Louisiana
Dec. 3rd, 2002

That is a very weird and seemingly arbitrary criteria to determine effectiveness….

660.   If I answer questions every time you ask one, expectations would be high. And as you know, I like to keep expectations low.

Washington DC
Dec 10th, 2002

> Reason and free inquiry are the only effectual agents against error.
>
> - Thomas Jefferson

661.   There's only one person who hugs the mothers and the
        widows, the wives and the kids upon the death of their loved
        one. Others hug, but having committed the troops, I've got an
        additional responsibility to hug and that's me and I know what
        it's like.

                        Washington DC
                        Dec 11th, 2002

                He's the hugger and the decider...
                a president's work is never done

662.   In other words, I don't think people ought to be compelled to
        make the decision which they think is best for their family.

                        Washington DC
                        Dec 11th, 2002

        Certainly not! They should be compelled to make the decision
                which they think is wrong.....awesome!

663.   I think the American people—I hope the American—I don't
        think, let me—I hope the American people trust me.

                        Washington D.C.
                        Dec. 18th, 2002

In my lifetime, we've gone from Eisenhower to George
W. Bush. We've gone from John F. Kennedy to Al Gore.
If this is evolution, I believe that in twelve years, we'll
be voting for plants.

                                        - Lewis Black

664. The goals for this country are peace in the world. And the goals for this country are a compassionate American for every single citizen.

Washington DC
Dec 19th, 2002

Do I need to feed and shelter my American like a pet Or is it more like a pen-pal-thing?...clearly we need more information on this program. But, I'll be working on my list.

665. BUSH:
Igor. In Ingles?

RUSSIAN FOREIGN MINISTER IVANOV
(English) Thank you for receiving us, first thing.

White House
Dec. 20th, 2002

I'm just wondering why he's asking the Russian Foreign Minister to speak English in Spanish?

666. You said we're headed to war in Iraq -- I don't know why you say that. I hope we're not headed to war in Iraq. I'm the person who gets to decide, not you.

To Reporter
Crawford Texas
Dec. 31st, 2002

667. The Iraqi regime is a threat to any American and to threats who are friends of America.

Fort Hood Texas
Jan. 3rd, 2003

244

668. All Texans are proud that our state is the home to so many fine military units, including the great 1st Calvary Division

Fort Hood Texas
Jan. 3rd, 2003

Cavalry - Troops trained to fight on horseback.
Calvary – the hill upon which Christ was crucified

669. He really doesn't care about the opinion of mankind.

On Saddam Hussein
Fort Hood Texas
Jan. 3rd, 2003

Strong criticism from the "I don't listen to polls" president.
Maybe Saddam feels it's his job to lead and set the tone.

670. And we also know that when somebody is looking for work who wants to work means we've got to continue to try to stimulate job growth.

Washington D.C.
Jan. 6th, 2003

671.   One year ago today, the time for excuse-making has come to an end.

Washington D.C.
Jan. 8th, 2003

672.   Some mom fixing to have a baby wonders out loud -- when she wonders out loud whether or not the doc is going to be there to deliver the baby, it's a -- we heard a story, by the way, about that -- it's a sad situation.

Scranton Pennsylvania
Jan. 16th, 2003

673.   And the time is getting worse. That's what people have got to understand up there in Washington or over there in Washington down there in Washington, whatever. Thought I was in Crawford for a minute.

Scranton Pennsylvania
Jan. 16th, 2003

674.   It's a law that'll recognize that an affordable and accessible
        health care system can best be had if we limit the la -- caps --
        put caps on non-economic and punitive damages. That's
        what it understands.

Scranton Pennsylvania
Jan. 16th, 2003

675.   Many of the punditry -- of course, not you -- but other punditry
        were quick to say, no one is going to follow the United States
        of America.

To a Reporter
Washington D.C.
Jan. 21st, 2003

With the situation in Iraq growing ever more dangerous,
the 34-member Coalition of The Willing are, one by
one, dropping out to join the other coalition known as
Most of The Rest of The World.

- Jon Stewart

676.   I mentioned early on that I recognize there are hurdles, and
        we're gonna achieve those hurdles.

St. Louis Missouri
Jan. 22nd, 2003

677.   Small business owners like Joe may have problems passing
        their business off to a child or somebody they choose to pass
        their business off of.

St. Louis Missouri
Jan. 22nd, 2003

678.   But there is a difference of opinion about who best to spend your money in Washington, D.C. Sometimes they forget whose money you're spending. Listen to the rhetoric.

St. Louis Missouri
Jan. 22nd, 2003

Rhetoric (noun).
a) Skill in using language effectively and
    persuasively.
b) A style of speaking or writing, especially the language of a particular subject:
c) Language that is elaborate, pretentious,
    insincere, or intellectually vacuous

679.   So I met a guy today named Joe.... He said, by allowing businesses to expense up to $75,000, it means somebody is more likely to buy a copying machine, or in this case, an architectural fancy machine.

St. Louis Missouri
Jan. 22nd, 2003

680.   No child in America should be left behind in this country.

St. Louis Missouri
Jan. 22nd, 2003

By all means, leave them behind
while you're abroad

248

681.   [Saddam Hussein] is adept at deception and delays and denying. He asked for more time so he can give the so-called inspectors more runaround.

St. Louis Missouri
Jan. 22nd, 2003

So called inspectors?

682.   Before September the 11th, many in the world believed that Saddam Hussein could be contained. But chemical agents, lethal viruses and shadowy terrorist networks are not easily contained. Imagine those 19 hijackers with other weapons and other plans -- this time armed by Saddam Hussein.

State of the Union Address
Jan. 28th, 2003

The leader of genius must have the ability to make different opponents appear as if they belonged to one category.

\- Adolf Hitler

683.   Mr. Speaker, Vice President Cheney, members of Congress, distinguished citizens and fellow citizens.

State of the Union Address
Jan. 28th, 2003

It's like damning himself with faint praise

684.   Ten million seniors receive dividends. It's a part of their retirement package. It's a part of making sure the quality of life is high. A dividend is a part of a dollar that has gone through our system that has been taxed twice

Grand Rapids Michigan
Jan. 29th, 2003

Dividend (noun).
a) share of a surplus; a bonus.
b) An unexpected gain, benefit, or advantage

685.   This great, powerful nation is motivated not by power for power's sake, but because of our values. If everybody matters, if every life counts, then we should hope everybody has the great God's gift of freedom.

Grand Rapids Michigan
Jan. 29th, 2003

We'll liberate you if it kills ..well…you.

686.   History has called the United States into action, and we will not let history down.

Grand Rapids Michigan
Jan. 29th, 2003

687.   The war on terror involves Saddam Hussein because of the nature of Saddam Hussein, the history of Saddam Hussein, and his willingness to terrorize himself.

Grand Rapids Michigan
Jan. 29th, 2003

250

688. It's a commission not only to convince our fellow citizens to love one another just like we like to be loved. It's a commission also to devise practical ways to encourage others to serve. And one practical way is for the development of an award that Americans from all walks of life all around our country will be able to post boldly on their wall, that says, I served this great country by loving somebody.

Washington D.C.
Jan. 30th, 2003

Yup, Love Awards....sounds practical to me!

689. Everybody is precious in the sight of the Almighty. Everybody has worth. That would be a philosophy that drives this government as we work to strive to make the American experience strong and hopeful for every single citizen.

Washington D.C.
Jan. 30th, 2003

690.   But Cecil decided to become a mentor. He brought his young mentoree with him today. I decided I'd trick the guy and say, you got any goals? He looked me right in the eye and said, I'm going to be an architect.

Washington D.C.
Jan. 30th, 2003

Wow, good trick Mr. President…

691.   And, most importantly, Alma Powell, Secretary of Colin Powell, is with us.

Washington D.C.
Jan. 30th, 2003

Mrs. Powell gets demoted

692.   And I also want to assure [Italian Prime Minister] Silvio [Berlusconi] that should we require military action, shortly after our troops go in, will go food and medicine and supplies to the Iraqi people. We will, of course, win militarily, if we have to.

Washington D.C.
Jan. 30th, 2003

So, losing is actually an option?

693.   Well, all due in modesty, I thought I did a pretty good job myself of making it clear that he's [Saddam Hussein's] not disarming and why he should disarm.

Washington D.C.
Jan. 31st, 2003

694.   Columbia carried in its payroll classroom experiments from
         some of our -- ah -- students in America.

National Institutes of Health
Bethesda Maryland
Feb. 3rd, 2003

695.   And as I said in my State of the Union, the idea is to see that
         a car born today -- I mean, a child born today will be driving a
         car, as his or her first car, which will be powered by hydrogen
         and pollution-free.

Washington D.C.
Feb. 6th, 2003

**White House Press Briefing with
Ari Fleisher - May 7, 2001**

Q - Is one of the problems with this, and the entire
energy field, American lifestyles? Does the President
believe that, given the amount of energy Americans
consume per capita, how much it exceeds any other
citizen in any other country in the world, does the
President believe we need to correct our lifestyles to
address the energy problem?

MR. FLEISCHER:- That's a big no. The President
believes that it's an American way of life, and that it
should be the goal of policy makers to protect the
American way of life. The American way of life is a
blessed one....

---

696.   We can also be confident in the ways of Providence, even
         when they are far from our understanding. Events aren't
         moved by blind change and chance. Behind all of life and all

of history, there's a dedication and purpose, set by the hand of a just and faithful God. And that hope will never be shaken.

Washington D.C.
Feb. 6th, 2003

I am convinced that nothing will happen to me, for I know the greatness of the task for which Providence has chosen me

- Adolf Hitler

---

697.   Well, the role of inspectors is to sit there and verify whether or not he's disarmed, not to play hide-and-seek in a country the size of California.

Washington D.C.
Feb. 7th, 2003

698.   In this country and in Australia people believe that everybody has got worth, everybody counts, that everybody is equal in the eyes of the Almighty. So the issue is not only peace, the issue is freedom and liberty. I made it clear in my State of the Union -- and the people of Australia must understand this -- I don't believe liberty is America's gift to the world. I believe it is God's gift to humanity.

Washington D.C.
Feb. 10th, 2003

699.   It's so inspirational to see your courage, as well as to see the great works of our Lord in your heart.

Nashville Tennessee
Feb. 10th, 2003

Bush takes his tent revival show on the road...

254

700.   So today I ask you to challenge your listeners to love
        somebody just like they'd like to be loved themselves, to
        remind them that one person can make a difference in
        somebody's life, to encourage them, to mentor, to encourage
        them to start a ministry, which will find the children of those
        who are incarsinated and love them.

Nashville Tennessee
Feb. 10th, 2003

There's laws against that.

701.   We face a continuing threat of terrorist networks that hate the
        very thought of people being able to live in freedom. They
        hate the thought of the fact that in this great country, we can
        worship the Almighty God the way we see fit. And what
        probably makes him even angrier is we're not going to
        change.

Nashville Tennessee
Feb. 10th, 2003

> But then I sigh, and with a piece of scripture,
> Tell them that God bids us do good for evil.
> And thus I clothe my naked villainy
> With odd old ends stolen forth of holy writ,
> And seem I a saint, when most I play the Devil.
>
> *-William Shakespeare,*
> *King Richard III*

702.   There was wars on other continents, but we were safe.

Washington D.C.
Feb. 10th, 2003

703.   I want to thank you, Sherry Jean, for representing all the decent people, whether they be foster moms or dads -- and by the way, being a foster parent is an incredibly important part of our society -- or whether being a mentor, or whether being somebody volunteering their time for after-school programs to help save lives, particularly lives of our children.

Nashville Tennessee
Feb. 10th, 2003

Bush introduces a dramatic new role for
after school programs

Stupidity is also a gift of God, but one mustn't misuse it

- Pope John Paul II

704.   I'm the person in this country that hugs the mothers and the widows if their son or husband dies.

Nashville Tennessee
Feb. 10th, 2003

Worse, the president hasn't attended funerals or memorials for the soldiers who have lost their lives, breaking with military tradition.

- Rev. Jesse Jackson

705.   Now, we talked to Joan Hanover. She and her husband, George, were visiting with us. They are near retirement—retiring—in the process of retiring, meaning they're very smart, active, capable people who are retirement age and are retiring.

Alexandria Virginia
Feb. 12th, 2003

256

706.   If we get rid of the double taxation of dividends, it means that one of the good investment vehicles for a child who is young today will be a dividend paying stock.

Alexandria Virginia
Feb. 12th, 2003

Daycare to Day Trading.

President Bush announced his new economic plan. The centerpiece was a proposed repeal of the dividends tax on stocks, a boon that could be worth millions of dollars to average Americans. Well, average stock owning Americans. Technically, Americans who own a significant amount of shares in dividend dealing companies. Well, rich people, that's what I'm trying to say. They're going to do really well with this.

- Jon Stewart

707.   Twenty-three million businesses will receive over $2,000 in income tax relief. Now, that means a lot when you start thinking about the implications. I mean, you've got a one-man shop. $2,000 may mean the capacity to buy a machine, leverage the money to buy a machine, which means another job.

Jacksonville Florida
Feb. 13th, 2003

Last night in his speech, President Bush called for a complete overhaul of the tax code. He said he was shocked to find out that some millionaires in this country were still paying taxes.

- Jay Leno

708. We owe it to our citizens to protect us within the Constitution that we're all sworn to uphold, and we will do that.

FBI Headquarters
Feb. 14th, 2003

> It behooves every man who values liberty of conscience for himself, to resist invasions of it in the case of others
> - Thomas Jefferson

709. And I think unless the United Nations shows some backbone and courage, it will render the -- it could render the Security Council irrelevant. And that's a danger, in dealing with the new threats that the civilized world faces. We face terrorism, we face the idea of people having nuclear arms.

Washington D.C.
Feb. 18th, 2003

> Too bad you can't buy a voodoo globe so that you could make the earth spin real fast and freak everybody out.
>
> - Jack Handy

710. REPORTER:
Given the size of the protests in England over the weekend, do you have any concerns that Tony Blair might pay a serious political price for supporting you on Iraq?

BUSH:
First of all, you know, size of protest, it's like deciding, well, I'm going to decide policy based upon a focus group.

Washington D.C.
Feb. 18th, 2003

> Politics, just like the tropical forest, feeds itself from its own waste.
>
> - Paul Carvel

711.   It used to be in our history that only a few would own stocks. I bet there's a lot of people in Georgia in the old days would look up at Wall Street and say, you know, they own stocks, what is that all about?

Kennesaw Georgia
Feb. 20th, 2003

712.   But as we insist that Congress be wise with your money, we're going to make sure we spend enough to win this war. And by spending enough to win a war, we may not have a war at all.

Kennesaw Georgia
Feb. 20th, 2003

713.   But it used to be that oceans -- we thought oceans could protect us, that we were guarded by the oceans. And that if there was a threat overseas, as a result of the protection from the oceans, we could decide whether to be involved or not. It might affect us overseas, but it couldn't affect us at home. And therefore, we have the luxury of kind of picking and choosing gathering threats.

Kennesaw Georgia
Feb. 20th, 2003

As fighting in Iraq intensifies, President Bush delivered his supplemental war budget to Congress. The money will cover 30 days of fighting, then we'll be sent one war every other month until we cancel our subscription.

—Craig Kilborn

714.   I know there's some concern about overstating of numbers, you know, invest in my company because the sky's the limit. We may not be cash flowing much, but the sky's the limit. Well, when you pay dividends, that sky's the limit business doesn't hunt. What only matters is whether or not they can distribute that cash they say they're going to distribute. It leads to conservative business practices. It leads to being people -- more businesses being responsible with your money.

Kennesaw Georgia
Feb. 20th, 2003

""not be cash flowing much", not be President thinking much and this statement infers that businesses being responsible with your money is a bad thing…

President Bush was on Wall Street giving a speech on corporate responsibility. He called for the doubling of punishment for corporate crime. That means they will slap you on both wrists apparently.

—Jay Leno

715.   I know there's a lot of young ladies who are growing up wondering whether or not they can be champs. And they see the championship teams from USC and University of Portland here, girls who worked hard to get to where they are, and they're wondering about the example they're setting. What is life choices about?

Meeting with NCAA Champions
White House
Feb. 24th, 2003

716.   There you are. You look just like yourself.

To ESPN analyst Kirk Herbstreit
White House
Feb. 24th, 2003

717.   The war on terror is recognizing that weapons of mass destruction, in the hands of brutal dictators, also threatens the American people.

Washington D.C.
Feb. 24th, 2003

The demagogue is one who preaches doctrines he knows to be untrue to men he knows to be idiots

- Henry Louis Mencken

---

718.   Saddam Hussein's refusal to comply with the demands of the
        civilized world is a threat to peace, and it's a threat to stability.
        ...It's a threat to the security of peace-leaving -- peace-loving
        people everywhere.

Washington D.C.
Feb. 24th, 2003

Chapter Seven

Master of Low Expectations

The dumber people think you are, the more surprised they're going to be when you kill them

William Clayton

> We are all capable of believing things which we know to
> be untrue, and then, when we are finally proved wrong,
> impudently twisting the facts so as to show that we
> were right. Intellectually, it is possible to carry on this
> process for an indefinite time: the only check on it is
> that sooner or later a false belief bumps up against
> solid reality, usually on a battlefield.
>
> - George Orwell

719.   I was disappointed that the Congress did not respond to the
$3.5 billion we asked for. They not only reduced the budget
that we asked for, they earmarked a lot of the money. That's
a disappointment, a disappointment when the executive
branch gets micromanaged by the legislative branch.

Washington D.C.
Feb. 24th, 2003

Micromanaged? Deciding how much $ and to whom
it goes is their job

720.   And you have an example now, as champs, to help solve
America's issues one person at a time.

Washington D.C.
Feb. 24th, 2003

721. As you know, appropriators are appropriators. They live up to their name, whether they be Republicans or Democrats. They like to appropriate. And our jobs as chief executives is to make sure they appropriate within reasonable levels.

Washington D.C.
Feb. 24th, 2003

722. It is important for the Iraqi leadership and Iraqi generals to clearly understand that if they take innocent life, if they destroy infrastructure, they will be held to account as war criminals.

Washington D.C.
Feb. 25th, 2003

723. Saddam Hussein could care less about human condition inside of Iraq.

Washington D.C.
Feb. 25th, 2003

724.   There is all kinds of estimates about the cost of war.

Washington D.C.
Feb. 25th, 2003

> I have a scheme for stopping war. It's this -- no nation is
> allowed to enter a war till they have paid for the last
> one
>   - Will Rogers

725.   The danger with Iraq is that he can strike in the
        neighborhood. And the danger with Iraq is that he has got the
        willingness and capacity to train al Qaeda-type organizations
        and provide them with equipment to hurt America.

Washington D.C.
Feb. 26th, 2003

726.   As I said in my State of the Union address, liberty is not
        America's gift to the world. Liberty is God's gift to human -- to
        the human -- mankind.

Washington D.C.
Feb. 26th, 2003

> Religion is regarded by the common people as true, by
> the wise as false, and by the rulers as useful
>   - Seneca (1AD)

727.   It's a war in which we will hunt down those who hate America,
        one person at a time.

Washington D.C.
Mar. 4th, 2003

For the record, I LOVE America!

728.   I went down to Mississippi, met a man who had moved to Mississippi to provide health care for some of our most neediest citizens.

Washington D.C.
Mar. 4th, 2003

729.   It's a different kind of war than we're used to in America. It's a war that requires patience and focus.

Washington D.C.
Mar. 4th, 2003

Different? Before now it's been kind of like Attention Deficit/Hyperactivity Disorder with ammunition?

730.   I want the United Nations to be effective. It's important for it to be a robust, capable body. It's important for it's words to mean what they say, and as we head into the 21st century, Mark, when it comes to our security, we really don't need anybody's permission.

To a Reporter at White House
Mar. 6th, 2003

> One of the principles that we operate on in this country is that leaders are held accountable. The simple truth is that we went into Iraq on the basis of some intuition, some fear, and some exaggerated rhetoric and some very, very scanty evidence.
>
> - Wesley Clark

268

731. I believe Saddam Hussein is a threat to the American people. I believe he's a threat to the neighborhood in which he lives. And I've got a good evidence to believe that..

White House
Mar. 6th, 2003

National Journal - March 2, 2006
Murray Waas

The second classified report, delivered to Bush in early January 2003, was also a summary of a National Intelligence Estimate, this one focusing on whether Saddam would launch an unprovoked attack on the United States, either directly, or indirectly by working with terrorists.

The report stated that U.S. intelligence agencies unanimously agreed that it was unlikely that Saddam would try to attack the United States -- except if "ongoing military operations risked the imminent demise of his regime" or if he intended to "extract revenge" for such an assault, according to records and sources. (continued below)

---

732. He has no intention of disarming -- otherwise, we would have known. There's a lot of talk about inspectors. It really would have taken a handful of inspectors to determine whether he was disarming -- they could have showed up at a parking lot and he could have brought his weapons and destroyed them.

White House
Mar. 6th, 2003

(...)When U.S. inspectors entered Iraq after the fall of Saddam's regime, they determined that Iraq's nuclear program had been dormant for more than a decade ...

733.   I've not made up our mind about military action.

White House
Mar. 6th, 2003

Bush Was Set on Path to War,
Memo by British Adviser Says
New York Times March 27, 2006

During a private two-hour meeting in the Oval Office on Jan. 31, 2003, he made clear to Prime Minister Tony Blair of Britain that he was determined to invade Iraq without the second resolution, or even if international arms inspectors failed to find unconventional weapons, said a confidential memo about the meeting written by Mr. Blair's top foreign policy adviser and reviewed by The New York Times.

"Our diplomatic strategy had to be arranged around the military planning," David Manning, Mr. Blair's chief foreign policy adviser at the time, wrote in the memo that summarized the discussion between Mr. Bush, Mr. Blair and six of their top aides.

"The start date for the military campaign was now penciled in for 10 March," Mr. Manning wrote, paraphrasing the president. "This was when the bombing would begin." [...]

734.   Nuclear weapons may end up in the hands of dictators,
        people who are not afraid of using weapons of mass
        destruction, people who try to impose their will on the world or
        blackmail free nations.

White House
Mar. 6th, 2003

735.   Saddam Hussein is a threat to our nation. September the
        11th changed the strategic thinking, at least, as far as I was
        concerned, for how to protect our country. My job is to protect
        the American people. It used to be that we could think that
        you could contain a person like Saddam Hussein, that oceans
        would protect us from his type of terror. September the 11th
        should say to the American people that we're now a
        battlefield, that weapons of mass destruction in the hands of
        a terrorist organization could be deployed here at home.

White House
Mar. 6th, 2003

736.   If I may, I'd like to remind you what I said at the State of the
        Union. Liberty is not America's gift to the world, it is God's gift
        to each and every person. And that's what I believe. I believe
        that when we see totalitarianism, that we must deal with it.

White House
Mar. 6th, 2003

Politics is the art of looking for trouble, finding it,
misdiagnosing it, and then misapplying the wrong
remedies.

- Groucho Marx

737. The price of doing nothing [in Iraq] exceeds the price of taking action, if we have to. We'll do everything we can to minimize the loss of life. The price of the attacks on America, the cost of the attacks on America on September the 11th were enormous. They were significant.

White House
Mar. 6th, 2003

9/11 Commission Testimony (March 22, 2004)
The president returned to the White House [on 9/11] and called me in and said, 'I've learned from George Tenet that there is no evidence of a link between Saddam Hussein and 9/11.'

Condoleeza Rice

738. The American people know that Saddam Hussein has weapons of mass destruction. By the way, he declared he didn't have any.

White House
Mar. 6th, 2003

Defense Secretary Donald Rumsfield said Wednesday that he still believes we will find weapons of mass destruction in Iraq. These statements used to make me angry, but now I just feel kinda sad for him. The way I feel when Linus waits for the Great Pumpkin.

—Tina Fey

739. I described them [Iraq] as the axis of evil once. I described them as an enemy until proven otherwise. They obviously, you know, desire weapons of mass destruction. I presume that he still views us as an enemy.

Waco Texas
Mar. 10th, 2003

272

740.   The American people appreciate Ireland's work... to help
        secure passage of Resolution 1441. ...We appreciate our own
        support for ensuring that the just demands of the world are
        enforced.

White House
Mar. 13th, 2003

741.   All of us need to step back and try to figure out how to make
        the U.N. work better as we head into the 21st century.
        Perhaps one way will be, if we use military force, in the post-
        Saddam Iraq the U.N. will definitely need to have a role. And
        that way it can begin to get its legs, legs of responsibility
        back.

Lajes Azores
Mar. 16th, 2003

742.   I was the guy that said they [the U.N.] ought to vote. And one
        country voted -- at least showed their cards, I believe. It's an
        old Texas expression, show your cards, when you're playing
        poker. France showed their cards.

Lajes Azores
Mar. 16th, 2004

On Sunday, the president flies to the Azores islands to
attend a summit with British Prime Minister Tony Blair
and Spanish Prime Minister Jose Aznar, and here's my
prediction: Bush gets voted off.

-Craig Kilborn

---

743. On my orders, coalition forces have begin striking selected targets of military importance to undermine Saddam Hussein's ability to wage war.

Announcing the War Against Iraq
Mar. 19th, 2003

War continues in Iraq. They're calling it Operation Iraqi Freedom. They were going to call it Operation Iraqi Liberation until they realized that spells 'OIL'
- Jay Leno

The problem is that the good Lord didn't see fit to put oil and gas reserves where there are democratically elected regimes friendly to the interests of the United States.
VP Dick Cheney on Nightline - April of 2002

744. Maybe between the time I left Camp David and here I'll learn more.

Camp David Maryland
Mar. 23rd, 2003

745. Fuck Saddam! we're taking him out.

Meeting with Senators and Condoleeza Rice
as reported in Time Magazine
Mar. 24th, 2003

746. We can help somebody who hurts by hugging a neighbor in need.

Camp Lejeune North Carolina
Apr. 4th, 2003

274

747.   There is such hope here in Northern Ireland that the past can
        be broken.

Belfast Northern Ireland
Apr. 8th, 2003

748.   We believe in freedom. We believe freedom is universal. We
        believe freedom is -- is a gift from the Almighty God for every
        person, regardless of their race or their religion.

Bethesda Maryland
Apr. 11th, 2003

749.   One of the great things about this country is a lot of people
        pray.

Washington D.C
Apr. 13th, 2003

A lot of people pray in Iraq too .In fact,
Muslims pray 5 times per day.

750.   I think that we believe there are chemical weapons
        in Syria.

Washington D.C
Apr. 13th, 2003

Condoleezza Rice was confirmed by a vote of 85, 13,
despite a contentious but futile protest vote by
democrats. By the way, for a fun second term drinking
game, chug a beer every time you hear the phrase
'contentious but futile protest vote by democrats.' By
the time Jeb Bush is elected, you'll be so wasted you
won't even notice the war in Syria.

                                                    - Jon Stewart

751.   You're free. And freedom is beautiful. And, uhh, you know, it'll take time to restore chaos, and order, but we -- but we will.

Washington D.C
Apr. 13th, 2003

752.   You know, it's amazing, the statue comes down on Wednesday and the headlines start to read: oh, there's disorder. Well, no kidding. It is a situation that is chaotic because Saddam Hussein created the conditions for chaos. He created conditions of fear and hatred. And it's going to take a while to stabilize the country.

Washington D.C,
Apr. 13th, 2003

753.   In Iraq, the regime of Saddam Hussein is no more. A month ago -- one month ago -- that country was a prison to its people, a haven for terrorists, an arsenal of weapons that endangered the world.

Washington D.C
Apr. 15th, 2003

You know we armed Iraq. I wondered about that too, you know during the Persian Gulf War those intelligence reports would come out: "Iraq: incredible weapons - incredible weapons." How do you know that? "Uh, well...we looked at the receipts"

- Bill Hicks

> Those who voluntarily put power into the hands of a tyrant or enemy, must not wonder if it be at last turned against themselves
>
> — Aesop

> **Congress Approves Aid for Former Soviet Republics, - Robert Shepard,**
>
> Rep. Dante Fascell, D-Fla., chairman of the House Foreign Affairs Committee, said ... that the United States could not 'make a claim for purity' on arms sales, since the U.S. government has sold weapons to Iran, Iraq and everybody else in the world.
>
> *United Press International,*
> *October 3, 1992.*

754. Well, you know, they were -- first of all, they were the encouraging people. They were the ones who offered encouragement. I was, believe this or not, somewhat taken aback when I was in their presence. And these guys were so uplifting and so positive, and so obviously thrilled to be here. They got in last night at midnight. They can speak for themselves. I think you can speak for yourselves. At least you did in my presence.

POW Homecoming
Fort Hood Texas
Apr. 20th, 2003

755. I don't bring God into my life to—to, you know, kind of be a political person.

Interview with Tom Brokaw
Air Force One,
April 24th, 2003

756.   You see, it wasn't all that long ago that our tanks were in
        Baghdad. It may seem like a lot of time -- there's a lot on our
        TV screens -- but it wasn't all that long ago that the people
        got the first whiff of freedom.

Lima Ohio
Apr. 24th, 2003

757.   And we had an emergency and a recession, which affected
        the revenue growth of the U.S. Treasury. I mean, the stock
        market went down. Some of the pie-in-the-sky projections
        didn't make, and the investors said, oops. The numbers
        weren't real. The investors said, well, it looks like the days of
        everything is going up may end. And so people started
        selling, and the markets went down. That affected the
        revenues coming into the U.S. Treasury. Recession --
        negative growth means less revenues. And so, of course,
        we've got a deficit.

Expert Assessment from MBA Grad
Canton Ohio
Apr. 24th, 2003

758.   But this nation has got a deficit because we have been
        through a war.

                            Canton Ohio
                            Apr. 24th, 2003

                            Past tense?

759.   Last year, this company paid out more than $30 million in
        dividends -- and a lot of that went to Timken employees. So
        when you hear politicians say the tax cut is only for the rich,
        they're talking about you.

                            Canton Ohio
                            Apr. 24th, 2003

760.   I also want to thank Tony Fauci. He works for the NIH. He is
        on the leading edge of finding the vaccines that will help
        those who suffer from AIDS.

                            White House
                            Apr. 29th, 2003

                Vaccines prevent illness, not cure it.
        Was his last program building a time machine?

```
Never ascribe to malice that which can adequately be
explained by incompetence
                                    - Napoleon Bonaparte
```

279

761.   When I picked the Secretary of Education I wanted somebody who knew something about public education.

Washington D.C.
Apr. 30th, 2003

As opposed to appointing someone who knows about....say....Arabian horses?

This is a considerable improvement, he used to pick people via Pillsbury Bake-Off...which was itself, an improvement over the previous policy
"eeny-meeny- miney-mo"

762.   Our greatest strength -- well, let me -- gas prices are coming down, which, by the way, is positive for the American consumer, American people.

Santa Clara California
May 2nd, 2003

763.   We also understand the habits of freedom are more likely to make the world a more peaceful and hopeful place.

Santa Clara California
May 2nd, 2003

764.   I know there's people hurting here in Silicon Valley.

Santa Clara California
May 2nd, 2003

765.   We got a recession because we went to war.

Santa Clara California
May 2nd, 2003

766.   For the sake of job growth, let's put those tax cuts we've already got in place, in place today so people can find work.

Santa Clara California
May 2nd, 2003

President Bush's economic plan will create 2.5 million new jobs. The bad news, they are all for Iraqi soldiers.
—Craig Kilborn

767. We ended the rule of one of history's worst tyrants, and in so doing we not only freed the American people, we made our own people more secure.

Crawford Texas
May 3rd, 2003

768. We got into deficit because the economy went into the recession -- is how we got into deficit.

Little Rock Arkansas
May 5th, 2003

769. Work is not done. There's still dangers and challenges to remain. A free society is one in which will mean more likely a peaceful partner in a troubled neighborhood.

Little Rock Arkansas
May 5th, 2003

770. You see, here's what America and Americans believe -- that freedom is not America's gift to the world, that freedom is the Almighty's gift to each and every individual who lives in the world.

Little Rock Arkansas
May 5th, 2003

The common curse of mankind, -- folly and ignorance.
- William Shakespeare

---

771. But one of the problems of being a productive economy is that a worker can -- one worker puts out -- there's better output per worker, let me put it to you that way.

Little Rock Arkansas
May 5th, 2003

See, there's laws about that…even if the worker puts out willingly….

772. Jim Davis, an Arkansas small business owner] was reminding me that by getting rid of the double-taxation of dividends, he would save $5,700 -- money, which, by the way, that he would seriously consider putting back into his insurance company. He'd like to hire two additional employees. The double-taxation -- getting rid of the double-taxation of dividends would make it more likely two people would find work in Jim's business.

Little Rock Arkansas
May 5th, 2003

That will be two very low paying jobs…by my calculations about $1.42/hr

773. I think war is a dangerous place.

Washington, D.C .
May 7th, 2003

Death has a tendency to encourage a depressing view of war.

- Donald Rumsfeld

774. Less than 60 days ago that we started our mission. And in that period of time, not only did we remove a regime which threatened our security and held the American people hostage -- not only did we remove a regime that brutalized their own people, but we will stay to make sure that the Iraqi people have got the security necessary.

Albuquerque New Mexico
May 12th, 2003

> You must look at the facts because they look at you
>
> - Winston Churchill

775. These despicable [suicide attacks] were committed by killers whose only faith is hate. And the United States will find the killers, and they will learn the meaning of American justice.

CNN
May 13th, 2003

776. If those killers, those criminals believe that their bloody criminal acts will shake even one hair off the body of our nation and its unity, then they are deceiving themselves.

CNN
May 13th, 2003

Too Late! The nation is completely bald. Bush already stripped national unity bare with hot wax and strips of the Constitution.

284

777.	Al Qaeda is a group of people that they don't care about taking innocent life.

To Reporters
May 13th, 2003

United Press Int'l   July 12, 2005

BAGHDAD -- An Iraqi humanitarian organization is reporting that 128,000 Iraqis have been killed since the U.S. invasion began in March 2003.

Mafkarat al-Islam reported that chairman of the 'Iraqiyun humanitarian organization in Baghdad, Dr. Hatim al-'Alwani, said that the toll includes everyone who has been killed since that time, adding that 55 percent of those killed have been women and children aged 12 and under.

Rise in Civilian Casualties Shows Troubling Shift
Associated Press - June 1, 2005
By Hamza Hendawi

... More than 4,000 Iraqis -- many of them civilians -- have been killed in war-related violence this year, including at least 936 in May alone, according to an Associated Press count.
...Eighty-two percent of the war-related Iraqi deaths recorded in May were civilians, compared with 61 percent in May 2005, when 746 Iraqis were killed
...Jassim's brother told the Associated Press. ` `People are shocked and fed up with the Americans. People in Samarra are very angry with the Americans not only because of the Haditha case but because the Americans kill people randomly, especially recently.'

778. The [military] academies are really important for a lot of reasons. Obviously, what you learn on the football field is even more important since we're still at war.

Washington D.C.
May 16th, 2003

779. What you -- the character you displayed in your drive to be the best will serve our nation well. Because we're still at war. We learned that lesson in Saudi Arabia the other day. An al Qaeda -- a group we think is al Qaeda killed innocent life just for the sake of killing them.

Washington D.C.
May 16th, 2003

780. First, let me make it very clear, poor people aren't necessarily killers. Just because you happen to be not rich doesn't mean you're willing to kill.

White House
May 19th, 2003

If I ever get real rich, I hope I'm not real mean to poor people, like I am now

- Jack Handy SNL

781. All up and down the different aspects of our society, we had meaningful discussions. Not only in the Cabinet Room, but prior to this and after this day, our secretaries, respective secretaries, will continue to interact to create the conditions necessary for prosperity to reign.

Washington D.C.
May 19th, 2003

286

782.   Oftentimes, we live in a processed world—you know, people focus on the process and not results.

Washington, D.C.
May 29th, 2003

> There is nothing wrong with America that the faith, love of freedom, intelligence, and energy of her citizens can not cure.
> - Dwight D Eisenhower

783.   I recently met with the finance minister of the Palestinian Authority, was very impressed by his grasp of finances.

Washington, D.C.
May 29th, 2003

It's gotta be better than his own...

> It's clearly a budget. It's got a lot of numbers in it.
> - GW Bush
> Reuters May 5th, 2000

784.   The first part of your question is that -- is whether or not the weapons of mass destruction question.

St. Petersburg Russia
Jun. 1st, 2003

785.   I believe that, as I told the Crown Prince, the Almighty God has endowed each individual on the face of the earth with -- that expects each person to be treated with dignity. This is a universal call.

Sharm el-Sheikh Egypt
Jun. 3rd, 2003

786.   I said you were a man of peace. I want you to know I took immense crap for that.

To Israeli Prime Minister Ariel Sharon
Reported in the Washington Post
Jun. 3rd 2003

787.   I'm the master of low expectations.

Air Force One
Jun. 4th, 2003

788.   I show up when they need me to call people to account, to praise, or to say, wait a minute -- you told me in Jordan that you would do this, you haven't done it, why? How come? What is it? It's to keep the thing moving, keep the processes moving. They've got the man on the ground that is going to -- he's just going to -- I used the expression, ride herd. I don't know if anybody understood the meaning. It's a little informal in diplomatic terms. I said, we're going to put a guy on the ground to ride herd on the process. See them all scratching their heads.

On his meeting with Palestinian and Israeli
leaders aboard Air Force One
Jun. 4th, 2003

789.   I'm also not very analytical. You know I don't spend a lot of time thinking about myself, about why I do things.

Air Force One
June 4th, 2003

That's OK, the rest of us spend a lot of time
wondering why you do things.

288

790.   Listen, I recognize there's going to be extremes, particularly
        in the Palestinian territories, that want to blow up peace.

Washington D.C.
Jun. 9th, 2003

791.   I talked about the visit to Poland and to Russia, where we've
        got good friends in both those countries -- at least in terms of
        their leaders.

Washington D.C.
Jun. 9th, 2003

792.   I am absolutely convinced with time we'll find out that they did
        have a weapons program.

Washington
D.C. Jun. 9th, 2003

793.   Since I was [last] here [in Chicago], thanks to the bravery of our military, and to friends and allies, the regime of Saddam Hussein is no more. The world is peaceful and free.

Chicago Illinois
Jun. 11th, 2003

> The president is focusing on his agenda for the next three years. One: finishing the war in Iraq. Two: starting the war in three other places.
>
> -Ed Helms

794.   The House of Representatives will take up this issue in the coming weeks, under the leadership of a man from Illinois, a guy who I've got a lot of respect from, Speaker Denny Hastert.

Chicago Illinois
Jun. 11th, 2003

795.   Wait for us to succeed peace. Wait for us to have two states, side by side -- is for everybody coming together to deny the killers the opportunity to destroy.

Kennebunkport Maine
Jun. 15th, 2003

796.   And in the meantime, before that state is established, it is clear that the free world, those who love freedom and peace, must deal harshly with Hamas and the killers. And that's just the way it is in the Middle East.

Kennebunkport Maine
Jun. 15th, 2003

290

797.   Now, there are some who would like to rewrite history—
        revisionist historians is what I like to call them.

Elizabeth New Jersey
June 16th, 2003

798.   I came to seize opportunities, and not let them slip away. We
        are meeting the tests of our time. Terrorists declared war on
        the United States and war is what they got.

Washington D.C.
Jun. 17th, 2003

In a presentation at Johns Hopkins School of Int'l
Studies, Condi Rice describes 9/11 as an "enormous
opportunity" and that "America and our friends and our
allies must move decisively to take advantage of these
new opportunities."

- Condoleezza Rice
April 29, 2002

---

799.   We've been through a terrorist attack and a national
        emergency, we've been through a recession, we've been
        through corporate scandals where CEOs forgot what it means
        to be a responsible citizen. People didn't tell the truth. They
        were not responsible to their shareholders and employees.
        They will be held to account for their irresponsible behavior.
        And that was a shock to our system. We've been through
        war.

Annandale Virginia
Jun. 17th, 2003

> After a long investigation the SEC has fined Halliburton
> $7.5 million for issuing fraudulent statements
> exaggerating their profits in 1998 and 1999 during which
> their CEO was — oh who was it? Oh that's right. ...
> Cheney himself has not been implicated in the scandal
> and according to Cheney's lawyer there is no allegation
> whatsoever that he acted in any way other than in the
> best interests of the company and its shareholders. And
> you know what? It's still true today.
>
> -Jon Stewart

800.　A lawsuit, which causes premiums to go up, which means
your bills go up. And it means many doctors in hospitals
practice preventative medicine, which means they prescribe
more than is necessary in order to make sure they cover
themselves in case of a lawsuit, which causes your costs to
go up.

Fridley Minnesota
Jun. 19th, 2003

> Dad always thought laughter was the best medicine,
> which I guess is why several of us died of tuberculosis.
> - Jack Handy

801.　The true strength of America is the fact that we've got millions
of fellow citizens who are willing to love a neighbor just like
they would like to be loved themselves. That's the real
strength of this country, because we're a deep and
compassionate nation.

Fridley Minnesota
Jun. 19th, 2003

802. We said loud and clear [to corporate scoundrels], if you cheat the shareholder and your employees, you will be held responsible for those decisions. The world is now more peaceful because we acted.

Fridley Minnesota
Jun. 19th, 2003

803. When you hear about war all the time on your TV screens, the speculation of war and the discussion of war, it's not conducive to a confident tomorrow.

Fridley Minnesota
Jun. 19th, 2003

Apparently ignorance is bliss

804. Together we work together.

Washington D.C.
Jun. 25th, 2003

805.   If only I could have heard Johnny Mathis sing, then I would
        have wished Laura were here again.

Los Angeles California
Jun. 27th, 2003

806.   I appreciate [Florida Governor] Jeb -- talk about swamping
        somebody, he knows the definition of 'swamp' when it comes
        to political campaigns.

Tampa Florida
Jun. 30th, 2003

> Florida's number three industry, behind tourism and skin
> cancer, is voter fraud
>
> - Dave Barry

807.   I think Jeb and I were touched by what it means to be sitting
        at a table with a daughter who has said, I've got a
        responsibility to my mom.

Miami Florida
Jun. 30th, 2003

808.   It means that doctors are practicing what they call
        preventative medicine. In other words, if you think
        somebody's going to sue you, if you're in a litigious society,
        then you'll take extra care by prescribing more and more
        either procedures, or whatever it may be.

Miami Florida
Jun. 30th, 2003

> Prevention is better than cure
>
> - Proverb

294

809. I mean, if somebody is practicing preventative medicine, it's going to mean Medicare costs go up. Medicaid costs will go up. Veterans health benefits go up.

Miami Florida
Jun. 30th, 2003

Preventative war is OK, preventative medicine is not? For one thing it's significantly cheaper to prevent disease than it is to cure it...This is consistent with Bush's "kill first, ask questions later" policy.

810. There are some who feel like that, uhh -- if they -- attack us, that we may decide to leave prematurely. They don't understand what they're talkin' about, if that's the case. Let me finish. Umm, there are some who, uhh -- feel like -- that, you know, the conditions are such that they can attack us there. My answer is bring 'em on.

Washington D.C.
Jul. 2nd, 2003

"[President Bush] recently challenged Iraqi soldiers still fighting U.S. troops like so: ... 'My answer is bring 'em on.' For those of you who may be criticizing Bush for acting like a movie cowboy, let me remind you. He's actually acting more like a movie cheerleader."
-Jon Stewart

An inglorious peace is better than a dishonorable war
- Mark Twain

811.   The best way to describe it is, we're really happy with what
        we've seen so far. But we're realists in this administration. We
        understand that there's been years of hatred and distrust, and
        we'll continue to keep the process moving forward.

Washington D.C.
Jul. 2nd, 2003

812.   And then we'll be going to Goree Island, where I'll be giving a
        speech about race, race in the world, race as it relates to
        Africa and America. And we're in the process of writing it. I
        can't give you any highlights of the speech yet because I,
        frankly, haven't seen it.

Washington D.C.
Jul. 3rd, 2003

813.   As to whether or not -- look, once the strategy is in place, I
        will let people know whether or not I'm airborne or not. In
        other words, I'm not trying to make any -- I don't need to
        dramatize the decision. It's getting plenty of attention here at
        home. But we've got -- and look, I'm just gathering enough
        information to be rational in what we do.

Washington D.C.
Jul. 3rd, 2003

Uhmmmm...why start now?

So they [the Government] go on in strange paradox,
decided only to be undecided, resolved to be irresolute,
adamant for drift, solid for fluidity, all-powerful for
impotence.

- Winston Churchill

296

814.   I appreciate the desire for flexibility, I support the governor's desire for flexibility so long as, one, federal monies going to the states are used only for Head Start. In other words, what we really don't want to do is say we're going to focus on Head Start, the Head Start money goes for, you know, the prison complex -- I know that won't happen with Governor Ehrlich, but there needs to be a guarantee that the federal money spent on Head Start, only go to Head Start. Secondly, states and local governments must put money into the program, which would lock in the Head Start money for Head Start. So, the flexibility given to the State would not allow the state's budget flexibility. Governors ought to have that flexibility to hope that Congress will provide that flexibility so that when the accountability systems kick in, fully kick in, that a governor can truthfully say, well, I've had the tools necessary to make sure the Head Start program fits into an overall comprehensive plan for literacy and math for every child in the state of Maryland, in Governor Ehrlich's case.

Landover Maryland
Jul. 7th, 2003

Jeff Gannon ... He is a White House correspondent who has been lobbing softball questions at the president and his press secretary, turns out he is actually a paid escort for wealthy homosexuals. ... He actually had two jobs -- one obviously was sleazy and shameful and the other was a gay male prostitute. ... I think I know what Bush meant now when he said he has a mandate.

- Bill Maher

815.   I'm not -- not any intention of second-guessing his tactics. We share the same outcome.

Pretoria South Africa
Jul. 9th, 2003

816.   REPORTER:
Do you still believe they [the Iraqis] were trying to buy nuclear materials in Africa?

BUSH:
Right now?

REPORTER:
No, were they? The statement you made --

BUSH:
One thing is for certain, he's not trying to buy anything right now.

Pretoria South Africa
Jul. 9th, 2003

817.   There's no doubt in my mind that when it's all said and done the facts will show the world the truth. There's going to be, you know, a lot of attempts to try to rewrite history, and I can understand that. But I'm absolutely confident in the decision I made.

On the failure to find WMD in Iraq
Pretoria South Africa
Jul. 9th, 2003

I heard some good news today, the FBI and the CIA are going to start cooperating. They are going to start working together. And if you don't know the difference between the FBI and the CIA, the FBI bungles domestic crime, the CIA bungles foreign crime.

—David Letterman

298

818. The larger point is, and the fundamental question is, did Saddam Hussein have a weapons program? And the answer is, absolutely. And we gave him a chance to allow the inspectors in, and he wouldn't let them in. And, therefore, after a reasonable request, we decided to remove him from power, along with other nations, so as to make sure he was not a threat to the United States and our friends and allies in the region.

Washington D.C.
Jul. 14th, 2003

The truth is incontrovertible, malice may attack it, ignorance may deride it, but in the end; there it is.
- Winston Churchill

---

819. I, I think the intelligy I get is darn good intelligence.

Washington D.C.
Jul. 14th, 2003

Senator Joe Lieberman said as far as these hijacking threats are concerned somebody should have put two and two together. Put two and two together? Well, that eliminates Bush right there.

—Jay Leno

---

820. I'll talk about the values that make our country unique and different. We love freedom here in America.

Washington D.C.
Jul. 16th, 2003

821. And we live in an amazing world. And yet, in the midst of our world, there's a lot of folks who are dying and will die.

Washington D.C.
Jul. 16th, 2003

> My young son asked me what happens after we die. I told him we get buried under a bunch of dirt and worms eat our bodies. I guess I should have told him the truth - that most of us go to Hell and burn eternally - but I didn't want to upset him.
>
> - Jack Handy SNL

822. Our country puts $1 billion a year up to help feed the hungry. And we're by far the most generous nation in the world when it comes to that, and I'm proud to report that. This isn't a contest of who's the most generous. I'm just telling you as an aside. We're generous. We shouldn't be bragging about it. But we are.

Washington D.C.
Jul. 16th, 2003

U.S. Aid Generous and Stingy

Los Angeles Times Dec 29 2004 ...the United States ranks among the least generous in the industrialized world." The article cited a 2004 study from the Center for Global Development and Foreign Policy magazine that "ranks 21 of the world's richest countries based on their dedication to policies that benefit the 5 billion people living in poorer nations worldwide." The study ranked the U.S. 19th out of 21 countries in terms of foreign aid. This measure combined public aid with private contributions attributable to tax breaks.

823.   And we've created these offices whose sole function it is to, one, recognize the power of faith and, two, recognize there are fantastic programs all throughout the country on a variety of subjects, all based upon faith, all changing lives, all making American life better, and therefore, folks would be enlisted in making sure the American dream extends throughout our society.

Washington D.C.
Jul. 16th, 2003

"Top" management is supposed to be a tree full of owls hooting when management heads into the wrong part of the forest. I'm still unpursuaded they even know where the forest is.

- Robert Townsend

---

824.   And one of the greatest societal needs is we have is to make sure our guys that spent time in the pen, not only receives spiritual guidance and love, but spiritual guidance and love can only go so far. And it's also helpful to have him be trained in a job which exists. In other words, there's practical application of taxpayers' money that we want to get into the hands of our faith-based organizations all throughout our society.

Washington D.C.
Jul. 16th, 2003

825.   There is no reason in the world why the great continent of Africa can't be self-sustaining in food. And not only self-sustaining, how about being -- the capacity to help others eat.

Washington D.C.
Jul. 16th, 2003

301

826.   People can read everything they want into it when they hear faith-based initiative. That all of a sudden opens everybody's imagination in the world to vast possibilities, some which exist and some which don't.

Washington D.C.
Jul. 16th, 2003

827.   Look, I fully understand the issue, the frustration some face. And it's a frustration based upon a long practice here at the federal level, and that is there's no place for faith-based programs and trying to help people in need. And therefore, we'll discriminate, shove out of the way, not deal with, make it hard for, create barriers to entry.

Washington D.C.
Jul. 16th, 2003

828.   So one of the things we've done here in the White House to deal with this issue is we've started -- and Jim Towey is -- we've got an office dedicated, by the way, to this faith-based initiative.

Washington D.C.
Jul. 16th, 2003

The Pope said that churches in countries like the United States are dying out. He said it's like they're going out of business. You know why? People used to need churches to help them understand the word of God. But, see, now that job has been transferred to the federal government.

-Jay Leno

829.   There's a lot of initiatives around from the faith-based program that track the child who needs to be mentored. And the best place to find mentors, of course, is you can find them every Sunday.

Washington D.C.
Jul. 16th, 2003

President Bush's parents called him this week and said, 'You cannot have another war until you've finished the ones you've started.'

- Bill Maher

---

830.   It makes it awfully hard for a society to function that is at war with itself, as you know.

Washington D.C.
Jul. 16th, 2003

831.   And we base it, our history, and our decision making, our future, on solid values. The first value is, we're all God's children.

Washington D.C.
Jul. 16th, 2003

President Bush nominated John Bolton as the new ambassador to the U.N. He did it while the Senate was in recess. Democrats say President Bush circumvented the system to get his way. And President Bush says that's ridiculous. I've never circumvented anything, I'm not even Jewish.

-Jay Leno

---

832.   Yeah, we will bring the weapons. And, of course, we will bring
         the information forward on the weapons when they find them.
         And that'll end up -- end all this speculation. I understand the
         -- there's been a lot of speculation over in Great Britain, we've
         got a little bit of it, about whether or not -- you know, whether
         or not the actions were based upon valid information. We can
         debate that all day long until the truth shows up.

                         Washington D.C.
                         Jul. 17th, 2003

President Bush even called Lance Armstrong after the
big victory. Not to congratulate him -- he wants Lance
to teach him how to back peddle even faster.

                                                    - Jay Leno

---

833.   We won't be proven wrong. I believe that we will find the
         truth.

                         Washington D.C.
                         Jul. 17th, 2003

834.   I like to talk about if you're a mother or a dad, reminding
         people you're responsible for loving your child, and really
         making sure your child understands the difference between
         right and wrong and what it means to make right choices in
         life if you're involved, if you're worried about your public
         school system.

                         Dallas Texas
                         Jul. 18th, 2003

304

835.   By making the right choices, we can make the right choice for
        our future.

Dallas Texas
Jul. 18th, 2003

When I found the skull in the woods, the first thing I did
was call the police. But then I got curious about it. I
picked it up, and started wondering who this person
was, and why he had deer horns.

- Jack Handy

---

836.   The only thing I know for certain is that they are bad people

On British detainees in Guantanamo
Meeting with British PM Tony Blair
Washington D.C.
Jul. 18th, 2003

The power of the Executive to cast a man into prison
without formulating any charge known to the law, and
particularly to deny him the judgment of his peers, is in
the highest degree odious and is the foundation of all
totalitarian government whether Nazi or Communist.

- Winston Churchill

---

837.   Paul Carrozza, who is an entrepreneur, a business
        entrepreneur, started with nothing except a good pair of legs,
        and started what they call RunTex.

Dallas Texas
Jul. 18th, 2003

305

838.   Secondly, the answer to your question about reconstruction efforts, the answer is, who can do the best job for the Iraqi people?

Crawford Texas
Jul. 21ˢᵗ, 2003

> President Bush is asking Congress for $80 billion dollars to re-build Iraq. And when you make out that check, remember there are two L's in Halliburton.
> —David Letterman
>
> He's like the Peanuts character Pigpen. Wherever he goes, he stirs up such a humongous mess, it can only be cleaned up by Halliburton.
> -Bill Maher

839.   The more people involved in Iraq, the better off we will be. And that's exactly what our intention is, to encourage people to participate in the -- making Iraq more secure and more free. A free Iraq is a crucial part of winning the war on terror. And now I'm going to go see to it that the Prime Minister is well fed. We're going to feed him some chicken.

With Italian Prime Minister Silvio Berlusconi
Crawford Texas
Jul. 21ˢᵗ, 2003

840.   And, obviously, the more help we can get, the more we appreciate it. And we are continuing to work with other nations to ask their help advice.

Crawford Texas
Jul. 21ˢᵗ, 2003

> We are made wise not by the recollection of our past,
> but by the responsibility for our future.
>
> - George Bernard Shaw

841.　He [the Palestinian Finance Minister] told me he would put the budget of the Palestinian Authority on the Web page, and he did, which means he's a man of his word.

White House
Jul. 25th, 2003

842.　And so, but these are all difficult issues. By the way, we are now discussing them, now, in a frank way which is progress unto itself.

White House
Jul. 25th, 2003

He is indeed the master of low expectations

307

Chapter Eight

Peeance, Freeance

Whatever that means...

It is more difficult to organize a peace than to win a war; but the fruits of victory will be lost if the peace is not organized.

Aristotle

> The cry has been that when war is declared, all opposition should therefore be hushed. A sentiment more unworthy of a free country could hardly be propagated. If the doctrine be admitted, rulers have only to declare war and they are screened at once from scrutiny . . . . In war, then, as in peace, assert the freedom of speech and of the press. Cling to this as the bulwark of all our rights and privileges.
>
> - William Ellery Channing
> 1780-1842

843.   Security is the essential roadblock to achieving the road map to peace.

White House
Jul. 25th, 2003

844.   Our opportunity in society must also be a compassionate society.

Pittsburgh Pennsylvania
Jul. 28th, 2003

845. Dr. Condoleezza Rice is an honest, fabulous person and America is lucky to have her service. Period

White House
Jul. 30ᵗʰ, 2003

> President Bush has reversed himself and decided to allow Condoleezza Rice to publicly testify before the 9/11 commission under oath. It was a little dicey for awhile because White House lawyers told Bush that they didn't want to set a dangerous precedent. Bush said 'Hey I'm the precedent, I'll decide what's dangerous around here.'
>
> —Jay Leno

846. Of course, it's important that the -- that Saddam's sons were brought to justice.

On the assassination of Saddam Hussein's sons
White House
Jul. 30ᵗʰ, 2003

> Where is the justice of political power if it executes the murderer and jails the plunderer, and then itself marches upon neighboring lands, killing thousands and pillaging the very hills?
>
> - Kalil Gibran

847. There's no need for any unrestrained yelling.

White House
Jul. 30ᵗʰ, 2003

By all means, keep the yelling restrained

848.   I am mindful that we're all sinners, and I caution those who may try to take the speck out of their neighbor's eye when they got a log in their own. I think it's very important for our society to respect each individual, to welcome those with good hearts, to be a welcoming country. On the other hand, that does not mean that somebody like me needs to compromise on an issue such as marriage.

White House
Jul. 30th, 2003

> Sen. Rick Santorum is causing a lot of controversy this week with remarks he made about gays. He said, 'I have no problem with homosexuals, I have a problem with homosexual acts.' Well maybe he's doing it wrong.
>
> —Jay Leno

849.   REPORTER:
Mr. President, with no opponent, how can you spend $170 million or more on your primary campaign?

BUSH:
Just watch.

White House
Jul. 30th, 2003

850.   As the economy kind of got going again, the enemy attacked us. September the 11th had a significant impact on our economy. And then we discovered some of our corporate CEOs forgot to tell the truth, and that affected confidence. And then as you may remember, Tom, we had the steady drumbeat to war. As I mentioned in my press conference the other day, on our TV screens there was a -- on some TV screens -- there was a constant

reminder for the American people, march to war. War is not a very pleasant subject in people's minds, it's not conducive for the investment of capital.

Washington D.C.
Aug. 1ˢᵗ, 2003

I'm sorry. Can I stop you here a moment?
They forgot to tell the truth???.
OK... Well that's understandable
After all, this administration accidentally invaded an entire country to save us from imaginary WMD. Heck, they even dropped the ball when it came to catching Osama bin Laden. Wait....oh no...they didn't drop the ball...it was bombs...yes, they dropped those bombs on Iraq...they forgot that Hussein was not involved in 9/11.

But, that's OK...it can happen to anybody.

It turns out Enron workers were not only shredding documents at work, they were having sex at work. Having sex and shredding documents. Those are two things you don't want to get mixed up.

—Jay Leno

---

851.   We got attacked in 9/11. And then corporate scandals started to bubble up to the surface, which created a -- a lack of confidence in the system. And then we had the drumbeat to war. Remember on our TV screens -- I'm not suggesting which network did this -- but it said, March to War, every day from last summer until the spring -- March to War, March to War. That's not a very conducive environment for people to take risk, when they hear, March to War all the time.

Washington D.C.
Aug. 1ˢᵗ, 2003

That's called blaming the messenger...

852.　We had a good Cabinet meeting, talked about a lot of issues.
Secretary of State and Defense brought us up to date about
our desires to spread freedom and peace around the world.

Washington D.C.
Aug. 1ˢᵗ, 2003

853.　Listen, this guy [Secretary of State Colin Powell] has done a
fabulous job. Washington, particularly in August, is a
dangerous period -- a dangerous time, because there's a lot
of speculation.

Crawford Texas
Aug. 6ᵗʰ, 2003

When I was a little girl I was terrified of the speculation hiding
under my bed. I had to sleep with a nightlight....My brother
used to dress up like speculation and leap out of my closet
and shout, "BOO". Then of course, at summer camp we'd sit
around the fire speculating....scared the bee-jeebers out of
me. Now I speculate that there isn't enough therapy in the
world to help me.

315

854.   We've got a year-and-a-while during my first term to make the world a more peaceful place and we'll deal with it. Washington loves speculation. Clearly, you love speculation. You love it. You love to speculate about... Let me finish, please, let me finish. You love to speculate about whether so-and-so is going to be a part of the administration or not. And I understand the game. But I have got to do my job, and I'm going to do it. And I'm going to do it with the Secretary of State.

Crawford Texas
Aug. 6th, 2003

Doing it with the Secretary of State

O'Neill also provided Suskind with several damming pre-9/11 memos including one entitled 'Foreign Suitors For Iraqi Oil Field Contracts' and another entitled 'Military Plan For Post-Saddam Iraq.' Said a Bush Administration official — 'So that's where the military plan for post-Saddam Iraq went! Can you fax that?'

- Jon Stewart

855.   The Vice President and I went fishing. We threw our first lure at about 6:20 a.m., this morning. Looks like -- turns out the fish like cooler weather than hot weather, probably the press corps feels the same way. Turns out this is our hundredth day since major military operations have ended, ended in Iraq.

Crawford Texas
Aug. 8th, 2003

Turns Out?...

856. Turns out this is our hundredth day since major military operations have ended, ended in Iraq. ...We've been there a hundred days. We've made a lot of progress in a hundred days, and I am pleased with the progress we've made, but fully recognize we've got a lot more work to do. ...The American people know that we laid out the facts, we based the decision on sound intelligence and they also know we've only been there for a hundred days.

Crawford Texas
Aug. 8th, 2003

Good news, the government's 'Don't Ask, Don't Tell' policy appears to be working. The bad news is that it is the FBI and the CIA. They're not really exchanging information.

—Jay Leno

857. We learned a lesson September the 11th, and that is, our nation is vulnerable to attack. The best way to secure America is to get the enemy before they get us, and that's what's happening in Iraq.

Crawford Texas
Aug. 8th, 2003

No, we've had no evidence that Saddam Hussein was involved with September the 11th.

- GW Bush
Sept 17, 2003

The great masses of the people will more easily fall victims to a big lie than to a small one.

- Adolf Hitler

858.   That's just the nature of democracy. Sometimes pure politics enters into the rhetoric.

Crawford Texas
Aug. 8th, 2003

859.   The Palestinians, the people in the neighborhood must deal with terror, must rout out those who would like to destroy the process. The fence, by the way, is a reaction to days when there were terror.

Crawford Texas
Aug. 8th, 2003

860.   I think it's interesting. I'm a follower of American politics.

On California Recall Crawford Texas
Aug. 8th, 2003

> Time was, our leaders were all veterans of World War II, the Korean conflict or even the struggle for civil rights. But now, with the election of Jesse Ventura in Minnesota and Arnold Schwarzenegger in California, it is clear that the next generation of political leaders will all come from the movie 'Predator.'
>
> —Stephen Colbert

861.   One of the people I've tasked with coming up with solutions to the problems we face is Secretary Ann Veneman. She's done a fabulous job on behalf of the people of the United States. She is a common sense purpose -person.

Summerhaven Arizona
Aug. 11th, 2003

318

862.   We want those objections heard, of course -- every citizen
        needs to hear a voice.

Summerhaven Arizona
Aug. 11th, 2003

*Perhaps the voice will tells them to fashion
headwear from tinfoil.*

863.   See, our job as policy people and members of Congress,
        have got to fix problems when we see them -- they don't
        ignore problems, they don't hope the problems go away.

Summerhaven Arizona
Aug. 11th, 2003

Congress just voted to give themselves a pay raise. This
is their fourth pay raise in four years. And yesterday ...
Leader Dick Armey -- he defended the congressional pay
raise. He said Congress works hard. And all that hard
work has certainly paid off, huh? Let's recognize a job
well done. We are at war, terrorists are all over the
place, Wall Street collapsing, people are out of work,
retirement funds are gone. ... I got an idea, let's put
Congress on commission, they don't get paid until they
do something right.

—Jay Leno

864.   Any skeptic about what I'm talking about ought to come and
        talk to the people who know what they're talking about.

Summerhaven Arizona
Aug. 11th, 2003

319

865.   See, when you hear, red tape, that means there's a lot of rules and regulations that generally are in place to prevent something from happening. And our job is to slice through the red tape to get thinning projects moving forward.

Summerhaven Arizona
Aug. 11th, 2003

If you tell a joke in the forest, but nobody laughs, was it a joke?

- Steven Wright

---

866.   REPORTER:
[The California recall is] the biggest political story in the country. Is it hard to go in there and say nothing about it?

BUSH:
It is the biggest political story in the country? That's interesting. That says a lot. That speaks volumes.

REPORTER:
You don't agree?

BUSH:
It's up to -- I don't get to decide the biggest political story. You decide the biggest political story. But I find it interesting that that is the biggest political story in the country, as you just said.

REPORTER:
You don't think it should be?

BUSH:
Oh, I think there's maybe other political stories. Isn't there, like, a presidential race coming up? Maybe that says something. It speaks volumes, if you know what I mean.

Crawford Texas
Aug. 13th, 2003

320

867.   Al Qaeda is still active, and they're still recruiting, and they're still a threat because we won't cower.

Miramar California
Aug. 14th, 2003

Really? The fact that you didn't catch Osama bin Laden doesn't have anything to do with it?
...it's the lack of cowering?

868.   Parts of Iraq are still dangerous because freedom has enemies inside of Iraq.

Miramar California,
Aug. 14, 2003

869.   These highway bills come in six-year increments. I proposed $30 billion more spending on highways over the next six, and the last six.

Richfield Ohio
Sept. 1st, 2003

870. I'm going to describe what we discussed a little earlier... We had a chance to visit with Teresa Nelson who's a parent, and a mom or a dad.

Jacksonville Florida
Sept. 9th, 2003

871. I learned some pretty interesting lessons as the governor. And one lesson is that in order for schools to succeed, you'd better have you a good principal.

Jacksonville Florida
Sept. 9th, 2003

872. 8,000 Florida teachers have now been retrained since the law came into being. They're retrained on curriculum which work.

Jacksonville Florida
Sept. 9th, 2003

California education officials said today that the state of California needs 52,000 more teachers. They say we are facing a huge teacher shortage. In fact, by the year 2007, they said many students will be forced to have sex with each other.

- Jay Leno

873. She is a fabulous First Lady. I was a lucky man when she said, yes, I agree to marry you. I love her dearly, and I'm proud of the job she's doing on behalf of all Americans. Just like I love my brother.

Jacksonville Florida
Sept. 9th, 2003

322

874.   Sometimes it's not easy to be the friend of George W. Bush --
        I know that. If you know what I mean.

                        Houston Texas
                        Sept. 12th, 2003

875.   Obviously, I think they're going badly for the soldiers who lost
        their lives, and I weep for that person and their family. But no,
        I think we're making good progress.

                        Interview on Fox
                        Sept. 21st, 2003

876.   I glance at the headlines just to kind of get a flavor for what's
        moving. I rarely read the stories, and get briefed by people
        who are ... probably read the news themselves.

                Interview with Brit Hume Fox News Channel
                        Washington D.C.
                        Sept. 21st, 2003

877.   I do think it would be helpful to get the United Nations in to
        help write a constitution. I mean, they're good at that.

                        Interview on Fox
                        Sept. 22nd, 2003

> After going to war against the U.N.'s expressed wishes,
> the U.S. is now admitting it needs the U.N.'s help. It's
> the geopolitical equivalent of the 2 a.m. phone call
> ever parent dreads: 'Mom, I'm not saying I wrecked the
> car, but I need a ride home.'
>   - Jon Stewart

> A small leak can sink a great ship
>
> - Benjamin Franklin

878.   Washington is a town where there's all kinds of allegations. You've heard much of the allegations. And if people have got solid information, please come forward with it. And that would be people inside the information who are the so-called anonymous sources, or people outside the information—outside the administration.

Chicago Illinois
Sept. 30th, 2003

879.   We'll get to the bottom of this and move on. But I want to tell you something -- leaks of classified information are a bad thing. And we've had them -- there's too much leaking in Washington. That's just the way it is. And we've had leaks out of the administrative branch, had leaks out of the legislative branch, and out of the executive branch and the legislative branch, and I've spoken out consistently against them and I want to know who the leakers are.

Chicago Illinois
Sept. 30th, 2003

www.thesmokinggun.com

APRIL 6, 2006--A former top aide to Vice President Dick Cheney told a federal grand jury that President George W. Bush authorized him to leak information from a classified intelligence report to a New York Times reporter.

> As of yesterday, the Bush administration still hadn't found the source of the White House leak that outed a woman as a CIA operative. To recap, here are the things President Bush can't find: The source of the leak, weapons of mass destruction in Iraq, Saddam Hussein, Osama bin laden, the link between Saddam and Osama bin laden, the guy who sent the anthrax through the mail, and his butt with two hands and a flashlight
>
> —Tina Fey, *SNL*

880.   As we hunt down the terrorists, we're committed to spending -- spreading freedom in all parts of the world, including the Middle East.

Washington D.C.
Oct. 1ˢᵗ, 2003

881.   I'm proud of the Sergeant. I'm proud to call him, citizen. I'm proud to call him, fellow citizen to America.

White House
Oct. 2ⁿᵈ, 2003

882.   Everybody needs to have a good abrogado

White House
Oct. 2ⁿᵈ, 2003

Apparently the 'r' turns the Spanish word for lawyer, into the word for abolished,

883.   Today when I landed, I met a fellow named Roy Bubeck. You don't know Bubeck at all, and I didn't either -- maybe some of you do.

Milwaukee Wisconsin
Oct. 3rd, 2003

884.   No, the attacks of September the 11th, and the march to war leading up to the Iraqi excursion, affected the psychology of the country. We had a recession, and we had the attacks, the national emergency, plus the march to war. But we're a strong country. We're a resilient country because the entrepreneurial spirit is strong and things seem to be okay.

Milwaukee Wisconsin
Oct. 3rd, 2003

> Bush advisers have long been worried that a lagging economy could hamper the president's re-election chances. They hope that the Cabinet shake-up will provide a needed jolt. If that doesn't work, North Korea has to go."
>
> -Jon Stewart

885.   REPORTER:
There's a poll out in which a lot of people today are wondering whether the war was really worth the cost.

BUSH:
Yes.

REPORTER:
How do you respond to that, sir?

326

BUSH:
Yes, I don't make decisions based upon polls. I make decisions based upon what I think is important for the security of the American people.

White House
Oct. 3rd, 2003

886.   As members of the press corps here know, I have, at times, complained about leaks of security information, whether the leaks be in the legislative branch or in the executive branch. And I take those leaks very seriously. ...I'd like to know who leaked, and if anybody has got any information inside our government or outside our government who leaked, you ought to take it to the Justice Department so we can find out the leaker. ... And, you know, there's a lot of leaking in Washington, D.C. It's a town famous for it. And if this helps stop leaks of -- this investigation in finding the truth, it will not only hold someone to account who should not have leaked -- and this is a serious charge, by the way.

Washington D.C.
Oct. 6th, 2003

..OOOOOH ...I know...ask Scooter Libby!

CNN Feb 9, 2006

WASHINGTON (CNN) -- Vice President Cheney's former chief of staff, I. Lewis "Scooter" Libby, told a grand jury he was "authorized by his superiors" to disclose classified information from an intelligence report to reporters, according to the special prosecutor in the CIA leak case.

887.   And, listen, we're making good progress in Iraq. Sometimes it's hard to tell it when you listen to the filter.

Washington D.C.
Oct. 6ᵗʰ, 2003

888.   You see, the enemies want to create a sense of fear and intrepidation.

Washington D.C.
Oct. 8ᵗʰ, 2003

889.   See, free nations do not develop weapons of mass destruction.

Washington D.C.
Oct. 8ᵗʰ, 2003

Our Hidden WMD Program by Fred Kaplan
Why Bush is spending so much
 on nuclear weapons?

The budget is busted; American soldiers need more armor; they're running out of supplies. Yet the Department of Energy is spending an astonishing $6.5 billion on nuclear weapons this year, and President Bush is requesting $6.8 billion more for next year and a total of $30 billion over the following four years. This does not include his much-cherished missile-defense program, by the way. This is simply for the maintenance, modernization, development, and production of nuclear bombs and warheads.

Slate.April 23, 2004

328

890.   I was not about to leave the security of the American people
        in the hands of a madman. I was not going to stand by and
        wait and trust the sanity and restraint of Mr. Saddam Hussein.

Washington D.C.
Oct. 8th, 2003

Blix Questions U.S. Honesty
CBS News Sept 21, 2003

(AP) Former U.N. chief weapons inspector Hans Blix
accused the United States of showing "questionable
honesty" over Iraq and said the country was attacked
despite posing no immediate threat.

Blix spent three years searching for Iraqi chemical,
biological and ballistic missiles as head of the U.N.
Monitoring, Verification and Inspection Commission. He
has been critical of the role played by the U.S. and
British governments in Iraq, in interviews since his
retirement on June 30.

"In Iraq, there was no sign of an immediate threat" from
weapons of mass destruction, Blix told the Athens daily
Kathimerini, in an interview published Sunday. "What
worries me is the questionable honesty of a government
that publicly presents certain arguments, but privately
has different thoughts."

---

891.   I love the story of America, I love the fact that people who
        started with nothing and have built a fantastic food processing
        business.

Fresno California
Oct. 14th, 2003

892.   REPORTER:
        Does the US actually see Australia as its deputy sheriff in
        Southeast Asia?

        BUSH:
        No, we don't see it as a deputy sheriff, we see it as a sheriff.
        There's a difference.

                            Bangkok Thailand
                            Oct. 19th, 2003

Sydney Morning Herald Oct 2003

US President George W Bush this week described
Australia as a sheriff, prompting an outcry from Malaysia
which described Australia as a puppet of the US.

"Can I make it very clear. I don't see this country as
being a sheriff, a deputy sheriff, as having any kind of
enforcement role in our region," John Howard, Prime
Minister Australia.

---

893.   There's a lot of things that there's misconceptions. Evidently
        it's a misconceptions that Americans believe that Muslims are
        terrorists.

                            Air Force One
                            Oct 22nd, 2003

894.   I remember when we had the discussion down in Crawford,
        one of reporters, fellow reporters, said, I hear you don't pay
        attention to the press. I said, not really. And he said, why?
        And I said, well, because sometimes your opinion matters to
        me and sometimes it doesn't, but I've got a job and I'm willing
        to   lead.   And   the   fellow   said,

330

well, how do you know what the people think? And I said, well -- I reminded the fellow that people don't make up their mind based upon what they write, and secondly, my job is to lead.

Air Force One
Oct 22nd, 2003

Democracy in action! Yay...

Unthinking respect for authority is the greatest enemy of truth.

-Albert Einstein

895.   I made it very clear, obviously -- I said this during the pool spray there -- that a treaty [with North Korea] is not going to happen, but there are other ways to affect, on paper, what I have said publicly -- we have no intention of invading.

Air Force One
Oct 22nd, 2003

It's been reported that in the event of an emergency situation with North Korea the U.S. is prepared to send 70% of the Marine Corps to the region. According to President Bush this will still allow us to send another 70% to Iran and keep our other 70% in Iraq.

- Tina Fey, SNL

896.   And it's interesting -- in the room there is something like 60 percent of all the world trade -- was affected -- was countries in that room, and therefore it was a, I think, a very positive and strong statement.

Air Force One
Oct 22nd, 2003

897. [Australian] Prime Minister [John Howard] was a distinguished visitor of ours in Crawford, Texas, at our ranch. You might remember that I called him a man of steel. That's Texan for fair dinkum.

Canberra Australia
Oct. 23rd, 2003

It's a bird! It's a plane!...No it's Superrman...no...crap
it's just the Prime Minister of Australia.

898. It's in the interest of long-term peace in the world that we -- uhh -- work for a free and secure and peaceful Iraq. A peeance, freeance secure Iraq in the midst of the Middle East will have enormous historical impact.

Oct. 27th, 2003

I too have always felt that peeance freeance was largely and
unfairly overlooked....I feel a headache coming on...

Historic in a good sense, not historic in a sense of 'so we dropped bombs on everyone.'

- Jon Stewart

---

899. The Ambassador and the General were briefing me on the....the vast majority of Iraqis want to live in a peaceful, free world. And we will find these people and we will bring them to justice.

White House
Oct 28th, 2003

900.   The world is more peaceful and more free under my leadership.

White House
Oct 28th, 2003

Defense Secretary Donald Rumsfeld had a press conference at the Pentagon. If you listen to him speak, it really makes you wonder what the *f**k* he's thinking. [Shows clip of Rumsfeld threatening to hold Syria and Iran accountable for hostile acts against the U.S.] Do you see what he just did there? We're in the middle of a war, and he's starting another war. We're already fighting Iraq and he's like, 'Syria, you want a piece?' ...There is nothing like a cantankerous old man who takes a hey-you-kids-get-off-my-lawn approach to foreign policy. The guy's literally just like drunk swinging a broken bottle at people. 'Hey Netherlands, you looking at me?'

\- Jon Stewart

901.   It is dangerous in Iraq because there are some who believe that we're soft, that the will of the United States can be shaken by suiciders -- and suiciders who are willing to drive up to a Red Cross center, a center of international help and aid and comfort, and just kill.... The strategy remains the same. The tactics to respond to more suiciders driving cars will alter on the ground.

White House
Oct 28th, 2003

I'm surprised that, despite his concerted effort to bring the term "suicider" into popular culture, the media and others have failed to climb on board...maybe he'll have better luck with misunderestimate or embetterment...

902.   She's doing a fine job of coordinating interagency. She's doing what her -- I mean -- it shouldnt'a -- the, the, the role of the National Security Advisor is to not only provide good advice to the President, which she does on a regular basis -- I value her judgment and her intelligence -- uhh -- but, uhh -- her job is also to deal interagency, and to help unstick things that may get stuck -- is the best way to put it. She's an unsticker. And -- is she listening? Okay, well, she's doing a fine job.

On National Security Advisor
Condoleezza Rice,
White House
Oct. 28th 2003

> As the New York Times noted, Rice is the president's closest adviser on foreign policy matters, so close in fact she can even sometimes finish his sentences — which makes one of them.
>
> —Jon Stewart

903.   The Mission Accomplished sign, of course, was put up by the members of the USS Abraham Lincoln, saying that their mission was accomplished. I know it was attributed some how to some ingenious advance man from my staff -- they weren't that ingenious, by the way.

White House
Oct. 28th 2003

> A strong nation, like a strong person, can afford to be gentle, firm, thoughtful, and restrained. It can afford to extend a helping hand to others. It's a weak nation, like a weak person, that must behave with bluster and boasting and rashness and other signs of insecurity.
>
> - Jimmy Carter

334

Mission Accomplished

Thank you all very much. Admiral Kelly, Captain Card, officers and sailors of the U.S.S. Abraham Lincoln, my fellow Americans: Major combat operations in Iraq have ended

The battle of Iraq is one victory in a war on terror that began on 11 September 2001...'The liberation of Iraq is a crucial advance in the campaign against terror. We've removed an ally of al-Qaida, and cut off a source of terrorist funding. And this much is certain: no terrorist network will gain weapons of mass destruction from the Iraqi regime, because the regime is no more. In these 19 months that changed the world, our actions have been focused and deliberate and proportionate to the offence. We have not forgotten the victims of 11 September: the last phone calls, the cold murder of children, the searches in the rubble. With those attacks, the terrorists and their supporters declared war on the United States. And war is what they got.'...

- President Bush
May 1, 2003

Relax and celebrate victory. The predictions of those who opposed this war can be discarded like spent cartridges.

- Richard Perle

We ought to look in a mirror and get proud and stick out our chests and suck in our bellies and say: "Damn, we're Americans."

- Gen. Jay Garner

904.   As you know, these are open forums, you're able to come and listen to what I have to say.

Washington D.C.
Oct. 28th, 2003

> It is a paradox that every dictator has climbed to power on the ladder of free speech. Immediately on attaining power each dictator has suppressed all free speech except his own
>
> - Herbert Hoover

905.   A President must set great goals, worthy of a great nation. We're a great nation. Therefore, a President must set big goals. I set a goal for this country to make the world more peaceful by spreading freedom. Freedom is not America's gift to the world, freedom is God's gift to each and every individual in the world. I set a great goal here at home.

Dallas Texas
Oct. 29th, 2003

> I believe today that my conduct is in accordance with the will of the Almighty Creator
>
> - Adolf Hitler

906.   By mentoring a child, you shape the character of a child. And it's a high calling in life, because that influence reaches to eternity.

Dallas Texas
Oct. 29th, 2003

907.   You need to have you a governor in the great state of Mississippi who understands what it means to create an environment for job growth, who hurts when he hears people are working, and that man is Haley Barbour.

Gulfport Mississippi
Nov. 1ˢᵗ, 2003

908.   America has got some wonderful citizenry who just refuse to be defeated.

Harbison Canyon California
Nov. 4ᵗʰ, 2003

909.   America stands for liberty, for the pursuit of happiness and for the unaliein-alien-able right of life.

Washington D.C.
Nov. 5ᵗʰ, 2003

910.   I'm sure there's a lot of people frightened -- biotechnology is a long word and it sounds -- they may say, well, I don't know if I'm smart enough to be in biotechnology, or it sounds too sophisticated to be in biotechnology.

Winston-Salem North Carolina
Nov. 7ᵗʰ, 2003

President Bush said for security reasons, he's sworn off all e-mail communication. He will not be using email at the White House at all. Is that a good idea? I mean, it's not like that speaking thing was working out so good.

- Jay Leno

---

911.   We want results in every single classroom so that one single child is left behind.

Little Rock Arkansas
Nov. 10th, 2003

That's the saddest thing I've ever heard!

912.   It's a little off the subject, but a responsible citizen is somebody who loves their child with all their heart, a citizen who says, I want to put my family -- is a citizen I'd love to have working for me -- a citizen who said, I want my family first, I weep when I think about the thought of missing my child's baseball games, the kind of guy I want working for me, the kind of guy I want working with me.

Greer South Carolina
Nov. 10th, 2003

It takes a big man to cry, but it takes a bigger man to laugh at that man.

- Jack Handy SNL

---

913.   We marched to war. I don't if you remember, on your TV screens, last summer it -- a year ago, summer -- it said, 'March to War'. You turn on the TV, and there it says: 'March to War'. That's not a very conducive environment in which people are willing to take risk. It's not a positive thought. It's a necessary, in my judgment, obviously, to make America secure.

Greer South Carolina
Nov. 10th, 2003

Wow!

338

> We will bankrupt ourselves in the vain search for absolute security.
>
> — Dwight D Eisenhower

914. Well, first of all, the goal of the terrorists -- whether they be Baathists, or mujahideen fighters, or al Qaeda-type fighters -- is to create terror and fear amongst average Iraqis -- is to create the conditions where people are just so fearful for their lives that they cannot think positively about freedom.

Washington D.C.
Nov. 13th, 2003

> It's amazing -- we invade a country, overthrow a dictator, and then boom, we have an election. Well, more like, boom, boom, boom.
>
> — Jay Leno

915. Marge says she's frustrated that Washington has not delivered a prescription drug benefit under Medicare. She says, 'I'm tired of the talk.' This is her words, not mine.

Orlando Florida
Nov. 13th, 2003

> Sometimes I think you have to march right in and demand your rights, even if you don't know what your rights are, or who the person is you're talking to. Then on the way out, slam the door
>
> — Jack Handy

916.   The second pillar of peace and security in our world is the
        willingness of free nations, when the last resort arrives, to
        retain aggression and evil by force.

London England
Nov. 20th, 2003

Yes you read it right!

917.   REPORTER *(asking if Bush will visit Iraq, pay attention to
        how it progresses into something else):*
        Did you look back at any precedence of any other president's
        trips?

        BUSH:
        There is no precedent in the war on terror. This is the first war
        of the 21st century, unique in its nature. But I don't know. I
        guess you all need to do that. I don't know whether or not -- I
        think Lyndon Johnson went as a Vice President, or as
        President. I don't know.

        REPORTER:
        He was in Asia and he made an unscheduled trip.

        BUSH:
        Into Vietnam as President?

        REPORTER:
        Eisenhower went to Korea as a --

        BUSH:
        Franklin Roosevelt went to North Africa, but the front was in
        Tunisia. I think, but maybe not.

        REPORTER:
        Abraham Lincoln went to Richmond a couple of days after --

        BUSH:
        He sure did. I got the picture of the White House of the --
        Lincoln with his generals and Admiral Porter talking about the
        peace. I think that's what you're talking about

REPORTER:
But he was mobbed by people when he went to -- this was a couple of days after he fell.

BUSH:
Right. And he was on a boat outside of Richmond -- unfortunately called the Peacemakers. It had a wonderful rainbow behind he and his generals. That's where he's talking about making sure the peace was fair and generous so that the United States would stay united. And, interestingly enough, the original is in the -- upstairs in the Trinity Room in the White House. And it is in the Pentagon, as well, a copy of it, which I found to be very -- so I remember going into the Pentagon and -- somebody took -- But thanks for honoring it.

Air Force One
Nov. 27th, 2003

918.   And then I obviously made the decision to go into Iraq. And by the way, a free and peaceful Iraq is in our nation's interest. It's in our security interest -- that affected the economy. When you turned on your TV, it said, America is marching to war. That's not very conducive for -- that's not a very positive statement. It doesn't build a lot of confidence -- people, you know, marching to war, why would I want to invest in my home? Or why would I want to come to Home Depot if we're fixing to go to war?

Halethorpe Maryland
Dec. 5th, 2003

> As a young boy, when you get splashed by a mud puddle on the way to school, you wonder if you should go home and change, but be late for school, or go to school the way you are; dirty and soaking wet. Well, while he tried to decide, I drove by and splashed him again.
> - Jack Handy

341

919.   BUSH:
        I don't know what you're talking about, about international
        law. I've got to consult my lawyer.

        REPORTER:
        Can I clarify one thing?

        BUSH:
        Yes, you may clarify something.

        REPORTER:
        Thank you very much.

        BUSH:
        Depends on what it is, though.

About awarding the
reconstruction contracts in Iraq,
Washington D.C.
Dec. 11th, 2003

920.   And the threat of Saddam Hussein was a unique threat in this
        sense -- the world recognized he was a threat for twelve
        years, and seventeen resolutions, I think it is -- I believe it
        was seventeen resolutions -- for the resolution counter, give
        me a hand here -- seventeen? Seventeen resolutions. And he
        ignored them.

Washington D.C.
Dec. 15th, 2003

BLIX - Those 17 violations were before 1998.

UN Weapons Inspector Hans Blix
O'Reilly Factor Fox Show
March 15, 2004

921.   It's going to be very important for the Iraqi authorities to reach out to those people and talk about a system that guarantees minority rights, and a system which says that for some the future is bright.

Washington D.C.
Dec. 15th, 2003

for SOME???

922.   There's what they call actionable intelligence, to which our military has responded on a quick basis is improving.

Washington D.C.
Dec. 15th, 2003

> True genius resides in the capacity for evaluation of uncertain, hazardous, and conflicting information.
> - Winston Churchill

923.   As you notice, when there's a hole in the ground and a person is able to crawl into it in a country the size of California, it means we're on a scavenger hunt for terror, and find these terrorists who hide in holes is to get people coming forth to describe the location of the hole, is to give clues and data. And we're on it.

Washington D.C.
Dec. 15th, 2003

> In Iraq, the U.S. military's whack-a-mole approach to killing Saddam Hussein may have finally paid off. The bombs destroyed the area and left behind a 60-foot crater, or as coalition forces prefer to call it: a freedom hole.
> -Jon Stewart

924. See, without the tax relief package, there would have been a deficit, but there wouldn't have been the comm -- commiserate -- the, the, the, the, not commiserate -- the, the, the -- kick to our economy that occurred as a result of the tax relief.

Washington D.C.
_Dec. 15th, 2003

> We contend that for a nation to try to tax itself into prosperity is like a man standing in a bucket and trying to lift himself up by the handle
> - Winston Churchill

925. I don't expect people to agree with every decision I make. But regardless of whether they do or not, I'm going to continue making the decisions in the way that I think is best for the country. There will be ample time to have the debate about whether or not it's the right strategy or not. I look forward to the debate.

Washington D.C.
Dec. 15th, 2003

> Criticism may not be agreeable, but it is necessary. It fulfils the same function as pain in the human body. It calls attention to an unhealthy state of things.
> - Winston Churchill
>
> Without Freedom of thought, there can be no such Thing as Wisdom; and no such thing as public Liberty, without Freedom of speech
> - Benjamin Franklin

926. I take my job seriously, I will do my job and I look forward to the political debate later on. So I'm confident during the numerous press conferences I'll be having next year -- just like I had this year -- that you'll be asking me questions about this political statement or that political statement, and my answer is going to be the same until I'm ready to engage, and that is, let me just tell you what the strategy is of this administration. Forget politics. The strategy that I've outlined in order to do my solemn duty -- and my duty is not only to keep the country more secure, but more prosperous and a better country, as well.

Washington D.C.
Dec. 15th, 2003

The greatness of every mighty organization embodying an idea in this world lies in the religious fanaticism and intolerance with which, fanatically convinced of its own right, it intolerantly imposes its will against all others

- Adolf Hitler

---

927. Justice was being delivered to a man who defied that gift from the Almighty to the people of Iraq.

Washington D.C.
Dec. 15th, 2003

Of all religions, Christianity is without a doubt the one that should inspire tolerance most, although, up to now, the Christians have been the most intolerant of all men.

- Voltaire

928.   And if you're interested in the quality of education and you're paying attention to what you hear at Laclede, why don't you volunteer? Why don't you mentor a child how to read?

St. Louis Missouri
Jan. 5th, 2004

First show him where you office, then mentor him how to read…teach him about nouns and verbs…it will embetter his life and make us a hopefuller.country.
You will feel more better.

And, on the way home, just for fun….go into a shut-in's house and say "I love you".

929.   So thank you for reminding me about the importance of being a good mom and a great volunteer as well.

St. Louis Missouri
Jan. 5th, 2004

930.   We had a problem that fall when it turned out some of our corporate citizens failed to live up to the responsibilities of leadership. They didn't tell the truth to their shareholders and their employees. That affected the psyche of the American investor. You know, capitalism is only as strong as the integrity of the people involved in the process. And these leaders will tell you that you've got to be open with your employees. Otherwise, they're not going to work for you very hard.

Washington DC
Jan 9th, 2004

And these leaders will tell you that now that they've been caught…

346

931.   I was a prisoner too, but for bad reasons.

To Argentine President Nestor Kirchner after being told that
all but one of the Argentine delegates to a summit meeting
were imprisoned during the military dictatorship

Monterrey Mexico
Jan. 13th, 2004

I didn't realize that sleeping it off in the
drunk tank qualified as "prisoner" status.

932.   I want to thank the astronauts who are with us, the
courageous spacial entrepreneurs who set such a wonderful
example for the young of our country.

Washington DC
Jan 14th, 2004

Welcome to President Bush, Mrs. Bush, and my fellow
astronauts.
- Dan Quayle

President Bush announced we're going to Mars, which
means he's given up on Earth.
-Jon Stewart

933.   It's not a dictatorship in Washington, but I tried to make it one
in that instance.

New Orleans LA
Jan 15th, 2004

Admitting it is the first step

934.   The Oval Office is an interesting place to meet, particularly, people who are beginning to struggle with democracy and freedom because it's a reminder that the institutions, at least in this country, are always bigger than the people. Sometime we've got an all-right President, sometimes not all right. But the presidency, itself, exists.

Roswell New Mexico
Jan 22nd, 2004

935.   If you want to be blunt about what has taken place, sometimes when you don't measure, you just shuffle kids through. Then you wake up at the high school level and find out that the illiteracy level of our children are appalling.

Washington DC
Jan 23rd, 2004

> If you want to be the most popular person in your class, whenever the professor pauses in his lecture, just let out a big snort and say, 'How do you figger that!' real loud. Then lean back and sort of smirk.
>
> - Jack Handy

936.   More Muslims have died at the hands of killers than—I say more Muslims—a lot of Muslims have died—I don't know the exact count—at Istanbul. Look at these different places around the world where there's been tremendous death and destruction because killers kill.

Washington D.C.
Jan. 29th, 2004

937.   See, one of the interesting things in the Oval Office - I love to bring people into the Oval Office - right around the corner from here - and say, this is where I office, but I want you to know the office is always bigger than the person.

Washington D.C.
Jan. 29th, 2004

If the office was smaller than the person there wouldn't be any room for furniture

Perhaps he was trying to express this...

> When you get to be President, there are all those things, the honors, the twenty-one gun salutes, all those things. You have to remember it isn't for you. It's for the Presidency.
>
> - Harry S Truman

938.   King Abdullah of Jordan, the King of Morocco, I mean, there's a series of places—Qatar, Oman—I mean, places that are developing—Bahrain—they're all developing the habits of free societies.

Washington D.C.
Jan. 29th, 2004

> After an attack at the American consulate, Saudi Arabia has renewed their fight against terrorism, and they're serious, this time they may actually stop funding them.
> -Jay Leno

939.   What we don't know yet is what we thought and what the Iraqi Survey Group has found, and we want to look at that.

Washington DC
Feb 2nd, 2004

940.   We're on an international manhunt for those who would do harm to America, or for anybody else who loves freedom.

Roswell New Mexico
Feb 2nd, 2004

Well, if crime fighters fight crime and fire fighters fight fire, what do freedom fighters fight? They never mention that part to us, do they?

- George Carlin

941.   I'm a war president. I make decisions here in the Oval Office in foreign policy matters with war on my mind.

NBC's Meet the Press
Feb 8th, 2004

He reminds me of the man who murdered both his parents, and then when sentence was about to be pronounced pleaded for mercy on the grounds that he was an orphan

- Abraham Lincoln

942.   I'm dealing with a world in which we have gotten struck by
        terrorists with airplanes, and we get intelligence saying that
        there is, you know, we want to harm America.

                        NBC's Meet the Press
                        Feb 8th, 2004

In Pakistan anti-American protestors set a Kentucky
Fried Chicken restaurant on fire. The protestors
mistaken-thought they were attacking high-ranking U.S.
military official Colonel Sanders.

—Jimmy Fallon SNL

---

943.   In my judgment, when the United States says there will be
        serious   consequences,   and   if   there   isn't   serious
        consequences, it creates adverse consequences.

                        NBC's Meet the Press
                        Feb 8th, 2004

944.   God loves you, and I love you. And you can count on both of
        us as a powerful message that people who wonder about
        their future can hear.

                        Los Angeles California.
                        March 3rd, 2004

If God dwells inside us like some people say, I sure hope
He likes enchiladas, because that's what He's getting

- Jack Handy

Months ago officials set August 15th as the due date for the country's new constitution and, as of August 11th, President Bush remained optimistic. [clip of Bush: 'I'm operating under the assumption that it will be agreed upon by August 15th.'] Well guess what? The assumption that the president was operating on was wrong -- bringing the number of false assumptions we were operating under to -- let's see: 1. Iraq has WMDs. 2. We'll be greeted as liberators. 3. No insurgency. 4. All q's followed by u's. 5. Oil revenue will pay for war. ... 19,021. Iraqi army training on schedule. 19,022. Hummus left out won't spoil. 19,023. Not everything explodes. 19,024. Constitution by August 15th. ... Is there a fuck up they can't make seem like it was their intention all along?

-Jon Stewart

Chapter Nine

Opposite of Optimistic

If you ever have to steal money from your kid, and later
on he discovers it's gone, I think a
good thing to do is to blame it on Santa Claus

Jack Handy

Today President Bush ordered an investigation into whether it is appropriate to have civilians with no experience running a Navy sub. Hey, how about an investigation into whether it's appropriate to have a civilian with no experience running the country?

—Jay Leno

Navy officials confirmed yesterday that a Texas oil magnate named John Hall was at the controls of the USS Greenville when it struck a Japanese fishing boat last week. Apparently Hall was participating in the Navy's 'Take Your Billionaire to Work Day.'

—Tina Fey, SNL

945.   TIM RUSSERT:
The General Accounting Office... did a computer simulation that shows that balancing the budget in 2040 could require either cutting total federal spending in half or doubling federal taxes. Why, as a fiscal conservative, as you like to call yourself, would you allow a $500 billion deficit and this kind of deficit disaster?

BUSH:
Sure. The budget I just proposed to the Congress cuts the deficit in half in five years. Now, I don't know what the assumptions are in the GAO report, but I do know that.

NBC's Meet the Press
Feb 8^{*th*}*, 2004*

946. *A* lot of times, this country talks about our strengths, and we should. We talk about the military strength of America. And that's important. And we're going to keep us strong.

Springfield Missouri
Feb 9th, 2004

947. The march to war affected the people's confidence. It's hard to make investment. See, if you're a small business owner or a large business owner and you're thinking about investing, you've got to be optimistic when you invest. Except when you're marching to war, it's not a very optimistic thought, is it? In other words, it's the opposite of optimistic when you're thinking you're going to war.

Springfield Missouri
Feb 9th, 2004

948. Yes, that's a -- first of all, Mom, you're doing -- that's tough. But it's -- I appreciate that. I appreciate the idea of you wanting to give your children the education from you and the mom.

Springfield Missouri
Feb 9th, 2004

949.   My views are one that speaks to freedom.

Washington DC
Feb 18th, 2004

> By and large, language is a tool for concealing the truth
> - George Carlin

950.   See, one of the interesting things in the Oval Office -- I love to
bring people into the Oval Office -- right around the corner
from here -- and say, this is where I office.

Washington DC
Feb 18th, 2004

Sometimes I take people into the kitchen and say,
"this is where I kitchen"

951.   But the Congress giveth, the Congress taketh away. And
these tax relief will be -- will expire on an irregular basis.

Washington DC
Feb 19th, 2004

952.   Hopefully, as the Georgia economy approves -- improves --
and I'm confident it will -- there will be opportunities for
business opportunities.

Washington DC
Feb 25th, 2004

953.   Saddam Hussein said, I'm not going to expose my weapons, I'm not going to get rid of my -- I'm not going to allow inspectors in, he said. But this is the same man who had used them. So I had to make a decision -- do I trust the word of madman, or do I remember the lessons of September the 11th?

Louisville Kentucky
Feb 26th, 2004

> The magician and the politician have much in common: they both have to draw our attention away from what they are really doing.
>
> - Ben Okri

> The events of September 11 were carried out by people armed not with weapons of mass destruction, but with blades you can buy at a newsagent
>
> - Philip Adams

954.   In spite of the fact that we've got large bankrolls and wealth, beyond imagination for many people in the world, in our own society there's darkness and loneliness and addiction and wonder

Los Angeles California
Mar 3rd, 2004

955.   Congress wouldn't act, so I signed an executive order -- that means I did it on my own. It says we're going to open up billions of dollars in grant money competition to faith-based charities.

Los Angeles California
Mar 3rd, 2004

358

956.   These stories are being written every day in America. Every, single day this is happening. We never hear half of them or any -- I never, but, you know -- I barely hear any of them, but I just know they're happening.

Los Angeles California
Mar 3rd, 2004

957.   I want to remind you right quick what this country has been through, and the challenges this economy had faced over the last three years. First, we went through a recession. That means we were going backwards.

Bakersfield California
Mar 4th, 2004

No, No, No it doesn't….A recession is an extended decline in general business activity. The National Bureau of Economic Research formally defines a recession as three consecutive quarters of falling real gross domestic product. "Backwards" doesn't enter into it…drivin' me nuts I tell ya...

> And I know this happens because I took economics, and I'd explain it to yea' - but I flunked that course. Not my fault. They taught it at 8 o'clock in the morning. And there is absolutely nothing you can learn out of one bloodshot eye.
>
> - Lewis Black

958.   REPORTER:
Mr. President, some firefighters and families of the 9/11 victims -- of the 9/11 victims want you to pull your campaign ad focusing on the tragedy. Are you prepared to honor their wishes?

BUSH:
First of all, I will continue to speak about the effects of 9/11 on our country and my presidency. I will continue to mourn the

loss of life on that day, but I'll never forget the lessons. The terrorists declared war on us on that day, and I will continue to pursue this war. I have an obligation to those who died. I have an obligation to those who were heroic in their attempts to rescue. And I won't forget that obligation.

Crawford Texas
Mar 6th, 2004

So, you are obliged to ignore the wishes of the victims
and families of 9/11

959.   I thought there's a lot of bull in Washington, D.C. But I'm really glad to be here at the livestock show. It's -- somebody said, what's it like when you come here? It's like being in a place with people who are willing to stand up to values that are important in this country.

Dallas Texas
Mar 8th, 2004

Ahhh yes, standing up to "values"...
we should do more of that.

960.   It's hard to be successful if you don't make something somebody doesn't want to buy.

Arlington Virginia
Mar 9th, 2004

961.   We can outcompete with anybody.

Bay Shore New York
Mar 11th, 2004

360

> One of the biggest changes in politics in my lifetime is that the delusional is no longer marginal. It has come in from the fringe, to sit in the seat of power in the Oval Office and in Congress. For the first time in our history, ideology and theology hold a monopoly of power in Washington. Theology asserts propositions that cannot be proven true; ideologues hold stoutly to a worldview despite being contradicted by what is generally accepted as reality. When ideology and theology couple, their offspring are not always bad but they are always blind. And there is the danger: voters and politicians alike, oblivious to the facts.
>
> - Bill Moyers

962. The march to war hurt the economy. Laura reminded me a while ago that remember what was on the TV screens -- she calls me, George W. -- George W. I call her, First Lady. No, anyway -- she said, we said, march to war on our TV screen.

Bay Shore New York
Mar 11th, 2004

963. There's two things I want to share with you on that. One, there's nothing better than a society which encourages people to own something, isn't there? Either to own your own business -- how about the fact that this is a fellow who is born in El Salvador, comes here to our country, and now owns his own home. Isn't that one of the spectacular aspects?

Bay Shore New York
Mar 11th, 2004

964. Earlier today, the Libyan government released Fathi Jahmi. She's a local government official who was imprisoned in 2002 for advocating free speech and democracy.

Washington DC
Mar 12th, 2004

Fathi Jahmi, as a MAN..was probably surprised to be honored as a part of Int'l Woman's Week

965. Dr. [Raja] Khuzai also was there to have Thanksgiving dinner with our troops. And it turned out to be me, as well.

Washington DC
Mar 12th, 2004

966. Alphonso and I have set a job. We want to close the minority homeownership gap in America. We want more people owning their own home, and we want more of our minorities owning their own home, as well.

Ardmore Pennsylvania
Mar 15th, 2004

People as well as minorities
….very progressive!

967. It's hard to be a manufacturer in the state of Pennsylvania if you're worried about where your next energy is coming from.

Ardmore Pennsylvania
Mar 15th, 2004

362

968.   We had some CEOs that weren't honest with their shareholders and their employees. And we passed tough laws that said, we're not going to tolerate dishonesty in the boardrooms of America. You're now beginning to see on your TV screens what we're talking about. People are being held to account. And that hurt our economy.

Ardmore Pennsylvania
Mar 15th, 2004

It's not the crimes that hurt the economy, it was catching the criminals and prosecuting them.

This past Sunday, former Enron CEO Ken Lay went to a church in Houston. On the way out, a reporter asked him how he thought it was going to work out. Lay said with God's help we'll get through it. To which the Devil said, 'Hey, I thought we had a deal.'"

—Jay Leno

969.   Homeownership is at the highest rate ever. That means there's more people ever in our history are able to say, I own something. I own my own home. I went to Pearl's home and it was pretty special. Really special, wasn't it? She said, This is my home. When I walked up the stairs, she didn't say this is anybody else's home, but her home. She said, Would you come into my home, please.

Ardmore Pennsylvania
Mar 15th, 2004

970.   BUSH:
Now, Judy is the co-founder of Genesis -- is that an accurate statement?

JUDY MEMBERG:
Yes, it is.

BUSH:

She's a social entrepreneur.

JUDY MEMBERG:
I've never been called that, but okay.

BUSH:
It's a plus.

Ardmore Pennsylvania
Mar 15th, 2004

971.   We got attacked by a bunch of cold-blooded killers. And the attack hurt. It hurt our psyche because we thought oceans could protect us. It hurt the fact -- we lost a million jobs after September the 11th.

Ardmore Pennsylvania
Mar 15th, 2004

> Consider the daffodil. And while you're doing that, I'll be over here, looking through your stuff.
>
> - Jack Handy

972.   We can compete with anybody -- at least, I think so.

Washington DC
Mar 16th, 2004

973.   Now, the advantage of this plan is -- the tax-free is an advantage, by the way.

Washington DC
Mar 16th, 2004

> Bush's new budget proposal's cut $1.1 billion from the federal food stamp program. I guess the president feels if rich people aren't going to get their full tax cut for a while, the poor people with food stamps should have to help out too.
>
> - Jay Leno

974. By the way, Patty is a 7-11 franchisee, owner. Pays taxes, by the way, business taxes at the individual income tax rate. So when you hear them talking about, going to run up these -- tax the rich, that's what you're talking about, right there.

Washington DC
Mar 16th, 2004

> President Bush asked Congress yesterday for an additional $82 billion in emergency spending for the wars in Iraq and Afghanistan. If granted, it would put the cost of the war in Iraq at about $200 billion, which I believe is around exactly what they told us the war would cost when they started the war two years ago. [Clip of USAID Administrator Andrew Natsios: 'The American part of this will be $1.7 billion. We have no plans for any further funding on this. ... In terms of the American tax payer contributions this is it for the U.S.'] Well, to be fair, 2003 dollars, if you adjust it for inflation, it is only $198 billion off, with a margin of error of we have no idea what we are doing.
>
> - Jon Stewart

MIA WMDs--For Bush, It's a Joke
David Corn *03/25/2004*   (excerpt)

It's standard fare humor. Bush says he is preparing for a tough election fight; then on the large video screens a picture flashes showing him wearing a boxing robe while sitting at his desk. Bush notes he spends "a lot of time on the phone listening to our European allies." Then we see a photo of him on the phone with a finger in his ear. There were funny bits about Skull and Bones, his mother, and Dick Cheney. But at one point, Bush showed a photo of himself looking for something out a window in the Oval Office, and he said, "Those weapons of mass destruction have got to be somewhere."

The audience laughed. I grimaced. But that wasn't the end of it. After a few more slides, there was a shot of Bush looking under furniture in the Oval Office. "Nope," he said. "No weapons over there." More laughter. Then another picture of Bush searching in his office: "Maybe under here." Laughter again

... Yet there was Bush--apparently having a laugh at his own expense, but actually doing so on the graves of thousands. This was a callous and arrogant display. For Bush, the misinformation--or disinformation--he peddled before the war was no more than material for yucks. As the audience laughed along, he smiled. The false statements (or lies) that had launched a war had become merely another punchline in the nation's capital.

My sincere thanks to David Corn
Washington editor of The Nation www.thenation.com

975.	The best way to protect us is to stay on the offensive and to find terrorists before they try to harm us again. And they will.

Nashua New Hampshire
Mar. 25th, 2004

> It is part of the general pattern of misguided policy that our country is now geared to an arms economy which was bred in an artificially induced psychosis of war hysteria and nurtured upon an incessant propaganda of fear
>
> - Douglas MacArthur

976.	We're really proud of you. I love the story. It's what I love about our country, isn't it?

Nashua New Hampshire
Mar. 25th, 2004

> Kind of a cute scene down in Washington, D.C. earlier today: A squirrel on the lawn of the White House, gathering shell casings. ... An armed gunman was caught shooting at the White House, you know? You're just going to have to get used to the fact that the election is over, Mr. Gore. ... Witnesses say that the gunman, the guy outside the White House, was middle-aged and confused. And I'm thinking, well coincidentally, that's how you can describe the guy inside the White House.
>
> —David Letterman

977.	He got him 175 employees, which is a good size company.

Nashua New Hampshire
Mar. 25th, 2004

> A little neglect may breed great mischief.
>
> —Benjamin Franklin

978.   Had I known that the enemy was going to use airplanes to strike America, to attack us, I would have used every resource, every asset, every power of this government to protect the American people.

Nashua New Hampshire
Mar. 25th, 2004

Excerpt from Presidential Daily Briefing Aug 6th, 2001

Bin Ladin Determined To Strike in US

Clandestine, foreign government, and media reports indicate Bin Ladin since 1997 has wanted to conduct terrorist attacks in the US. Bin Ladin implied in US television interviews in 1997 and 1998 that his followers would follow the example of World Trade Center bomber Ramzi Yousef and "bring the fighting to America."

We have not been able to corroborate some of the more sensational threat reporting, such as that from a ▮▮▮▮▮▮▮▮▮▮ service in 1998 saying that Bin Ladin wanted to hijack a US aircraft to gain the release of "Blind Shaykh" 'Umar 'Abd al-Rahman and other US-held extremists.

Nevertheless, FBI information since that time indicates patterns of suspicious activity in this country consistent with preparations for hijackings or other types of attacks, including recent surveillance of federal buildings in New York.

The FBI is conducting approximately 70 full field investigations throughout the US that it considers Bin Ladin–related. CIA and the FBI are investigating a call to our Embassy in the UAE in May saying that a group of Bin Ladin supporters was in the US planning attacks with explosives.

979.   We increased the child credit to $1,000 per child. That helps
        people raising their families. If you've got children, it helps a
        lot.

Nashua New Hampshire
Mar. 25th, 2004

980.   You can't see what you think is a threat and hope it goes
        away. You used to could when the oceans protected us, but
        the lesson of September the 11th is, is when the President
        sees a threat, we must deal with it before it -- before it comes
        to fruition through death on our own soils, for example.

Albuquerque New Mexico
Mar 26th, 2004

Humanity should question itself, once more, about the
absurd and always unfair phenomenon of war, on
whose stage of death and pain only remain standing
the negotiating table that could and should have
prevented it.

- Pope John Paul II

981.   Lori is -- when I met her backstage -- the kind of person that
        you want really owning a home because she's so thrilled with
        the idea. We helped her. I say we -- people here in this part of
        the world did.

Albuquerque New Mexico
Mar 26th, 2004

982. I looked at the intelligence and saw a threat in Iraq. The United States Congress looked at the same intelligence, and they saw a threat. The United Nations Security Council looked at the intelligence, and it saw a threat. In fall of 2002, I went back to the United Nations, I said, look, why don't we deal with this threat together? We all see a threat, so why don't we get Saddam Hussein to do what the world has been demanding to do for over a decade, which is to reveal the weapons programs and get rid of him, for the sake of the security of the world. Your choice, Mr. Saddam. He said, no, I'm not interested. You see, given that choice whether to trust the word of a madman, a man who had used chemical weapons on his own people, or to defend our country, I will choose to defend America every time.

Albuquerque New Mexico
Mar 26th, 2004

> The art of leadership. . . consists in consolidating the attention of the people against a single adversary and taking care that nothing will split up that attention. . .
> - Adolf Hitler

> Today at a speech in New Hampshire, President Bush defended the war in Iraq saying, 'I was not about to leave the security of American people in the hands of madman.' So, I guess he's firing Donald Rumsfeld.
> —Jay Leno

983. We want people owning something in America. That's what we want. The great dream about America is, I can own my own home, people say.

Albuquerque New Mexico
Mar 26th, 2004

370

984.   I urge others to take time out of your life to make a difference in a child who may be lonely.

Albuquerque New Mexico
Mar 26th, 2004

985.   I laid out a doctrine that said, if you harbor a terrorist, you're just as guilty as the terrorist. By the way, when the President says something, you better mean it. It turns out in this job -- I, of course, meant it.

Appleton Wisconsin
Mar. 30th, 2004

Because if you're the Vice President, Press Secretary, Secretary of Defense etc...it doesn't matter if you say stuff you don't mean...

Vice President Cheney continues his whirlwind 11-nation Middle Eastern tour designed to bring America's anti-terror message to the region. That message: Help us fight terror or ...*Is that oil?*

—Jon Stewart

986.   We're still being challenged in Iraq and the reason why is a free Iraq will be a major defeat in the cause of freedom.

Charlotte North Carolina
Apr 5th, 2004

It's the unguarded moments, a slip of the tongue or unintended turn of phrase that offers us a glimpse of truth or hidden intentions...
...but then again, he may just be an idiot.

987.   BUSH:
It was my way to -- to help kick off the baseball season.

SPORTSCASTER:
That's neat.

BUSH:
I, I really think it's, an integral part of the -- fabric of our society, and, I'm, I'm gonna try to do my part to make sure baseball gets the notoriety it deserves.

St. Louis Missouri
Apr. 5th, 2004

988.   Obviously, every day I pray there is less casualty, but I know what we are doing in Iraq is right.

Fort Hood Texas
Apr. 11th, 2004

> It is more honorable to repair a wrong than to persist in it
>
> - Thomas Jefferson

989.   REPORTER:
Mr. President, I'd like to follow up on a couple of these questions that have been asked. One of the biggest criticisms of you is that whether it's WMD in Iraq, postwar planning in Iraq, or even the question of whether this administration did enough to ward off 9/11, you never admit a mistake. Is that a fair criticism? And do you believe there were any errors in judgment that you made related to any of those topics I brought up?

BUSH:
Well, I think, as I mentioned, it's -- the country wasn't on war footing, and yet we're at war. And that's just a reality, Dave. I mean, that's -- that was the situation that

372

existed prior to 9/11, because the truth of the matter is, most in the country never felt that we'd be vulnerable to an attack such as the one that Osama bin Laden unleashed on us. We knew he had designs on us, we knew he hated us. But there was a -- nobody in our government, at least, and I don't think the prior government, could envision flying airplanes into buildings on such a massive scale. The people know where I stand. I mean, in terms of Iraq, I was very clear about what I believed. ***And, of course, I want to know why we haven't found a weapon yet.*** But I still know Saddam Hussein was a threat, and the world is better off without Saddam Hussein. I don't think anybody can -- maybe people can argue that. I know the Iraqi people don't believe that, that they're better off with Saddam Hussein -- would be better off with Saddam Hussein in power. I also know that there's an historic opportunity here to change the world. And it's very important for the loved ones of our troops to understand that the mission is an important, vital mission for the security of America and for the ability to change the world for the better.

Prime Time Press Conference
White House
Apr. 13th, 2004

We've found the weapons of mass destruction. You know, we found biological laboratories. You remember when Colin Powell stood up in front of the world and he said Iraq has got laboratories, mobile labs to build biological weapons. They're illegal. They're against the United Nations' resolutions and we've so far discovered two. And we'll find more weapons as time goes on. But for those who say we haven't found the banned manufacturing devices or banned weapons, they're wrong. We found them

- President GW Bush
On Polish TV May 30th, 2003

990.   REPORTER:
You, yourself, have acknowledged that Osama bin Laden
was not a central focus of the administration in the months
before September 11th. I was not on point, you told the
journalist, Bob Woodward, I didn't feel that sense of urgency.
Two-and-a-half years later, do you feel any sense of personal
responsibility for September 11th?

BUSH:
Let me put that quote to Woodward in context. He had asked
me if I was -- something about killing bin Laden. That's what
the question was. And I said, compared to how I felt at the
time, after the attack, I didn't have that -- I also went on to
say, my blood wasn't boiling, I think is what the quote said. I
didn't see -- I mean, I didn't have that great sense of outrage
that I felt on September the 11th. I was -- on that day I was
angry and sad. Angry that al Qaeda had -- well, at the time --
thought al Qaeda -- found out shortly thereafter it was al
Qaeda -- had unleashed this attack. Sad for those who lost
their life.

Prime Time Press Conference
White House
Apr. 13th, 2004

Did you see the Osama bin Laden dinner party tape?
He's having dinner with a legless sheik. We can't even
catch that guy.
—David Letterman

374

991.   The -- the -- frankly mood of the world would have been astounded had the United States acted unilaterally in, uh, trying to deal with al Qaeda in that part of the world.

Prime Time Press Conference
White House
Apr. 13th, 2004

992.   One of my hardest parts of my job is to console the family members who have lost their life.

Prime Time Press Conference
White House
Apr. 13th, 2004

You don't need me to point out that it's hard to communicate with the dead right?

993.   REPORTER:
Mr. President, why are you and the Vice President insisting on appearing together before the 9/11 Commission? And, Mr. President, who will you be handing the Iraqi government over to on June 30th?

BUSH:
We will find that out soon. That's what Mr. Brahimi is doing.

He's figuring out the nature of the entity we'll be handing sovereignty over. And, secondly, because the 9/11 Commission wants to ask us questions, that's why we're meeting. And I look forward to meeting with them and answering their questions.

REPORTER:
I was asking why you're appearing together, rather than separately, which was their request.

BUSH:
Because it's a good chance for both of us to answer questions that the 9/11 Commission is looking *forward to asking us, and I'm looking forward to answering them.*

Prime Time Press Conference
White House
Apr. 13th, 2004

Excellent non-answer

President Bush and Vice President Dick Cheney are scheduled to testify before the 9/11 commission. I guess right now they're finalizing the seating arrangements. Should Bush sit on Cheney's right knee or his left knee

—Jay Leno

994.   BUSH:
John.

REPORTER:
Thank you, Mr. President. Two weeks ago, a former counter terrorism official at the NSC, Richard Clarke, offered an unequivocal apology to the American people for failing them prior to 9/11. Do you believe the American people deserve a similar from you, and would you be prepared to give them one?

376

BUSH:
Look, I can understand why people in my administration anguished over the fact that people lost their life. I feel the same way. I mean, I'm sick when I think about the death that took place on that day. And as I mentioned, I've met with a lot of family members and I do the best I do to console them about the loss of their loved one. As I mentioned, I oftentimes think about what I could have done differently. I can assure the American people that had we had any inkling that this was going to happen, we would have done everything in our power to stop the attack. Here's what I feel about that. The person responsible for the attacks was Osama bin Laden. That's who's responsible for killing Americans. And that's why we will stay on the offense until we bring people to justice.

Prime Time Press Conference
White House
Apr. 13th, 2004

Self Test for Paranoia: You know you have it when you can't think of anything that's your own fault

- Anonymous

You know if I had nickel for every time Bush has mentioned 9/11, I could raise enough reward money to go after bin Laden.

- Jon Stewart

---

995.   REPORTER:
In the last campaign, you were asked a question about the biggest mistake you'd made in your life, and you used to like to joke that it was trading Sammy Sosa. You've looked back before 9/11 for what mistakes might have been made. After 9/11, what would your biggest mistake be, would you say, and what lessons have you learned from it?

BUSH:
I wish you would have given me this written question ahead

of time, so I could plan for it. John, I'm sure historians will look back and say, gosh, he could have done it better this way, or that way. You know, I just -- I'm sure something will pop into my head here in the midst of this press conference, with all the pressure of trying to come up with an answer, but it hadn't yet.

Press Conference White House
Apr. 13th, 2004

He told me that as a leader, you can never admit to a mistake, that was one of the keys to being a leader.

- Mickey Herskowitz Biographer

996.   REPORTER:
With public support for your policies in Iraq falling off the way they have -- quite significantly over the past couple of months -- I guess I'd like to know if you feel in any way that you've failed as a communicator on this topic? Because --

BUSH:
Gosh, I don't know. I mean --

REPORTER:
Well, you deliver a lot of speeches and a lot of them contain similar phrases, and they vary very little from one to the next. And they often include a pretty upbeat assessment of how things are going ...I guess I just wonder if you feel that you have failed in any way? You don't have many of these press conferences, where you engage in this kind of exchange. Have you failed in any way to really make the case to the American public?

BUSH:
I guess if you put it into a political context, that's the kind of thing the voters will decide next November. That's what elections are about. They'll take a look at me and my opponent and say, let's see, which one of them can better win

the war on terror? Who best can see to it that Iraq emerges as a free society? Don, if I tried to fine-tune my messages based upon polls, I think I'd be pretty ineffective. I know I would be disappointed in myself. I hope today you've got a sense of my conviction about what we're doing. If you don't, maybe I need to learn to communicate better.

Prime Time Press Conference
White House
Apr. 13th, 2004

President Bush said catching a 7.5 pound fish was his best moment since becoming president. You know the sad thing, a lot of historians would agree with that.
-Jay Leno

---

997.   We have an obligation to lead the fight on AIDS, on Africa

.Prime Time Press Conference
White House
Apr. 13th, 2004

998.   The United Nations Security Council looked at the intelligence and said, Saddam is a threat. And so, for about the -- I can't remember how many times they said it, but they said, disarm. See, you're a threat. Disarm. There's a reason why a lot of people made the conclusion. It was not only based upon intelligence, it was based upon the fact that he hated America, that he's willing to pay suiciders to go kill people in Israel, that he actually used weapons of mass destruction on his own people.

Hershey Pennsylvania
Apr. 19th, 2004

999.   Freedom frightens people who are terrorists.

Hershey Pennsylvania
Apr. 19th, 2004

> We have been the cowards lobbing cruise missiles from
> 2,000 miles away. That's cowardly. Staying in the
> airplane when it hits the building, say what you want
> about it, it's not cowardly.
>
> - Bill Maher

1000.   The enemy can't stand the thought of free societies. That's
         why they attacked us, see.

Buffalo New York
Apr. 20th, 2004

1001.   There is no doubt in my mind that this country cannot achieve
         any objective we put our mind to.

Buffalo New York
Apr. 20th, 2004

1002.   So that's what -- there's some ideas. And the -- it's my job is
         to like, think beyond the immediate.

Washington D.C.
Apr. 21st, 2004

> Lance Armstrong is going on a bike ride with President
> Bush. Apparently Armstrong's mom called the
> president's mom and they set the whole thing up.
> They're going to have a sleep over, build a tent, maybe
> eat s'mores.
>
> - Conan O'Brien

380

1003.　One sure way to hold things up is that the federal lands say, you can't build on us.

Minneapolis Minnesota
Apr. 26th, 2004

Impossible strategy, but if it works I'd like to watch
..or listen at least

1004.　I'm working with Congress to pass the Striving Reader and Math Initiative Program, and that's a fancy word for saying we're going to intervene quickly with struggling middle-class - - middle grade and high school students.

Minneapolis Minnesota
Apr. 26th, 2004

1005.　I'm glad I did it. I'm glad I took the time. This is an important commission, and it's important that they ask the questions they ask so that they can help make recommendations necessary to better protect our homeland. It was -- I enjoyed it.

On meeting with 9/11 Commission
White House
Apr. 29th, 2004

If once the people become inattentive to the public affairs, you and I, and Congress and Assemblies, Judges and Governors, shall all become wolves. It seems to be the law of our general nature, in spite of individual exceptions

- Thomas Jefferson

1006.   REPORTER:
Mr. President, as you know, a lot of critics suggested that you wanted to appear jointly with the Vice President so that you two could keep your stories straight, or something --

BUSH:
Yes --

REPORTER:
Can you tell us what you think of the value of appearing together and how you would answer those critics?

BUSH:
Yes -- first of all, look, if we had something to hide we wouldn't have met with them in the first place. We answered all their questions. And as I say, I think I -- I came away good about the session, because I wanted them to know how I set strategy, how we run the White House, how we deal with threats. The Vice President answered a lot of their questions -- answered all their questions. And I think it was important for them to see our body language, as well, how we work together. But it was -- you know, the commissioners will speak for themselves over time. They will let you know whether they thought it was a fruitful series of discussions. I think they did. I think they found it to be useful.

White House
Apr. 29th, 2004

Today the White House admitted that President Bush was warned last summer that Al Qaeda may have been planning hijackings in the U.S. Of course now Congress is demanding answers. They want to know what did George Bush know, and when did Dick Cheney explain it to him.

—Jay Leno

382

1007.   You know, there's a lot of people in the world who don't believe that -- that people whose skin color may not be the same as ours can be free, and self-govern. I reject that. I reject that strongly. I believe that people who practice the Muslim faith can self-govern. I believe that people whose skins aren't necessarily -- are, you know -- a different color than white can self-govern. And, the Prime Minister (Canadian PM Paul Martin) -- I don't want to put words in his mouth, but -- I think he shares that great sense of optimism and possibility.

White House
Apr. 30th, 2004

1008.   I also understand that many problems can be only solved by love. Many problems can only be solved when a decent citizen takes time out of their lives and says, how can I help you, brother? What can I do to make your life better? The job of the President is to understand the proper relationship between the government and the strength of the country.

Kalamazoo Michigan
May 3rd, 2004

> Did you hear about this? According to a recent poll, three out of five Americans believe George W. Bush should be impeached. And when he heard that, the president said, 'Cool, I love peaches.'
> -David Letterman

1009.   What the country needs is a leader who speaks clearly.

Kalamazoo Michigan
May 3rd, 2004

1010.   I'm also running [for re-election] because I want to keep us --
         I want to enable us to be the innovative society that we are.

Kalamazoo Michigan
May 3rd, 2004

I hope some animal never bores a hole in my head and
lays its eggs in my brain, because later you might think
you're having a good idea but it's just eggs hatching.
                                                    - Jack Handy

1011.   You can't tax the rich enough to pay for his promises. Guess
         who he's going to tax? He's going to tax me and you.

Lebanon Ohio
May 4th, 2004

That's President Bush, just an ordinary guy
from an ordinary working class family

Analysis of President Bush's tax plan has revealed that
several elaborate tricks and gimmicks were used to
make it look like a $1.35 trillion cut, but in reality it's
going to be closer to costing $1.8 trillion. Critics claim
it's math so fuzzy, you have to squint to see our nation's
future of subsistence farming and post-apocalyptic
roving motorcycle gangs.
                                                    - Jon Stewart

1012.   I saw a threat in Afghanistan. I looked at the intelligence and saw a threat. The Congress looked at the intelligence. Members of both political parties looked at that same intelligence and saw and threat. The United Nations Security Council looked at the intelligence and it saw a threat. The United Nations Security Council, like me, remembered -- we saw more than a threat, we remembered that Saddam Hussein had used weapons of mass destruction against his own people and against his neighborhood, that Saddam Hussein professed hatred for America, that he had terrorist ties, that he paid suiciders to kill innocent citizens in the Middle East. We remembered all that.

Lebanon Ohio
May 4th, 2004

> The soldier, above all other people, prays for peace, for he must suffer and bear the deepest wounds and scars of war.
>
> - Douglas MacArthur

1013.   And so the people in the Middle East must understand that this [the abuse of Iraqi prisoners] was horrible.

Washington D.C.
May 5th, 2004

1014.   And so long as I'm the President, we will be determined, steadfast, and strong as we pursue those people who kill innocent lives because they hate freedom.

Washington D.C.
May 5th, 2004

1015.   Iraqis are sick of foreign people coming in their country and
         trying to destabilize their country.

Washington D.C.
May 5th, 2004

Hmmm...ya don't say...

1016.   So as I told His Majesty [King Abdullah of Jordan], I said, we
         will -- people will be brought to justice in a way commiserate
         with how our system works.

Washington D.C.
May 6th, 2004

Bush is talking about bringing US soldiers to
justice here....not Saudi hijackers...

These days it's good to know we still have friends in the
Middle East, friends like Saudi Arabia. That's right
where, may I remind you, four of the 19 September
11th hijackers were not from.

—Jon Stewart

1017.   For example, if a school -- a child is trapped in a school for
         several years that is -- that's not meeting standards, the
         federal government will pay for after-school tutoring, and the
         parent can choose all kind of tutoring options, whether they
         be public or private. One parent -- a parent can send the
         school -- a child to a different public school. In other words,
         when -- there has to be accountability in order for a -- I mean,
         there has to be a consequence in order for an accountability
         system to work.

Van Buren Arkansas
May 11th, 2004

1018. Ehud Olmert is with us. Ehud, it's good to see you again.
Thank you, sir. I remember the first time we visited in 1998. I
had just been re-elected as the Governor of Texas. I went to
Israel, and Ehud welcomed me and three over governors to, I
guess, your office. You were the Mayor, if I'm not mistaken at
that point in time. And you were focused on filling potholes
and emptying the garbage of the people.

Washington D.C.
May 18th, 2004

1019. And I call upon the Iraqi people to reject violence, band
together to insist that the country move toward a peaceful
tomorrow. Iraq is changing for the better. I mean, look at the
soccer team.

Washington D.C.
May 20th, 2004

387

1020.   Under the dictator, prisons like Abu Gar -- reb -- were symbols of death and torture. That same prison became a symbol of disgraceful conduct by a few American troops who dishonored our country and disregardered our values. America will fund the construction of a modern, maximum security prison. When that prison is completed, detainees at Abu Garomp will be relocated. Then, with the approval of the Iraqi government, we will demolish the Abu Garab prison, as a fitting symbol of Iraq's new beginning.

United States Army War College
Carlisle Pennsylvania
May 24th, 2004

Watching him flounder is akin to driving slowly past the scene of an accident. It's disturbingly mesmerizing. Actually, the same holds true for this entire presidency.

1021.   I'm honored to, shake the hand -- of a brave Iraqi citizen who had his hand cut off by Saddam Hussein.

White House
May 25th, 2004

1022.   I want to thank my friend, Sen. Bill Frist, for joining us today. ... He married a Texas girl, I want you to know. (Laughter.) Karyn is with us. A West Texas girl, just like me.

Nashville Tennessee
May 27th, 2004

One out of forty American men wears women's clothing. We've had more than forty presidents. One of these guys has been dancing around the Oval Office in a prom dress.
Allison Janney

388

1023.   REPORTER:
Could you understand -- your political action is inspired by
God, you say a number of times --

BUSH:
I said what?

REPORTER:
Is inspired by God, I mean, your --

BUSH:
My political action? I've never said that.

REPORTER:
You've never said that? I mean, I'm not quoting you?.

BUSH:
No, I've never said that.

REPORTER:
I said, in general, you relate to God as a --

BUSH:
You said, my political action is caused by God, I think.

REPORTER:
No, no, no, no, I said your political action is inspired by God.

BUSH:
No, my political action is -- my life is inspired by God.

Paris Match Magazine
Rome Italy
Jun. 4th, 2004

I've heard the call. I believe God wants me to run for
President
George Magazine Interview
September 2000

I feel like God wants me to run for President. I can't explain it, but I sense my country is going to need me. Something is going to happen [...] I know it won't be easy on me or my family, but God wants me to do it

Reported in London Observer
November 2, 2003

I trust God speaks through me. Without that, I couldn't do my job.

July 9, 2004

God would tell me, 'George, go and fight those terrorists in Afghanistan.' And I did, and then God would tell me, 'George, go and end the tyranny in Iraq ...' And I did. And now, again, I feel God's words coming to me, 'Go get the Palestinians their state and get the Israelis their security, and get peace in the Middle East.' And by God I'm gonna do it.

- President Bush, as quoted by former Palestinian foreign minister Nabil Shaath, during a top-level meeting with Bush in June 2003

1024. And there are a lot of nations working in Afghanistan and in Iraq to not only deal with terror -- the immediate effects of terror -- and that is, finding people before they hurt somebody again -- but also to spread freedom. Free societies are peaceful societies, free societies are hopeful societies. And there's a lot of nations working to get her to do so.

Paris Match Magazine
Rome Italy
Jun. 4th, 2004

390

1025.   REPORTER:
The whole world remembers you addressing the firemen in the ruins of the World Trade Center. You were healing the wounds and uniting the world at that time. Today, your message through the megaphone doesn't reach the world. Don't you feel isolated?

BUSH:
No, I feel very comfortable with what I'm doing.

REPORTER:
Yes, but all the nations --

BUSH:
Let me finish my -- you ask a question, I give you the answers. And then if you want to ask another question, you're allowed to do so.

Paris Match Magazine
Rome Italy
Jun. 4th, 2004

1026.   REPORTER:
Once, President Kennedy said, Everyone has two countries, their own, and France. And why is it that your policy tends to be pushing your country and France to divorce? Second point, some in public opinion have accused you of state terrorism, and do you not believe that what has happened in Abu Ghraib has put you in the same basket, as it were, of Saddam Hussein, especially in the eyes of an international tribunal, and especially in light of the unfound weapons of mass destruction?

BUSH:
To paraphrase President Kennedy, there's America, and then there's Texas. We have great relations with France. We work closely with the French government on a lot of issues.

Paris France
Jun. 5th, 2004

American tourists in Paris are reported to being yelled at, spit upon, and attacked by the French. Thank God things are getting back to normal.

—Jay Leno

1027.   REPORTER:
So when you say that you want the U.S. to adhere to international and U.S. laws, that's not very comforting. This is a moral question. Is terr -- torture ever justified?

BUSH:
Look, I'm gonna say it one more time. I
can -- if I can -- maybe -- maybe I can be
more clear. The instructions went out to our people to adhere to law. That oughta comfort you. We -- we're a nation of law. We adhere to laws. We have laws on the books. You might look at those laws. And that might provide comfort for you. And those were the instructions out of -- from me to the government.

Savannah Georgia
Jun. 10th, 2004

Cheney Plan Exempts CIA From Bill Barring Abuse of Detainees

By R. Jeffrey Smith and Josh White
Washington Post Staff Writers
Tuesday, October 25, 2005; A01

The Bush administration has proposed exempting employees of the Central Intelligence Agency from a legislative measure endorsed earlier this month by 90 members of the Senate that would bar cruel and degrading treatment of any prisoners in U.S. custody.

392

WASHINGTON Nov 28, 2005 - A top aide to former Secretary of State Colin Powell said Monday that wrongheaded ideas for the handling of foreign detainees arose from White House and Pentagon officials who argued that "the president of the United States is all-powerful" and the Geneva Conventions irrelevant... Cheney's office, Rumsfeld aides and others argued "that the president of the United States is all-powerful, that as commander in chief the president of the United States can do anything he damn well pleases,"

ANNE GEARAN, AP Diplomatic Writer

White House Press Briefing.
October 31st, 2005

Re: Exemption to Torture Law Sought by Cheney as noted in previous article...

Enjoy...

Q I'd like you to clear up, once and for all, the ambiguity about torture. Can we get a straight answer? The President says we don't do torture, but Cheney --

MR. McCLELLAN: That's about as straight as it can be.

Q Yes, but Cheney has gone to the Senate and asked for an exemption on --

MR. McCLELLAN: No, he has not. Are you claiming he's asked for an exemption on torture? No, that's

Q He did not ask for that?

MR. McCLELLAN: -- that is inaccurate.

Q Are you denying everything that came from the Hill, in terms of torture?

MR. McCLELLAN: No, you're mischaracterizing things. And I'm not going to get into discussions we have --

Q Can you give me a straight answer for once?

MR. McCLELLAN: Let me give it to you, just like the President has. We do not torture. He does not condone torture and he would never --

Q I'm asking about exemptions.

MR. McCLELLAN: Let me respond. And he would never authorize the use of torture. We have an obligation to do all that we can to protect the American people. We are engaged --

Q That's not the answer I'm asking for --

MR. McCLELLAN: It is an answer -- because the American people want to know that we are doing all within our power to prevent terrorist attacks from happening. There are people in this world who want to spread a hateful ideology that is based on killing innocent men, women and children. We saw what they can do on September 11th --

Q He didn't ask for an exemption --

MR. McCLELLAN: -- and we are going to --

Q -- answer that one question. I'm asking, is the administration asking for an exemption?

MR. McCLELLAN: I am answering your question. The President has made it very clear that we are going to do --

Q You're not answering -- yes or no?

MR. McCLELLAN: No, you don't want the American people to hear what the facts are, Helen, and I'm going to tell them the facts.

Q -- the American people every day. I'm asking you, yes or no, did we ask for an exemption?

MR. McCLELLAN: And let me respond. You've had your opportunity to ask the question. Now I'm going to respond to it.

Q If you could answer in a straight way.

MR. McCLELLAN: And I'm going to answer it, just like the President -- I just did, and the President has answered it numerous times.

Q -- yes or no --

MR. McCLELLAN: Our most important responsibility is to protect the American people. We are engaged in a global war against Islamic radicals who are intent on spreading a hateful ideology, and intent on killing innocent men, women and children.

Q Did we ask for an exemption?

MR. McCLELLAN: We are going to do what is necessary to protect the American people.

Q Is that the answer?

MR. McCLELLAN: We are also going to do so in a way that adheres to our laws and to our values. We have made that very clear. The President directed everybody within this government that we do not engage in torture. We will not torture. He made that very clear.

Q Are you denying we asked for an exemption?

MR. McCLELLAN: Helen, we will continue to work with the Congress on the issue that you brought up. The way you characterize it, that we're asking for exemption from torture, is just flat-out false, because there are laws that are on the books that prohibit the use of torture. And we adhere to those laws.

Q We did ask for an exemption; is that right? I mean, be simple -- this is a very simple question.

MR. McCLELLAN: I just answered your question. The President answered it last week.

Q What are we asking for?
Q Would you characterize what we're asking for?

MR. McCLELLAN: We're asking to do what is necessary to protect the American people in a way that is consistent with our laws and our treaty obligations. And that's what we --

Q Why does the CIA need an exemption from the military?

MR. McCLELLAN: David, let's talk about people that you're talking about who have been brought to justice and captured. You're talking about people like Khalid Shaykh Muhammad; people like Abu Zubaydah.

Q I'm asking you --

MR. McCLELLAN: No, this is facts about what you're talking about.

Q Why does the CIA need an exemption from rules that would govern the conduct of our military in interrogation practices?

MR. McCLELLAN: There are already laws and rules that are on the books, and we follow those laws and rules. What we need to make sure is that we are able to carry out the war on terrorism as effectively as possible, not only --

Q What does that mean --

MR. McCLELLAN: What I'm telling you right now -- not only to protect Americans from an attack, but to prevent an attack from happening in the first place. And, you bet, when we capture terrorist leaders, we are going to seek to find out information that will protect -- that prevent attacks from happening in the first place. But we have an obligation to do so. Our military knows this; all people within the United States government know this. We have an obligation to do so in a way that is consistent with our laws and values.

Now, the people that you are bringing up -- you're talking about in the context, and I think it's important for the American people to know, are people like Khalid Shaykh Muhammad, Abu Zubaydah, Ramzi Binalshibh -- these are -- these are dangerous killers.

Q So they're all killers --
Q Did you ask for an exemption on torture? That's a simple question, yes or no.

MR. McCLELLAN: No. And we have not. That's what I told you at the beginning.

Q You want to reserve the ability to use tougher tactics with those individuals who you mentioned.

MR. McCLELLAN: Well, obviously, you have a different view from the American people. I think the American people understand the importance of doing everything within our power and within our laws to protect the American people.

Q Scott, are you saying that Cheney did not ask

Q What is it that you want the -- what is it that you want the CIA to be able to do that the U.S. Armed Forces are not allowed to do?

MR. McCLELLAN: I'm not going to get into talking about national security matters, Bill. I don't do that, because this involves --

Q This would be the exemption, in other words.

MR. McCLELLAN: This involves information that relates to doing all we can to protect the American people. And if you have a different view -- obviously, some of you on this room -- in this room have a different view, some of you on the front row have a different view.

Q We simply are asking a question.
Q What is the Vice President -- what is the Vice President asking for?

MR. McCLELLAN: It's spelled out in our statement of administration policy in terms of what our views are. That's very public information. In terms of our discussions with members of Congress --

Q -- no, it's not --

MR. McCLELLAN: In terms of our members -- like I said, there are already laws on the books that we have to adhere to and abide by, and we do. And we believe that those laws and those obligations address these issues.

Q So then why is the Vice President continuing to lobby on this issue? If you're very happy with the laws on the books, what needs change?

MR. McCLELLAN: Again, you asked me -- you want to ask questions of the Vice President's office, feel free to do that. We've made our position very clear, and it's spelled out on our website for everybody to see.

Q We don't need a website, we need you from the podium.

MR. McCLELLAN: And what I just told you is what our view is.

Q But Scott, do you see the contradiction --

MR. McCLELLAN: Jessica, go ahead.

The United States is a nation of laws: badly written and randomly enforced

- Frank Zappa

1028. REPORTER:
Thank you, Mr. President. You do have now the personal gun of Saddam Hussein. Are you willing to give it to President al-Yawar as a symbolic gift, or are you keeping it?

BUSH:
What she's referring to is a -- members of a Delta team came to see me in the Oval Office and brought with me -- these were the people that found Saddam Hussein, the dictator of Iraq, hiding in a hole. And, by the way, let me remind everybody about Saddam Hussein, just in case we all forget. There were mass graves under his leadership. There were torture chambers. Saddam Hussein -- if you -- we had seven people come to my office. Perhaps the foreign press didn't see this story. Seven people came to my -- they had their

hands cut off because the Iraqi currency had devalued. And Saddam Hussein needed somebody to blame, so he blamed small merchants. And their hands were chopped off, their right hand.

Savannah Georgia
Jun. 10th, 2004

So, is that a 'yes'?

1029.   And I am an optimistic person. I guess if you want to try to find something to be pessimistic about, you can find it, no matter how hard you look, you know?

Washington D.C.
Jun. 15th, 2004

1030.   The reason I keep insisting that there was a relationship between Iraq and Saddam and al Qaeda, because there was a relationship between Iraq and al Qaeda.

Washington D.C.
Jun. 17th, 2004

We've had no evidence that Saddam Hussein was involved with the September 11th

.-President George W. Bush
September 15, 2003

The president returned to the White House [on 9/11] and called me in and said, 'I've learned from George Tenet that there is no evidence of a link between Saddam Hussein and 9/11.'

- Condoleeza Rice
9/11 Commission Testimony

GEN. CLARK: I think it was an effort to convince the American people to do something, and I think there was an immediate determination right after 9/11 that Saddam Hussein was one of the keys to winning the war on terror. Whether it was the need just to strike out or whether he was a linchpin in this, there was a concerted
effort during the fall of 2001 starting immediately after 9/11 to pin 9/11 and the terrorism problem on Saddam Hussein.

MR. RUSSERT: By who? Who did that?

GEN. CLARK: Well, it came from the White House, it came from people around the White House. It came from all over. I got a call on 9/11. I was on CNN, and I got a call at my home saying, "You got to say this is connected. This is state-sponsored terrorism. This has to be connected to Saddam Hussein." I said, "But--I'm willing to say it but what's your evidence?" And I never got any evidence. And these were people who had-- Middle East think tanks and people like this and it was a lot of pressure to connect this and there were a lot of assumptions made. But I never personally saw the evidence and
didn't talk to anybody who had the evidence to make that connection.

Meet the Press, 7/13/2003

1031. This disease leaves suffering and orphans and fear wherever it reaches. Every man and woman and child who suffers from this addiction, from the streets of Philly to the villages of Africa, is a child of God who deserves our love and our help.

AIDS is an addiction now.
Philadelphia Pennsylvania
Jun. 23rd, 2004

1032.   The Prime Minister brought up the Abu Garef ---- si --
        situation.

Washington D.C.
Jun. 22nd, 2004

1033.   But we've got a big border in Texas, with Mexico, obviously --
        and we've got a big border with Canada -- Arizona is affected.

Washington D.C.
Jun. 22nd, 2004

I'd like a peek at his atlas

1034.   It's amazing with the software that has been developed these
        days that enable a camera to distinguish the difference
        between a squirrel and a bomb.

Washington DC
June 24th, 2004

We actually need software for this?

1035.   We actually misnamed the war on terror, it ought to be the
        'struggle against ideological extremists who do not believe in
        free societies who happen to use terror as a weapon to try to
        shake the conscience of the free world.'

Charleston West
Virginia Jul. 4th, 2004

But, it wouldn't look as good on a T-shirt

402

1036.   Americans are serving and sacrificing to keep this country safe and to bring freedom to others. After the attacks of September the 11th, 2001, this nation resolved to fight terrorists where they dwell. We resolved to arm the terrorist enemy.

Charleston West Virginia
Jul. 4th, 2004

Complex problems have simple, easy to understand, wrong answers.

- Henry Louis Mencken

1037.   I went to the United Nations and said, he's a threat. And they agreed with the fact that he was a threat, by a 15 to nothing vote in the United Nations Security Council. See, the world spoke. Not only America speak, the world spoke.

Kutztown Pennsylvania
Jul. 9th, 2004

Bush administration officials were reported to be actively seeking a link between Iraq and al Qaeda. Bush administration lawyers had concluded that linking Iraq to the group responsible for the September 11 terrorist attacks would provide the legal justification the administration needs to launch a strike without congressional approval, based on the congressional resolution passed on September 14, 2001 authorizing Bush "to use all necessary and appropriate force against those nations, organizations, or persons he determines planned, authorized, committed, or aided" in the attack. An al Qaeda link also would allow the administration to bypass the United Nations

Washington Times, 8/4/02

403

1038.   I trust God speaks through me. Without that, I couldn't do my job.

Lancaster County Pennsylvania
Jul. 9th, 2004

Gott Mit Uns - God With Us

It's Called "Faith-Based" Dummy

No one ever told me that Hitler was a Christian. It never came up. I assumed he was Godless and certainly no - one ever tried to inform me otherwise. I guess Christians hate to acknowledge that heinous crimes have been committed by their own in the name of their God too. What I have learned through watching events unfold during the Bush presidency and research has cemented my belief that we must consciously maintain the active separation between Church and State. No good comes from the belief that you hold special favor with God above all others.

Now...Let's look at some curious parallels between George W and Adolf.

Hitler believed that God chose him to lead Germany saying, "I would like to thank Providence and the Almighty for choosing me of all people to be allowed to wage this battle for Germany." and "I am convinced that nothing will happen to me, for I know the greatness of the task for which Providence has chosen me." - Hitler

Bush told Dr Richard Land on the day he was inaugurated as Gov of Texas that "God wants me to be president". He also told Evangelist James Robinson, "I feel like God wants me to run for President. I can't explain it, but I sense my country is going to need me. Something is going to happen . . . I know it won't be easy on me or my family, but God wants me to do it".

404

Hitler was also responsible for implementing programs that diverted government funds to the Christian churches to fund social programs because the State had previously been seen as hostile towards religion...He believed that the government had a responsibility to support and spread Christian doctrine for the good of it's people...

"...public monies derived from taxation through the organs of the State have been placed at the disposal of both churches [Protestant and Catholic]." in addition he said, "Amongst the accusations which are directed against Germany in the so-called democracy is the charge that the National Socialist State is hostile to religion"

In direct contravention of the Constitutional Separation of Church and State, and because Congress sought to maintain that tradition, Bush acted unilaterally and imposed his Faith Based Initiatives, saying, "...but spiritual guidance and love can only go so far. .... In other words, there's practical application of taxpayers' money that we want to get into the hands of our faith-based organizations all throughout our society.". "This government of yours must welcome faith, not discriminate faith, as we deal with the future of this great country." and "Congress wouldn't act, so I signed an executive order -- that means I did it on my own. It says we're going to open up billions of dollars in grant money competition to faith-based charities."

Although Bush touts the "freedom to worship an Almighty God" as we see fit, and while appearing friendly to Muslims, he seems ignorant or indifferent to the notion that not every religion worships an Almighty God, or that freedom to worship includes the right to not worship. He calls Islam a "false religion" and Lt Gen Boykin, a Bush friend and the man he personally appointed to track down Osama bin Laden (stellar job by the way) has been quoted as saying to audiences on several occasions that he told a Muslim warlord in Somalia, "I knew my God was bigger than his. I knew that my God was a real God and his was an idol.". He also paints the war on terror as a battle of Christians against Satan" Bush has said many times that his "administration has a job to do. We will rid the world of evildoers". He also speaks often of God-given values of freedom as his reason for war. He is doing God's work. So, much for the First Amendment.

This is frighteningly similar to Hitler's scary and yet contradictory rhetoric about Jews. Hitler wrote: "I believe that I am acting in accordance with the will of the Almighty Creator: by defending myself against the Jew, I am fighting for the work of the Lord.." But in stark contrast, Hitler also said, "...For the Jew was still characterized for me by nothing but his religion, and therefore, on grounds of human tolerance, I maintained my rejection of religious attacks in this case as in others. Consequently, the tone, particularly that of the Viennese anti-Semitic press, seemed to me unworthy of the cultural tradition of a great nation."

Perhaps even more telling, both leaders seized an opportunity to capitalize on the fears and prejudices of their nation after tragedy struck.

For Hitler, it was the Reichstag Fire.

For Bush it was 9/11.

Hitler immediately claimed that the fire was an attack orchestrated by Communists and had party leaders arrested. Then he rounded up Jews and sent them to concentration camps.

Bush immediately started looking for ways to pin the WTC attack on Iraq and simultaneously began rounding up and detaining citizens suspected of being terrorists or having terrorist ties. Many of these were Muslims and Middle Eastern people who were/are held, years hence, without charges, without lawyers and in direct contravention of their civil rights.

406

Both leaders orchestrated a campaign of propaganda to convince their countrymen that their beloved nation was under imminent threat and that they must take preemptive military action to protect themselves.

Bush implemented the hysterical color chart of terror-alert status and takes every opportunity to remind us that as long as we "love freedom" that we are never safe and that we must fight them "over there" before it results in "death on our own soils." It is an unsophisticated , but effective form of psychological warfare. It has been a technique used for centuries that is summed up best by Nazi Official Herman Georing with, "Voice or no voice, the people can always be brought to do the bidding of the leaders. All you have to do is tell them they are being attacked and denounce the pacifists for lack of patriotism and exposing the country to danger. It works the same way in any country."

Seizing on the fears of a nation still reeling from tragedy, both leaders capitalized on an opportunity to increase their power and erode civil liberties by endowing themselves with sweeping new powers. Hitler implemented the "Reichstag Fire Decree" to undermine civil liberties and human rights. Bush called his the "Patriot Act".

Hitler was bent on demonstrating that the fire was caused by the Communists.

Bush was determined to show that Iraq was behind 9/11.

Hitler invaded Poland and France, devastating Europe.

Bush invaded Iraq.

Both men waged war for God, with God's blessings and in Bush's case, under direct instructions from the Almighty himself.

"I follow the path assigned to me by Providence with the instinctive sureness of a sleepwalker" -Hitler

Bush said "God told me to strike at al Qaida and I struck them, and then He instructed me to strike at Saddam, which I did, ..."

Both men felt that they were justified, with or without public support.

"I must repeat, no pretext was needed for taking measures against the Communists. I already had a number of perfectly good reasons in the forms of murders, etc." - Hitler

"I want the United Nations to be effective. It's important for it to be a robust, capable body. It's important for it's words to mean what they say, and as we head into the 21st century, Mark, when it comes to our security, we really don't need anybody's permission." -Bush

Both men believed their country curried God's special favor.

"But there is something else I believe, and that is that there is a God. . . . And this God again has blessed our efforts during the past 13 years." - Hitler

"...Since America's founding, prayer has reassured us that the hand of God is guiding the affairs of this nation. We have never asserted a special claim on His favor, yet we've always believed in God's presence in our lives. This has always been true." - Bush

"Providence withdrew its protection and our people fell, fell as scarcely any other people heretofore. In this deep misery we again learn to pray. - *Hitler*

"We feel our reliance on the creator who made us. We place our sorrows and cares before him, seeking God's mercy." - Bush

"The mercy of the Lord slowly returns to us again. And in this hour we sink to our knees and beseech our almighty God that he may bless us, that He may give us the strength to carry on the struggle for the freedom, the future, the honor, and the peace of our people. So help us God." -Hitler

"We can also be confident in the ways of Providence, even when they are far from our understanding. Events aren't moved by blind change and chance. Behind all of life and all of history, there's a dedication and purpose, set by the hand of a just and faithful God. And that hope will never be shaken." -Bush

Although clearly demented, Hitler was an intelligent man and a powerful public speaker.

Bush, also demented...is intell....oh wait....as a speaker he's........scratch that. Apparently Hitler was charismatic. Bush's ability to woo people in this enlightened and informed age, frankly, I don't understand.

Add to these the Skull and Bones affiliation.

Skull and Bones is an off-shoot of Hitler's Thule Society introduced to the US at Yale by Bush's grandfather and fundraiser for the Third Reich, Prescott Bush. The entire picture is deeply disturbing, not only because of the picture it paints but, because we are still unable or unwilling to address it.

There are many more interesting quotes by these two men, but I had to stop somewhere....

Why are we still fooled by trickery that's been employed by leaders since Ancient Greece? They are Chicken Little - You are Turkey Lurkey.

The sky is falling! The sky is falling! Danger! War! Treason!

Lemmings may be easily led off the proverbial cliff but, we are educated, informed and intelligent. Why are we still seduced by fairy tales? How do we quell this tide of lies and fear-mongering masked as democracy? Did Bush and his cronies pull up to the White House in a Trojan Horse built of Christian values and governmental accountability? I have no doubt that this Administration will go down in history as the single most corrupt, incompetent and hypocritical ever. Their promises, their respect for their respective offices, purported respect for life, their faith and their rhetoric is as empty as the Goddamn horse they rode up on.

Some parting thoughts.....

Those who do not learn from history are condemned to repeat it.

- George Santayana

The most heinous and the most cruel crimes of which history has record have been committed under the cover of religion or equally noble motives

- Mahatma Gandhi

We are not makers of history. We are made by history.

- Martin Luther King Jr

If history repeats itself, and the unexpected always happens, how incapable must man be of learning from experience.

- George Bernard Shaw

1039.   Pennsylvania's unemployment rate is 5.1 percent. That's good news for people who are trying to find jobs.

Smoketown Pennsylvania
Jul. 9th, 2004

410

1040.   One good reason to put me back in there for four more years is so that Laura will be the First Lady. Thank you. I married well. What a fabulous woman she is.

Kutztown Pennsylvania
Jul. 9th, 2004

> If you go to a costume party at your boss's house, wouldn't you think a good costume would be to dress up like the boss's wife? Trust me, it's not.
>
> - Jack Handy

1041.   And traveling with me today is one of our daughters, a newly-graduate from college, Barbara Bush. Thanks for coming, Barbara.

Marquette Michigan
Jul. 13th, 2004

> I think flying planes into a building was a faith-based initiative. I think religion is a neurological disorder.
>
> - Bill Maher

1042.   I don't think you order suiciders to kill innocent men, women, and children if you're a religious person.

Fond Du Lac Wisconsin
Jul. 14th, 2004

Demonstrating his profound understanding of the motivations of the enemy in this War on Terror.

411

> We--with God's help--call on every Muslim who believes in God and wishes to be rewarded to comply with God's order to kill the Americans and plunder their money wherever and whenever they find it. We also call on Muslim ulema, leaders, youths, and soldiers to launch the raid on Satan's U.S. troops and the devil's supporters allying with them, and to displace those who are behind them so that they may learn a lesson.
>
> Osama Bin Laden
> Feb. 1998

> We should fully understand our religion. Fighting is a part of our religion and our Sharia [an Islamic legal code]. Those who love God and his Prophet and this religion cannot deny that. Whoever denies even a minor tenet of our religion commits the gravest sin in Islam
> - Osama Bin Laden

1043.   That's one of the goals we're on, is to encourage programs, community-based -- you don't have to be a faith-based program, although it turns out faith-based programs are pretty good places to find people who want to love a neighbor just like they'd like to be loved themselves.

Cedar Rapids Iowa
Jul. 20th, 2004

Damn, I was using sports bars and Internet dating.

412

1044. By the way, to whom much has been given, much is owed. Not only are we leading the world in terms of encouraging freedom and peace, we're feeding the hungry. We're taking care of, as best as we possibly can, the victims of HIV/AIDS.

Cedar Rapids Iowa
Jul. 20th, 2004

Actually, to whom much has been given, much is expected...Especially revealing Freudian slip

1045. It reads like a mystery, a novel. It's well written.

On the 9/11 Commission's report
Crawford Texas
Jul. 26th, 2004

1046. We phased out the death tax, so America's family farmers can stay in the family.

Davenport Iowa
Aug. 5th, 2004

1047. Our enemies are innovative and resourceful, and so are we. They never stop thinking about new ways to harm our country and our people, and neither do we.

Washington D.C.
Aug. 5th, 2004

1048.   REPORTER:
What do you think tribal sovereignty means in the 21st
century, and how do we resolve conflicts between tribes and
the federal and state governments?

BUSH:
Yeah -- tribal sovereignty means that, it's sovereign. It's --
you're a -- you're a -- you've been given sovereignty, and
you're -- viewed as a sovereign entity. [Laughter from the
audience]

REPORTER:
Okay.

BUSH:
And, therefore, the relationship between the federal
government and tribes is one between -- sovereign entities.

Washington D.C.
Aug. 6th, 2004

1049.   I'm impressed with the number of words, but no, I think we
should stick with War on Terror. It's easier to remember.

Washington D.C.
Aug. 6th, 2004

1050.   4TH GRADE TEACHER:
What can you do for our children in public education, private
education, that will make a difference in America today?

BUSH:
Here's what we're going to do. We're going to continue to
challenge the soft bigotry of low expectations, is what we're
going to do.

Annandale Virginia
Aug. 9th, 2004

414

> I'm the master of low expectations.
>
> I like to keep expectations low
>
> — President GW Bush

1051. That's why you've got to be careful about this rhetoric, we're only going to tax the rich. You know who the -- the rich in America happen to be the small business owners. That's what that means.

Annandale Virginia
Aug. 9th, 2004

> Vice President Dick Cheney's getting a tax refund of $1.9 million. How do you get a $1.9 million refund when your salary is $205,000 a year? How does that work? ... Apparently, he's writing off the guns and ammo as business expenses.
>
> —Jay Leno

1052. BUSH:
Don't get me wrong. Don't get me wrong. You said, against affirmative action, is what you said. You put words in my mouth. What I am for is —

MARTIN:
I just read the speech, Mr. President.

BUSH:
What speech?

MARTIN:
In terms of when you came out against the Michigan affirmative action policy, and --

BUSH:
No, I said was against quotas.

MARTIN:
So you support affirmative action, but not quotas.

BUSH:
I support colleges affirmatively taking action to get more minorities in their school.

Unity Journalists of Color Convention
Washington D.C.
Aug. 6th, 2004

Some would argue that the president himself benefited from a form of affirmative action because as a C student, he only got into Yale because his father was a wealthy alumnus. But the White House counters that Saddam is a menace and must be stopped."
-Jon Stewart

1053.   Health savings accounts are new. Anything new in society, when it comes to health, requires a certain amount of education. Now, if you're a small business like Sharon is, I want you to listen to these accounts.

Annandale Virginia
Aug. 9th, 2004

1054.   Had we to do it over again, we would look at the
         consequences of catastrophic success, being so successful
         so fast that an enemy that should have surrendered or been
         done in escaped and lived to fight another day.

Time Magazine
Aug. 2004

President Bush visited with soldiers yesterday in an
effort to f*ck up morale. I'm sorry, that's buck up
morale. ... [Video of President Bush: 'Today's war on
terror will not end with a ceremony on the deck of a
battleship.'] Mr. President, if you're asking me not to
trust ceremonies on the deck of battleships, I'm way
ahead of you.

-Jon Stewart

Chapter Ten

Mission Accomplished

Broken promises don't upset me. I just think, why did they believe me?

- Jack Handy

> Maybe every other American movie shouldn't be based on a comic book. Other countries will think Americans live in an infantile fantasy land where reality is whatever we say it is and every problem can be solved with violence.
>
> - Bill Maher

1055. Secondly, the tactics of our—as you know, we don't have relationships with Iran. I mean, that's—ever since the late '70s, we have no contacts with them, and we've totally sanctioned them. In other words, there's no sanctions—you can't—we're out of sanctions

Annandale Virginia
Aug. 9th, 2004

1056. So community colleges are accessible, they're available, they're affordable, and their curriculums don't get stuck. In other words, if there's a need for a certain kind of worker, I presume your curriculums evolved over time.

Niceville Florida.
Aug. 10th, 2004

1057.   I didn't join the International Criminal Court because I don't
         want to put our troops in the hands of prosecutors from other
         nations. Look, if somebody has done some wrong in our
         military, we'll take care of it. We got plenty of capability of
         dealing with justice.

Niceville, Florida
Aug. 10^{th,} 2004

Defense Secretary Donald Rumsfeld, facing growing
demands that he resign or be fired, apologized to
Congress on Friday for the abuse of Iraqi prisoners.
Rumsfeld said, 'I take full responsibility. This happened
on my watch. I feel terrible.' He went on to add, 'My
heart goes out, yada yada yada, you had me at hello,
blah blah blah, I'm a genius you're all morons, you can't
handle the truth, can I go now, ahhh.'

—Tina Fey SNL

Secretary of Defense Donald Rumsfeld said that he was
responsible for the abuse of the Iraqi prisoners. And
today President Bush said the abuse was cruel and
disgraceful and an affront to the most basic standards of
morality and decency. And then he told Rumsfeld that
he was doing a superb job. Then Rumsfeld said, 'What
the hell do I gotta do to get fired?''

—Jay Leno

Donald Rumsfeld made a surprise visit to Baghdad this
week where he told reporters, 'If anyone thinks I'm here
to throw water on a fire, they're wrong.' So, more bad
news for Iraqi prisoners who are on fire.

—Jimmy Fallon

1058.   You know what else I think? You know what else I think when
         they say, tax the rich? Most rich people are able to avoid
         taxes, and if you can't raise enough money from taxing the
         rich, guess who pays the taxes? Yes, you do.

Albuquerque New Mexico
Aug. 11th, 2004

422

1059.　　Government can hand out money, but government cannot put
hope in a person's heart, or a sense of purpose in a person's
life. Government happens when a loving neighbor puts their
arm around somebody who hurts and says, I love you and
can I help you?.

Sioux City Iowa
Aug 14th 2004

That's when government "happens"? Maybe beaurocracy isn't the
problem…It's all that government-lovin'

1060.　　Even though we didn't find the stockpiles we affected -- to
find, Saddam Hussein had the capability of making weapons.

Hedgesville West Virginia
Aug. 17th, 2004

In the lead up to the Iraq war and its later conduct, I
saw at a minimum, true dereliction, negligence and
irresponsibility, at worse, lying, incompetence and
corruption.

-Anthony Zinni

1061.　　Investment means you're purchasing something, and
somebody has to make that which you purchase and sell that
which you purchase. And that's how the economy works.

Hudson Wisconsin
Aug. 18th, 2004

423

1062.　　Your fellow citizens ought to worry about somebody who is out there making promise after promise after promise, like over $2 trillion worth of new promises, and not telling you how he's going to pay for it. You know, he says, well, we can pay for it because we'll tax the rich. Well, we've heard that kind of language before. And you know what happens with this kind of tax the rich deal. That's why they've got accountants and lawyers. So the rich figure out ways not to pay, and you get stuck with the tab.

Hudson Wisconsin
Aug. 18th, 2004

President Bush said yesterday it doesn't make any sense to raise taxes on the rich because rich people can figure out how to dodge taxes. Then Dick Cheney said 'Shut up! You're ruining everything.'
- Jay Leno

1063.　　REPORTER 1:
You're not going to Athens this week, are you?

BUSH:
Athens, Texas?

REPORTER 1:
Ol -- the Olympics, in Greece.

BUSH:
Oh, the Olympics? No, I'm not.

REPORTER 2:
Have you been watching them?

BUSH:
Oh, yeah, yeah, it's been exciting.

424

REPORTER 2:
Any particular moment stand out?

BUSH:
Umm -- particular moment? I like the -- let's see -- uhhhm --
Iraqi soccer. I liked -- I liked seein' the Afghan woman carryin'
the flag comin' in. I loved, uhh -- you know, our gymnasts. I've
been watching the swimming. I like th' -- I've seen a lot, yeah.
Listen, thank you all.

Crawford Texas
Aug. 23rd, 2004

A Dairy Queen cashier in Danville, Kentucky accidentally
gave change for a novelty $200 bill with George W.
Bush's picture on it. Reached for comment, Bush said,
'Well, if I am not on the $200 bill, who the hell is?'
—Craig Kilborn

1064. Last weekend we're continuing to implement our strategy of
la verdad, the truth.

Miami Florida
Aug. 27th, 2004

OK, obvious problems with his tense aside…
I suppose if honesty can be the best policy,
truth can be a strategy that must be implemented.

The men the American people admire most
extravagantly are the most daring liars; the men they
detest most violently are those who try to tell them the
truth

- Henry Louis Mencken

1065. They've seen me make decisions, they've seen me under trying times, they've seen me weep, they've seen me laugh, they've seen me hug. And they know who I am, and I believe they're comfortable with the fact that they know I'm not going to shift principles or shift positions based upon polls and focus groups.

USA Today
Aug. 27th, 2004

1066. Once you figure out the nature of the enemy, and know that they hide in caves and dark resorts of the city, it requires a universal effort to find them.

Lima Ohio
Aug. 28th, 2004

Dark resorts of the city? Uhmmm..is that like a Radisson?

1067. Laura] was a public school librarian when I asked her to marry me. She said, I'll marry you just so long as I don't have to give any speeches. It's the only political promise I've ever broken. And thankfully, I broke it. What a fabulous, articulate woman she is.

Lima Ohio
Aug. 28th, 2004

Librarians, Dusty, possess a vast store of politeness. These are people who get asked regularly the dumbest questions on God's green earth. These people tolerate every kind of crank and eccentric and mouth-breather there is.

- Garrison Kiellor

426

1068. I love the entrepreneurial spirit of America, don't you? Good job. There's nothing better. There is nothing better, is it, to be in an ownership society. Don't you love the idea of somebody saying, this is my business? How about the fact that home ownership rates in America are at an all-time high? More people -- and it's a fantastic statistic. It is a fantastic statistic of our society. It means more people are opening up that front door, saying, welcome to my home. Come into my piece of property. See, I love an ownership society.

Lima Ohio
Aug. 28th, 2004

1069. QUESTION:
Can we win the war on terrorism?

BUSH:
I don't think you can win it. But I think you can create conditions so that the -- those who use terror as a tool are -- less acceptable in parts of the world.

NBC Today Show
Aug. 30th, 2004

Not only will we win the war on terror to secure the peace in the world, we will show the world that a diverse nation from all walks of life and all religions can be compassionate and kind and hopeful for everyone who's lucky enough to be an American citizen.

President Bush
Mar. 19th, 2002

1070. It's only fair if other countries treat us the way they treat them.

Columbus Ohio
Sept. 1st, 2004

1071.   Like generations before us, we have a calling from beyond the stars to stand for freedom.

Republican National Convention
New York New York
Sept. 2nd, 2004

In the speech President Bush said that as a country we have a calling from 'beyond the stars.' You know what this means? He's drinking again.

- David Letterman

1072.   Senator Kerry opposed Medicare reform and health savings accounts. After supporting my education reforms, he now wants to tilute them.

Republican National Convention
New York New York
Sept. 2nd, 2004

1073.   We will make sure our troops have all that is necessary to complete their missions. That's why I went to the Congress last September and proposed fundamental -- supplemental funding, which is money for armor and body parts and ammunition and fuel.

Erie Pennsylvania
Sept. 4th, 2004

428

> Will Rumsfeld take personal responsibility for this problem? Clip: Rumsfeld: "I talked to the General coming out here about the pace at which the vehicles are being armored and it is essentially a matter of physics. It isn't a matter of money or on the part of the Army of desire. It is a matter of production and capability to do it."] Stewart: A matter of...physics. Don't you soldiers driving with no armor get it? Mass times velocity squared equals force. Damn you Einstein! Rumsfeld quickly moved from physics to philosophy. Clip: Rumsfeld: "You go to war with the Army you have not the Army you might want or wish to have." Stewart: "Actually they go to war, the Army. You fly in occasionally."
>
> - Jon Stewart

1074.   We got an issue in America. Too many good docs are gettin' out of business. Too many OB/GYNs aren't able to practice their -- their love with women all across this country.

Poplar Bluff Missouri
Sept. 6th, 2004

Funny, funny...FUN-EEEE Every time I read it...

1075.   I'm telling you, too many good docs are getting sued time and time and time again by frivolous lawsuits.

Sedalia Missouri
Sept. 7th, 2004

Well maybe if they stopped "practicing their love"....

1076.   ...There's a gap between what he promises and what he says he's going to do.

Johnstown Pennsylvania
Sept. 9th, 2004

1077. If you're a baby boomer, you don't have to worry about Social
Security. And by the way, you'll hear the same rhetoric you
hear every campaign, believe me, you know. Oh, don't worry,
they're going to take away your Social Security check. It is
the most tired, pathetic way to campaign for the presidency.
So you don't have to worry about that. And baby boomers are
fine. We're in good shape, you know. The people who aren't
in good shape are the children and grandchildren in this
country, because there's a lot fewer payer-inners than there
are recipients when it comes to Social Security checks.

Muskegon Michigan
Sept. 13th, 2004

"Payer-Inners!!" OH COME ON!
...payer inners....good grief. he's got an MBA!

From its birth in the 1630s, the Guard protected the early
colonists and helped win the War on Independence.

Las Vegas Nevada
Sept. 14th, 2004

Heralding the defeat of Independence!
Everybody now.."Hip Hip Hoor.....heh?"

430

> Government is not reason, it is not eloquence, it is
> force; like fire, a troublesome servant and a fearful
> master. Never for a moment should it be left to
> irresponsible action.
>
> - George Washington

1078.　Free societies are hopeful societies. And free societies will be allies against these hateful few who have no conscience, who kill at the whim of a hat.

Washington D.C.
Sept. 17ᵗʰ, 2004

Yes, damn those whimsical hats!

> President Bush spent last night calling world leaders to
> support the war with Iraq and it is sad when the most
> powerful man on earth is yelling, 'I know you're there,
> pick up, pick up.'
>
> - Craig Kilborn

1079.　Listen, the other day I was asked about the National Intelligence Estimate, which is a National Intelligence Estimate.

Washington D.C.
Sept. 23ʳᵈ, 2004

1080.　It breaks my heart to see the loss of innocent life and to see brave troops in combat lose their life. It just breaks my heart. But I understand what's going on. These people are trying to shake the will of the Iraqi citizens, and they want us to leave. That's what they want us to do. And I think the world would be better off if we did leave. If we didn't -- if we left, the world would be worse.

Derry New Hampshire
Sept. 20th, 2004

The question in my mind is how many additional American casualties is Saddam worth? And the answer is: not that damned many.'

- Dick Cheney
Secretary of Defense 1992

BAGHDAD, Iraq (CNN) -- The U.S. military death toll in Iraq reached 2,000 Tuesday with the reports of three new deaths, and President Bush prepared the nation for more casualties, saying the "defense of freedom is worth our sacrifice."

October 26, 2005

1081.   We know that dictators are quick to choose aggression, while free nations strive to resolve differences in peace.

U.N. General Assembly
Sept. 21st, 2004

Let mortals beware of words
For with words we lie
Can speak peace
When we mean war

- WH Audin

432

1082.   I'm not the expert on how the Iraqi people think, because I live in America, where it's nice and safe and secure.

Washington D.C.
Sept. 23rd, 2004

1083.   I think it's very important for the American President to mean what he says. That's why I understand that the enemy could misread what I say. That's why I try to be as clearly I can.

Washington D.C.
Sept. 23rd, 2004

Thank God he's able to "be clearly"…cause we don't want any misunderestimations

1084.   You can't lead this country if your ally in Iraq feels like you question his credibility.

Janesville Wisconsin
Sept. 24th, 2004

1085.   You've got to be able to speak clearly in order to make this world a more peaceful place.

Springfield Ohio
Sept 27th, 2004

A joke is a very serious thing

\- Winston Churchill

1086.	JIM LEHRER:
New question, Mr. President, two minutes. Do you believe the election of Senator Kerry on November the 2nd would increase the chances of the U.S. being hit by another 9/11-type terrorist attack?

BUSH:
I don't believe it's gonna happen. I believe I'm gonna win because the American people know I know how to lead. I've shown the American people I know how to lead.

First Presidential Debate
Coral Gables Florida
Sept. 30th, 2004

The prisoner scandal is yet another election year problem for President Bush. And, with the economy still struggling, combat operations in Iraq dragging on, and the 9-11 hearings revealing damning information, even an opponent of limited political skill should be able to capitalize on those problems. The Democrats, however, chose to nominate John Kerry.

-Jon Stewart

1087.	My concerns about the Senator is that, in the course of this campaign I've been listening very carefully to what he says, and he changes positions on the war on Iraq. It's a -- changes positions on something as ff -- fundamental as what you believe in your core, in your heart of hearts is right for -- in Iraq. I -- you cannot lead if you send mexed miss -- mixed messages.

First Presidential Debate
Coral Gables Florida
Sept. 30th, 2004

434

1088.   But I, again, I wanna tell the American people, we're doin'
        everything we can at home, but you better have a president
        who chases these terrorists down and bring 'em to justice
        before they hurt us again.

First Presidential Debate
Coral Gables Florida
Sept. 30th, 2004

The urgent necessity to disband terrorist networks
abroad and to secure the American homeland has been
replaced by the Bush administration's puzzling
preoccupation with Saddam Hussein. He has become
George Bush's White Whale, an obsession that has cost
us international solidarity in eradicating terrorism, the
goodwill of tens of millions of people worldwide and the
role of benign democratic world leader....

Former Senator Gary Hart
March 9, 2003

1089.   In Iraq, no doubt about it, it's tough. It's hard work. It's
        incredibly hard. You know why? Because an enemy realizes
        the stakes. The enemy understands a free Iraq will be a
        major defeat in their ideology of hatred. That's why they're
        fighting so vociferously.

First Presidential Debate
Coral Gables Florida
Sept. 30th, 2004

Those who can win a war well can rarely make a good
peace and those who could make a good peace would
never have won the war.

- Winston Churchill

1090.　　And you know, I think about -- Missy Johnson's a fantastic young lady I met in Charlotte, North Carolina, she and her son, Bryan. They came to see me. Her husband, P.J., got killed. He'd been in Afghanistan, went to Iraq. You know, it's hard work to try to love her as best as I can, knowing full well that the decision I made caused her -- her loved one to be in harm's way.

First Presidential Debate
Coral Gables Florida
Sept. 30th, 2004

There were some verbal gaffes. Bush said he had met with a war widow, and quote, 'tried to love her as best I could.' Which isn't easy when there's a guy at the foot of the bed playing 'Taps.'

- Bill Maher

1091.　　JIM LEHRER:
Does the Iraq experience make it more likely or less likely that you would take the United States into another preemptive military action?

BUSH:
I would hope I'd never have to. I understand how hard it is to commit troops. I never wanted to commit troops. I never -- when I was running -- when we had the debate in 2000, I never dreamt I'd be doing that. But the enemy attacked us, Jim, and -- ah -- I have a solemn duty to protect the American people, to do everything I can to protect us.

First Presidential Debate
Coral Gables Florida
Sept. 30th, 2004

436

60 Minutes Interview w/ Paul O'Neill
Jan 11, 2004

From the very beginning, there was a conviction, that Saddam Hussein was a bad person and that he needed to go.... going after Saddam was topic "A" 10 days after the inauguration - eight months before Sept. 11.

From the very first instance, it was about Iraq. It was about what we can do to change this regime. Day one, these things were laid and sealed.

The thing that's most surprising, I think, is how emphatically, from the very first, the administration had said 'X' during the campaign, but from the first day was often doing 'Y'.

1092.   Senator Kerry opposed Medicare reform and health savings accounts. After supporting my education reforms, he now wants to tilute them.

First Presidential Debate
Coral Gables Florida
Sept. 30th, 2004

...Strike Two!

1093.   Americans spend 6 billion hours a year filling out their tax reforms.

Manchester New Hampshire
Oct. 1st, 2004

1094.   Mr. Chairman -- you probably think I've come here to sign an important piece of legislation. Actually, I'm here for a different reason. The south lawn of the White House has a lot of grass -- I'm looking for somebody to mow it. And so Mr. Chairman, you shall now be known as 'Grass-mower.' And, by the way, when you're through using that car -- I've always liked an old Olds. I appreciate you being here, Mr. Chairman. Proud to call you friend. ...And I really do appreciate working with Mr. Chairman.

Des Moines Iowa
Oct. 4th, 2004

George W Bush is like a bad comic working the crowd, a moron, if you'll pardon the expression.

- Martin Sheen

1095.   I am sure many of you stayed up to watch the vice presidential debate last night. America saw two very different visions of our country, and two different hairdos. I didn't pick my Vice President for his hairdo. I picked him for his judgment, his experience.

Wilkes-Barre Pennsylvania
Oct. 6th, 2004

Which sadly, is as good as his hairdo

- Jon Stewart

438

1096.   After September the 11th, America had to assess every potential threat in a new light. Our nation awakened to an even greater danger, the prospect that terrorists who killed thousands with hijacked airplanes would kill many more with weapons of mass murder. We had to take a hard look at every place where terrorists might get those weapons. And one regime stood out, the dictatorship of Saddam Hussein.

Wilkes-Barre Pennsylvania
Oct. 6th, 2004

The powers in charge keep us in a perpetual state of fear keep us in a continuous stampede of patriotic fervor with the cry of grave national emergency. Always there has been some terrible evil to gobble us up if we did not blindly rally behind it by furnishing the exorbitant sums demanded. Yet, in retrospect, these disasters seem never to have happened, seem never to have been quite real.

- Douglas McArthur

1097.   And we've heard that rhetoric, haven't we, tax the rich? The rich hire lawyers and accountants for a reason, to stick you with the tab.

Wilkes-Barre Pennsylvania
Oct. 6th, 2004

GOP strategists hope the revelation of Kerry's wealth might debunk his status as a, quote, man of the people, and reveal him to be a bit of a fat cat. Unlike the President who — as we all know — before attending Andover and Yale, was a Cockney matchstick girl dying of tuberculosis.   - Jon Stewart

---

1098.   KERRY
We're going to build alliances. We're not going to go
unilaterally. We're not going to go alone like this president
did.

GIBSON:
Mr. President, let's extend for a minute...

BUSH:
Let me just -- I've got to answer this.

GIBSON:
Exactly. And with Reservists being held on duty...
(CROSSTALK)

BUSH:
Let me answer what he just said, about around the world.

GIBSON:
Well, I want to get into the issue of the back-door draft...

BUSH:
You tell Tony Blair we're going alone. Tell Tony Blair we're
going alone. Tell Silvio Berlusconi we're going alone. Tell
Aleksander Kwasniewski of Poland we're going alone. There
are 30 countries there. It denigrates an alliance to say we're
going alone, to discount their sacrifices. You cannot lead an
alliance if you say, you know, you're going alone. And people
listen. They're sacrificing with us.

GIBSON:
Senator?

440

KERRY:
Mr. President, countries are leaving the coalition, not joining. Eight countries have left it. If Missouri, just given the number of people from Missouri who are in the military over there today, were a country, it would be the third largest country in the coalition, behind Great Britain and the United States. That's not a grand coalition.

Second Presidential Debate
St. Louis Missouri
Oct. 8th, 2004

Spain's new Prime Minister Jose Luis Rodriguez Zapatero announced he will soon call back Spain's 1300 troops from Iraq — meaning the coalition of the willing is fast turning into a duet of the stubborn.

-Jon Stewart

1099.   I wasn't happy when we found out there wasn't weapons, and we've got an intelligence group together to figure out why.

Second Presidential Debate
St. Louis Missouri
Oct. 8th, 2004

President Bush has appointed a commission to answer one big question about pre-war Iraq: How did our oil get under their sand?

—Craig Kilborn

441

1100.   JOHN KERRY:
Ninety-eight percent of America, I'm giving you a tax cut and
I'm giving you health care.

CHARLES GIBSON:
Mr. President, a minute-and-a-half.

BUSH:
Let me see where to start here. First, the National Journal
named Senator Kennedy the most liberal senator of all. And
that's saying something in that bunch. You might say that
took a lot of hard work.

Second Presidential Debate
St. Louis Missouri
Oct. 8th, 2004

So, the Democrat is liberal....wow, good burn!
Would you like to answer the question now?

1101.   I'm going to tell you what I really think is going to happen over
time is technology is going to change the way we live for the
good for the environment. That's why I proposed a hydrogen
automobile -- hydrogen-generated automobile. We're
spending 1 billion dollars to come up with the technologies to
do that.

Second Presidential Debate
St. Louis Missouri
Oct. 8th, 2004

President Bush paid a visit to a hydrogen fueling
station. He said that hydrogen will provide the power
for our automobiles in the future. You know I'm not sure
president Bush really understands hydrogen. Like he
kept trying to take a hit off the pump to see if it would
make him talk funny.

- Jay Leno

442

1102. JAMES HUBB:
Mr. President, how would you rate yourself as an
environmentalist? What specifically has your administration
done to improve the condition of our nation's air and water
supply?

BUSH:
Off-road diesel engines. We have reached an agreement to
reduce pollution from off-road diesel engines by 90 percent.
I've got a plan to increase the wetlands by three million.

Second Presidential Debate
St. Louis Missouri
Oct. 8th, 2004

1103. JOHN KERRY:
Ladies and gentlemen, that's just not true what he said. The
Wall Street Journal said 96 percent of small businesses are
not affected at all by my plan. And you know why he gets that
count? The president got $84 from a timber company that he
owns, and he's counted as a small business. Dick Cheney's
counted as a small business. That's how they do things.
That's just not right.

BUSH:
I own a timber company? [LAUGHTER] That's news to me.
[LAUGHTER] Need some wood?

Second Presidential Debate
St. Louis Missouri
Oct. 8th, 2004

1104. I wouldn't pick a judge who said that the Pledge of Allegiance
couldn't be said in a school because it had the words under
God in it. I think that's an example of a judge allowing
personal opinion to enter into the decision-making process,
as opposed to strict interpretation of the Constitution. Another
example would be the Dred Scott case, which is where
judges years ago said that the Constitution allowed slavery
because of personal property rights. That's personal opinion.
That's not what the Constitution says. The Constitution of the
United States says we're all -- it doesn't say that, it doesn't
speak to the equality of America.

Second Presidential Debate
St. Louis Missouri
Oct. 8ᵗʰ, 2004

So, it's "do as I say, not as I do" again.
He's wrong about the Constitution though, according to Bush the
Constitution affords him some extraordinary rights, not extended
to anyone else, including other presidents.

1105. On the tax cut, it's a big decision. I did the right decision.

Second Presidential Debate
St. Louis Missouri
Oct. 8ᵗʰ, 2004

444

It was a big, huge, powerful win for the Republicans, and now they're saying that the Democrats could not articulate a message. You know you're in trouble when you are out-articulated by President Bush.

—David Letterman

1106.   John Kerry complains about the fact our troops don't have adequate equipment, yet he voted against the $87 billion supplemental I sent to the Congress, and then issued one of the most amazing quotes in political history: I actually did vote for the $87 billion before I voted against it.

Second Presidential Debate
St. Louis Missouri
Oct. 8th, 2004

Stupid Quote Score Kerry – 1 Bush 4703…still counting

There are photographs of President Bush from the first debate and he's got some kinda lump in the back of his coat, and the rumors are flying that he had a special radio receiver and he was getting answers from someone off stage. Wow, it's like he's back at Yale.

—David Letterman

We still don't know what the deal is what that thing in Bush's back, but I tell you, if God has a sense of humor, it is something that can only be cured with stem cell research.

-Bill Maher

Problems at Kerry debate prep: They keep trying to tell him he doesn't talk like a regular average Joe and he said, 'Au contraire!'

-Jay Leno

1107.   The truth of the matter is, if you listen carefully, Saddam
         would still be in power if he [John Kerry] were the President of
         the United States, and the world would be a lot better off.

Second Presidential Debate
St. Louis Missouri
Oct. 8th, 2004

> The loyalties which center upon number one are
> enormous. If he trips, he must be sustained. If he make
> mistakes, they must be covered. If he sleeps, he must
> not be wantonly disturbed. If he is no good, he must be
> pole-axed.
>
> - Winston Churchill

1108.   After listening to the litany of complaints and the dour
         pessimism, I did all I could not to make a bad face.

Second Presidential Debate
St. Louis Missouri
Oct. 8th, 2004

> Last night was the first presidential debate and it lasted
> a full 90 minutes. Or, as President Bush calls it, three
> Sponge Bobs.
>
> -Conan O'Brien

1109.   We spend money on research and development to expand
         the use of renewables, technologies to help us live different
         ways at the same lifestyle we're accustomed to.

Colorado Springs Colorado
Oct. 12th, 2004

1110.　See, I have a different philosophy. I'm a compassionate conservative. I think government ought to help people realize their dreams, not tell them how to live their lives.

Colorado Springs Colorado
Oct. 12th, 2004

> This week George W. Bush reversed his campaign pledge to limit carbon dioxide emissions and proposed cutting anti-drug programs for public housing residents, saying the addicts should just be evicted instead — which brings the tally up to: conservative 97, compassionate 0.
>
> —Tina Fey *Saturday Night Live*

1111.　As a matter of fact, when we gave [Saddam Hussein] the final chance, he continued to deceive and evade. So I have a choice to make at this point in our history. Do I forget the lessons of September the 11th and take the word of a madman, or do I take action to defend this country?

Colorado Springs Colorado
Oct. 12th, 2004

> One cannot wage war under present conditions without the support of public opinion, which is tremendously molded by the press and other forms of propaganda.
> - Douglas McArthur

1112.　Uhh -- Gosh, I -- don't think I ever said I'm not worried about Osama bin Laden. It's kind of one of those, uhh, exaggerations.

Third Presidential Debate
Tempe Arizona
Oct. 13th, 2004

1113.   BOB SCHIEFFER:
Suddenly we find ourselves with a severe shortage of flu
vaccine. How did that happen?

BUSH:
Uhhh -- Bob, we relied upon a company
out of England to provide about half of
the flu vaccines for the United States citizen,
and it turned out that the vaccine they were producing was
contaminated. And so we took
the right action and didn't allow contamidated medicine into
our country.

Third Presidential Debate
Tempe Arizona
Oct. 13th, 2004

The company "out of England" is Chiron based in California.
Their England facility was shut down by British health
authorities and 50 million units were seized so, Bush's "right
action" wasn't exactly by choice.......... and ya, he said "con-
tam-id-ated"

America had its third and final chance to watch the two
major presidential candidates discuss the issues in a
town hall format debate which, from the GOP
perspective, looked less like debates one and two and
more like the heartbreaking scene at the end of *Flowers
for Algernon* when Charley, the moron-turned-genius,
began visibly turning back into a moron.

—Jon Stewart

448

1114. The last debate, my opponent said well they only -- those lawsuits only caused costs to go up by 1 percent. Well, he didn't -- he didn't in -- include the defensive practice of medicine, that costs the federal government some 28 billion dollars a year and costs our society between 60 and 100 billion dollars a year. Uhh, thirdly, one of the reasons why there's still high cost in, in medicine is because this is -- the, the, the, they don't use an information technology. It's like if you looked at the -- it's the equivalent of the -- of the buggy and horse days.

Third Presidential Debate
Tempe Arizona
Oct. 13th, 2004

1115. In all due respect, I'm not so sure it's credible to quote leading news organizations about -- oh, never mind.

Third Presidential Debate
Tempe Arizona
Oct. 13th, 2004

1116. I believe part of a hopeful society is one in which somebody owns something.

Third Presidential Debate
Tempe Arizona
Oct. 13th, 2004

1117. Laura is out campaigning along with our girls. And she speaks English a lot better than I do.

Tempe Arizona
Oct. 13th, 2004

1118.   We will not have an all-volunteer army. And yet, this week ----
we will have an all-volunteer army!

Daytona Beach Florida
Oct. 16th, 2004

1119.   The last two years, the American people have come to know
me. They know my blunt way of speaking.

Daytona Beach Florida
Oct. 16th, 2004

1120.   One of the most amazing events of my life, at least as the
presidency, was to go to the NASCAR Race here at the
Daytona 500.

Daytona Beach Florida
Oct. 16th, 2004

This Sunday, President Bush will be at the Daytona 500
for the start of NASCAR season. President Bush is a big
fan of NASCAR. Bush says if it weren't for NASCAR, man
never would have stepped foot on the moon. Finally,
somebody said, "Uh, sir ... that's NASA."

- Jay Leno

1121.   We need a safety net for those with the greatest needs. I
believe in community health centers, where low and poor can
get their preventative and care.

Daytona Beach Florida
Oct. 16th, 2004

450

1122.   We will stand up for terror. We will stand up for freedom.

Marlton New Jersey
Oct. 18th, 2004

1123.   And then came the attack on the USS Cole in 2000, which
cost the lives of 17 American sailors. In this period, America's
response to terrorism was generally piecemeal and symbolic.
The terrorists concluded this was a sign of weakness, and
their plans became more ambitions.

Marlton New Jersey
Oct. 18th, 2004

> What a cruel thing is war: to separate and destroy
> families and friends, and mar the purest joys and
> happiness God has granted us in this world; to fill our
> hearts with hatred instead of love for our neighbors,
> and to devastate the fair face of this beautiful world. -
> letter to his wife, 1864
>
> - General Robert E Lee

1124.   I have a record in office, as well, and all Americans have
seen that record. September the 4th, 2001, I stood in the
ruins of the Twin Towers. It's a day I will never forget.

Marlton New Jersey
Oct. 18th, 2004

Never forget?

> We have to do the best we can. This is our sacred
> human responsibility.
>
> - Albert Einstein

1125.   DUANE ALBERTS OF PINE SHELTER FARMS:
        Well, Mr. President, it's time to kill the death tax. I just want to
        start out that way.

        BUSH:
        Well, he's got -- the man's got an opinion. We've got it -- it's
        on its way to extinction. Unfortunately, it pops back up. It's
        going to be an odd year in 2010. You can imagine people -- I
        mean, it goes away in 2010, it pops back up in 2011. So
        people are going to have some weird choices in 2010 when it
        comes to the death tax. But never mind. It's a little morbid.

        Rochester Minnesota
        Oct. 20th, 2004

1126.   Saddam Hussein was a threat. He was a threat because he
        hated America. He was a threat because he was shooting
        missiles at American airplanes. He was a threat because he
        harbored terrorists. He was a threat because he invaded his
        neighbors. He was a threat because he had used weapons of
        mass destruction. He was a threat. Now, we didn't find the
        stockpiles we all thought were there. That includes me and
        my opponent.

        Rochester Minnesota
        Oct. 20th, 2004

1127.   When I came into public office too many republic schools
        were passing children, grade to grade, year after year,
        without learning the basics.

        Mason City Iowa
        Oct. 20th, 2004

        The basics like, the difference between
        "republic" and "public"

452

1128.   I think the job of a problem is to confront problems, not to pass them on to future Presidents and future generations.

Cuba City Wisconsin
Oct. 26th, 2004

1129.   I want to remind the American people, if Senator Kerry had his way, we would still be taking our global test. Saddam Hussein would still be in power. He would control all those weapons and explosives and could have shared them with our terrorist enemies.

Vienna Ohio
Oct. 27th, 2004

He could share those weapons that don't exist?

1130.   September the 11th changed me. I remember the day I was in the -- at Ground Zero, on September the 4th, 2001. It's a day I will never forget.

Lititz Pennsylvania
Oct. 27th, 2004

...and again

1131.   And a political candidate who jumps to conclusions without knowing the facts is not the person you want as the Commander-in-Chief.

Vienna Ohio
Oct. 27th, 2004

(Ring-Ring)
Uhhh, Is this the Kettle?
Ya,….it's the Pot here…
I've got something to tell you…

1132.   The Senator's willingness to trade principle for political convenience makes it clear that John Kerry is the wrong man for the wrong job at the wrong time.

Westlake Ohio
Oct. 28th, 2004

1133.   Thank you all. Thanks for coming out to say hello. I got to tell me, you have lifted my spirits, for which I am grateful.

Saginaw Michigan
Oct. 28th, 2004

1134.   [John Kerry] voted against that tax relief at a vital time. Plus, he's decided to raise $2.2 million in new federal spending. He's going to spend it. That's what he said.

Saginaw Michigan
Oct. 28th, 2004

454

1135.   And next Tuesday, the American people will go to the polls.
        They will be voting for vision. They will be voting for
        consistency. They will be voting for conviction. And no doubt
        in my help, they'll be voting for Bush/Cheney.

Grand Rapids Michigan
Oct. 30th, 2004

If not conviction, then at least indictment.

In our age there is no such thing as 'keeping out of
politics.' All issues are political issues, and politics itself
is a mass of lies, evasions, folly, hatred and
schizophrenia.

- George Orwell

1136.   Perhaps the most important reason to put me back in is so
        that Laura will be the First Lady for four more years. ...We
        were campaigning together tomorrow.

Burgettstown Pennsylvania
Nov. 1st, 2004

1137.   My opponent says that America must submit to what he has
        called a global test before we take action to defend ourselves.
        I'm not making that up. I heard it during one of the debates.
        As far as I can tell, my opponent's global test means America
        must get permission to defend our country.

Sioux City Iowa
Nov. 1st, 2004

> Kerry said, "No president, through all of American history, has ever ceded, and nor would I, the right to preempt in any way necessary to protect the United States of America. But ...you have to do it in a way that passes the test, that passes the global test where your countrymen, your people understand fully why you're doing what you're doing and you can prove to the world that you did it for legitimate reasons."

1138. I want to thank you all for your hard work. I was impressed every day by how hard and how skillful our team was.

Washington D.C.
Nov. 3rd, 2004

Either get me phone numbers or.....fine,
just write your own dirty joke

1139. And so Prime Minister Allawi and his government, which fully understands that, are working with our generals on the ground to do just that. We will work closely with the government. It's their government, it's their country. We're there at their invitation.

Washington D.C.
Nov. 4th, 2004

That's a little like a bank robber saying, "If you didn't
want me to rob the bank, why did you have all that money?"

1140. We must continue the work of education reform, to bring high standards and accountability not just to our elementary and secondary schools, but to our high schools, as well.

Washington D.C.
Nov. 4th, 2004

456

1141.　You covered me when I was the governor of Texas. I told you that I was going to do that as a governor. There was probably skepticism in your beady eyes there. But you might remember -- you might remember, we did -- we were able to accomplish a lot by -- and Washington is different from Austin, no question about it. Washington -- one of the disappointments of being here in Washington is how bitter this town can become and how divisive. I'm not blaming one party or the other. It's just the reality of Washington, D.C., sometimes exacerbated by you, because it's great sport. It's really -- it's entertaining for some. It also makes - is difficult to govern at times.

Washington D.C.
Nov. 4th, 2004

When in doubt, blame the press

No government ought to be without censors; and where the press is free no one ever will.

- Thomas Jefferson

1142.　I always jest to people, the Oval Office is the kind of place where people stand outside, they're getting ready to come in and tell me what for, and they walk in and get overwhelmed in the atmosphere, and they say, man, you're looking pretty.

Washington D.C.
Nov. 4th, 2004

This, I'm sure is absolutely true and I'm actually surprised that he has enough awareness to recognize that. After all, what's a naked Emperor to do?

1143.   The deficit is less than we thought because the revenues is
         exceeding projections. And the reason why the revenues --
         the revenues are exceeding projections -- sometimes I
         mangle the English language. I get that.

Washington D.C.
Nov. 4th, 2004

1144.   I earned capital in the campaign, political capital, and now I
         intend to spend it. It is my style. That's what happened in the
         -- after the 2000 election, I earned some capital.

Washington D.C.
Nov. 4th, 2004

1145.   It's such a comforting sense for me to be able to tell a loved
         one, your person hurt, your loved one will get the best care
         possible.

Walter Reed Army Medical Center
Washington D.C.
Nov. 9th, 2004

Now we must focus attention on our veterans and
military retirees who have seen the government cut
medical benefits, close VA hospitals, double tax
disability payments, and more than double prescription
drug co-payments, while requiring veterans to pay an
annual enrollment fee of $250 to use government health
services in the 2006 budget.

- General Wesley Clark (ret.)
Introducing his GI Bill of Rights

458

1146.   And the reason why I'm so strong on democracy is democracies don't go to war with each other.

White House
Nov. 12th, 2004

No, but apparently they go to war
with everybody else

1147.   TOUR GUIDE:
[Looking across the Arkansas River...]
Usually, you might see some bass
fishermen out there.

BUSH:
A submarine could take this place out.

Dedication of the Clinton Presidential Center
Little Rock Arkansas
Nov. 18th, 2004

President Bush actually was excited to be there because he had never been to a library before.

-David Letterman

1148.   You know, what's interesting about our country is that for years we were isolated from the world by two great oceans, and for a while we got a false sense of security as a result of that. We thought we were protected forever from trade policy or terrorist attacks because oceans protected us. What's interesting about today's world is that the oceans now connect us.

Santiago Chile
Nov. 20th, 2004

1149. The president and I also reaffirmed our determination to fight
terror, to bring drug trafficking to bear, to bring justice to those
who pollute our youth.

With Chilean President Ricardo Lagos
Santiago Chile
Nov. 21st, 2004

1150. REPORTER:
In the days after September 11th, thousands of Canadians
went to Parliament Hill to demonstrate solidarity with the U.S.
-- and, in fact, in cities across the country. Yet, public opinion
polls and other evidence suggest that now, today, our
peoples are, in fact, diverging. That, in fact, our peoples are
drifting apart. Why do you think that is? And do you have any
responsibility for it?

BUSH:
You know, I haven't seen the polls you look at,
and we just had a poll in our country where
people decided that the foreign policy of the
Bush administration ought to be -- stay in
place for four more years.

Ottawa Canada
Nov 30th, 2004

460

Chapter Eleven

We Still At War

The two pillars of 'political correctness' are

    a) willful ignorance
    b) steadfast refusal to face the truth

                George MacDonald

> In response to the escalating violence in Iraq, President Bush is delaying the return home of 25,000 troops and will actually add reinforcements to the south. Then in a symbolic gesture he pulled down the mission accomplished banner, put on a flight suit, walked backwards to a jet fighter and flew it in reverse off an aircraft carrier.
>
> —Tina Fey, *Saturday Night Live*

1151.   I don't view relations as one that there's a score card that says, you know, well, if we all fight terror together, therefore, somebody owes somebody something.

White House
Dec 4th, 2004

1152.   Tommy [Thompson] was commenting on the fact that we're a large company -- country, with all kinds of avenues where somebody can inflict harm.

White House
Dec 4th, 2004

1153.   And so during these holiday seasons, we thank our blessings.

Fort Belvoir Virginia
Dec. 10th, 2004

1154.   George is rightly -- rightly proud of the people of the Agency, and I have been proud to work with George. George has carried great authority without putting on airs, because he remembers his roots. There's still a lotta Queens in George Tenet.

White House
Dec 14th, 2004

> Senate committee on Thursday approved a constitutional amendment banning same sex marriage, apparently forgetting that our forefathers wore wigs and satin Capri pants.
>
> -Tina Fey

1155.   There's a trade deficit. That's easy to resolve: People can buy more United States products if they're worried about the trade deficit.

Oval Office
Dec. 15th, 2004.

1156.   And we will continue to make it clear to both Syria and Iran that -- as will other nations in our coalition, including our friend, the Italians, that meddling in the internal affairs of Iraq is not in their interest.

Washington DC
Dec 15th, 2004

> Alan Greenspan, our Fed chairman, said that Bush's budget is such a mess that we're going to have to either cut spending, raise taxes or start a national sales tax. You know what that means -- war with Syria.
>
> - Bill Maher

464

1157.   I really appreciate the different backgrounds of the people who spoke. We had your entrepreneur, we had your academic, we had your corporate leader, we just had plain old citizens show up.

Washington DC
Dec 16th, 2004

1158.   I want you to know that the death tax takes up more than 300 pages of laws and regulations in the current tax code. By getting rid of the death tax forever, we have simplified the code by 300 pages.

Washington DC
Dec 16th, 2004

...Demonstrating his understanding of what
concerns Americans about tax code

1159.   We started to change the system here in Washington with the No Child Left Behind Act. I understand that it's created some consternation. And it's created consternation because, in return for increased federal spending, we finally started asking the question, can you read and write and add and subtract? It's never seemed to me -- For some, that's called an unfunded mandate. To me, that's called a necessary mandate -- to make sure our children can learn.

Washington D.C.
Dec. 16th, 2004

Bush's "Straw Man" runs amok

465

Two Can Play That Game
Bush loves his imaginary friends

It's called the "Straw Man Fallacy" It's a debate technique whereby a fictional opponent is ascribed an opposing viewpoint so that the speaker can refute it. In short, a Straw Man is set up specifically so that he can be shot down, putting the shooter on the 'right' side. He is victorious in a contrived conflict that he orchestrated to bolster his own opinion and/or public image. The opposing side may or may not exist. It's irrelevant because that point of view is provided no opportunity to engage. (like Iraq, without the improvised exploding devices)

<u>Some people say that the Straw Man is an excellent debate technique. I say it's a cheap manipulative ploy that stunts any honest discourse</u>

Bush loves to say he won't "debate himself", yet he is constantly trotting out his silent opponent and ascribing him ridiculous criticisms so, that Bush can object to them.

The No Child Left Behind program is an excellent example. Bush claims that "'some' call it an unfunded mandate" and describe that criticism as an objection to the accountability requirements. The criticism of real live educators actually centers on the lack of funding provided to the schools to implement the program.

A cringe-worthy favorite, at a press conference with PM Paul Martin of Canada, Bush says "some people don't think people whose skin is not necessarily white can self-govern" Eeeeek! Have you ever heard anyone actually say that? (someone that matters)

Bush needs to retire his buddy the "Straw Man" and start honest debate with real people and handle their tangible objections. No more screened attendees asking approved questions in townhall meetings. If he believes he is defending the best side of an argument, there is no need for disambiguation.
In the meantime, Bush and his Straw Man should go see the Wizard. I'm sure he could spare another brain.

1160.	You know, polls change, Dave. Polls go up. Polls go down. I can understand why people -- they're looking on your TV screen and seeing indiscriminate bombing where thousands of innocent, or hundreds of innocent Iraqis are getting killed, and they're saying whether or not we're able to achieve the objective.

Washington DC
Dec 20th, 2004

Stunning admission!

1161.	The principles I laid out in the course of the campaign, and the principles we laid out at the recent economic summit are still the principles I believe in. And that is nothing will change for those near our Social Security, payroll -- I believe you were the one who asked me about the payroll tax, if I'm not mistaken -- will not go up. And I know there's a big definition about what that means. Well, again, I will repeat. Don't bother to ask me. Or you can ask me. I shouldn't -- I can't tell you what to ask. It's not the holiday spirit.

Washington DC
Dec 20th, 2004

As you know President Bush has been traveling around the country trying to sell his new Social Security plan. He wants to take our retirement money and invest it in the stock market. He says nothing can go wrong. I'll mention that to Martha Stewart the next time I see her.
- Jay Leno

467

1162.   That if somebody who is here working wants to be a citizen, they can get in line like those who have been here legally and have been working to become a citizenship in a legal manner.

Washington DC
Dec 20th, 2004

1163.   ... And so I am -- I just want to try to condition you. I'm not doing a very good job, because the other day in the Oval when the press pool came in I was asked about this -- a series of question on -- a question on Social Security with these different aspects to it. And I said, I'm not going to negotiate with myself.

Washington DC
Dec 20th, 2004

> I care about our young people, and I wish them great success, because they are our hope for the future, and some day, when my generation retires, they will have to pay us trillions of dollars in social security
> - Dave Barry

1164.   The idea of a democracy taking hold in what was a place of tyranny and hatred and destruction is -- is such a hopeful moment in the history of the world.

Washington DC
Dec 21st, 2004

1165.   Today, we had a rocket attack that took a lot of lives. Any time of the year it's a time of sorrow and sadness when we lose a loss of life.

Washington DC
Dec 21st, 2004

> That peace was better than war; because in peace the
> sons did bury their fathers, but in wars the fathers did
> bury their sons
>
> — Francis Bacon

1166.   People sometimes say what's more important than the
country is my politics.

Washington DC
Jan 3rd, 2005

1167.   I believe we are called to do the hard work to make our
communities and quality of life a better place.

Collinsville Illinois
Jan 5th, 2005

1168.   That's been the proven example around the world.
Democracies equal peace.

White House
Jan 7th, 2005

> Naturally the common people don't want war; neither in
> Russia, nor in England, nor in America, nor in Germany.
> That is understood. But after all, it is the leaders of the
> country who determine policy, and it is always a simple
> matter to drag the people along, whether it is a
> democracy, or a fascist dictatorship, or a parliament, or
> a communist dictatorship. Voice or no voice, the people
> can always be brought to the bidding of the leaders.
> That is easy. All you have to do is to tell them they are
> being attacked, and denounce the pacifists.
>
> — Hermann Goering

1169.   Who could have possibly envisioned an erect-sh -- an election in Iraq at this point in history?

White House
Jan 10th, 2005

1170.   SONYA STONE:
I would like to introduce my mom. This is my mother, Rhoda Stone. And she is grandmother of three, and originally from Helsinki, Finland, and has been here over 40 years.

BUSH:
Fantastic. Same age as my mother.

SONYA STONE: Just turned 80.

Washington DC
Jan 11th, 2005

Wow it's like read her mind!....

1171.   We've got to make sure education systems actually educate willing workers for the jobs which exist. And that's why I'm here at the community college system today.

Jacksonville Florida
Jan 14th, 2005

Reminding us not to pursue imaginary jobs.

470

1172.   I'm also mindful that it takes a while for democracy to take hold. Witness our own history. We weren't -- we certainly were not the perfect democracy and are yet the perfect democracy.

Air Force One
Jan 14th, 2005

> At the bottom of all the tributes paid to democracy is the little man walking into the little booth with a little pencil, making a little cross on a little bit of paper.
> - Albert Einstein

1173.   It's important for people to know that I'm the president of everybody.

Air Force One
Jan 14th, 2005

1174.   WASHINGTON POST:
In Iraq, there's been a steady stream of surprises. We weren't welcomed as liberators, as Vice President Cheney had talked about. We haven't found the weapons of mass destruction as predicted. The postwar process hasn't gone as well as some had hoped. Why hasn't anyone been held accountable, either through firings or demotions, for what some people see as mistakes or misjudgments?

BUSH:
Well, we had an accountability moment, and that's called the 2004 election. And the American people listened to different assessments made about what was taking place in Iraq, and they looked at the two candidates, and chose me, for which I'm grateful

Air Force One
Jan 14th, 2005

1175.   WASHINGTON POST:
Why do you think Bin Laden has not been caught?

BUSH:
Because he's hiding.

Air Force One
Jan 14th, 2005

We do know, of certain knowledge, that (Bin Laden) is either in Afghanistan or in some other country or dead.
- Donald Rumsfeld

1176.   I'm also mindful that man should never try to put words in God's mouth. I mean, we should never ascribe natural disasters or anything else, to God. We are in no way, shape, or form should a human being, play God..

ABC's 20/20
Washington D.C.
Jan. 14th, 2005

According to Palestinean Prime Minister Abbas, immediately thereafter Bush said: "God told me to strike at al Qaida and I struck them, and then he instructed me to strike at Saddam, which I did, and now I am determined to solve the problem in the Middle East. If you help me I will act, and if not, the elections will come and I will have to focus on them.-
Haaretz Ireali News
June 25th, 2003

472

1177.   REPORTER:
I seem to remember a time in Texas on another problem --
taxes -- where you tried to get out in front and tell people it's
not a crisis now, it's going to be a crisis down the line. You
went down in flames on that one. Why is there –

BUSH:
Actually, I -- let me -- let me, if I might -- I don't think a billion
dollar tax relief that permanently reduced property taxes on
senior citizens was flames -- but since you weren't a senior
citizen, perhaps that's your definition of flame. Yeah –

REPORTER:
What is there about government --

BUSH:
'Cause you're not a senior citizen yet.

REPORTER:
I'm getting there. What is there
about government that makes it hard --

BUSH:
Acting like one, however. Go ahead.

REPORTER: --
that makes it hard for government to get -

BUSH:
Faulty memory.

Washington DC
Jan 26th, 2005

Politicians are dumb, but they can count to 50% plus 1.
- Will Rogers

473

1178.   BUSH:
         How old is your child, Carl?

         CARL:
         Fourteen years old.

         BUSH:
         Yes, 14. Well, if she were --

         CARL:
         He, sir.

         BUSH:
         He, excuse me. I should have done the
         background check. She will -- when she gets
         ready to -- when she's 50, the system will be
         broke, if my math is correct.

                        Washington DC
                        Jan 26th, 2005

1179.   But in my meetings with Chinese leadership in the past, in my
         meetings with Chinese leadership in the future, I will
         constantly remind them of the benefits of a society that
         honors their people and respects human rights and human
         dignity.

                        Washington DC
                        Jan 26th, 2005

1180.   REPORTER:
         Mr. President, I'd like to ask you about the Gonzales
         nomination, and specifically, about an issue that came up
         during it, your views on torture. You've said repeatedly that
         you do not sanction it, you would never approve it. But there
         are some written responses that Judge Gonzales gave to his
         Senate testimony that have troubled some people, and
         specifically, his allusion to the fact that cruel, inhumane and
         degrading treatment o

474

f some prisoners is not specifically forbidden so long as it's conducted by the CIA and conducted overseas. Is that a loophole that you approve?

BUSH:
Listen, Al Gonzales reflects our policy, and that is we don't sanction torture. He will be a great Attorney General, and I call upon the Senate to confirm him.   (pointing to another reporter...]

Washington DC
Jan 26th, 2005

> Alberto Gonzales, nominee for the U.S. attorney general, answered some tough questions from Congress today about his role in the Iraqi prison torture scandal. But afterwards he said to make himself relax he used that old trick of imagining your audience in their underwear -- with hoods over their heads being led around on a dog leash by a women. It just helps to get your mind clear.
>
> - Jav Leno

1181.   The United States has no right, no desire, and no intention to impose our form of government on anyone else. That is one of the main differences between us and our enemies.

State of the Union Address
Washington DC
Feb 2nd, 2005

1182.   We are in Iraq to achieve a result. A country that is democratic.

State of the Union Address
Washington DC
Feb 2nd, 2005

1183. A bunch of baby boomers who are going to live longer and
have been promised greater benefits are fixing to retire. And
so the system goes into the red. And it goes into the red --
that means negative, that means losing money -- quite
dramatically. In the year 2027, it will be $200 billion in the red
-- $200 billion for one year alone. And in 3032, it's like $300
billion. And in 20 -- I mean, 2032. And in 2042, it's bust.

Fargo North Dakota
Feb 3rd, 2005

1184. The President needs a lot of advice.

White House
Feb. 4th, 2005

1185. WOMAN   IN   AUDIENCE:
I don't really understand. How is it the new [Social Security]
plan   is   going   to   fix   that   problem?

BUSH:
Because the -- all which is on the table begins to address the
big cost drivers. For example, how benefits are calculated, for
example, is on the table. Whether or not benefits rise based
upon wage increases or price increases. There's a series of
parts of the formula that are being considered. And when you
couple that, those different cost drivers, affecting those --
changing those with personal accounts, the idea is to get
what has been promised more likely to be -- or closer
delivered to what has been promised. Does that make any
sense to you? It's kind of muddled. Look, there's a series of
things that cause the -- like, for example, benefits are
calculated based upon the increase of wages, as opposed to
the increase of prices. Some have suggested that we

476

calculate -- the benefits will rise based upon inflation, as opposed to wage increases. There is a reform that would help solve the red if that were put into effect. In other words, how fast benefits grow, how fast the promised benefits grow, if those -- if that growth is affected, it will help on the red.

Tampa Florida
Feb 4th, 2005

Thanks for clearing that up...

Over the weekend, President Bush threw out the first pitch at a Little League play off game, and that must have been exciting. I mean that's something those kids will remember until they are old and gray and have no Social Security.

\- Jay Leno

1186.   And it's not only having no retirement system. It is how are we going to pay for people like George W. when he gets ready to retire? That's as big a burden as having no system at all, see? And that's the dilemma we're faced with.

Little Rock Arkansas
Feb 4th, 2005

1187.   Now, there's some rules, and it's important for you to know the rules. One, you can't take your money that you set aside in the personal account and go to the race track. ...Secondly, you can't pull it all out when it comes time to your -- you can't take it all and then go to the track.

Tampa Florida
Feb 4th, 2005

1188.   Now, if you're a worker who earns 35 dollars a year over your lifetime, and this system were in effect where you could put 4 percent of your payroll taxes in a personal account, and you started at age 20, by the time you retired, your personal account would grow to 250,000 dollars. That's compounding rate of interest.

Raleigh North Carolina
Feb 10th, 2005

And it's confounding math!

1189.   Can you imagine if my name had been Mungo Bush?

White House
Feb 18th, 2005

1190.   The United States and the U.S. stand together in support of the Iraqi people and the new Iraqi government, which will soon come into action.

Brussels Belgium
Feb 22nd, 2005

That Coalition of the Willing gets smaller every day.

478

1191.   This notion that the United States is getting ready to attack Iran is simply ridiculous. And having said that, all options are on the table.

Brussels Belgium
Feb 22nd, 2005

Bush is denying reports today that he plans to invade Iran. Oh, we're still going to invade, we just don't have any plans.

- Jay Leno

1192.   You know, you can't discriminate. Freedom is not a discriminatory thought, at least in the White House -- in other words, if you say, certain people should be free, but others shouldn't free. It's a universal thought, as far as I'm concerned.

Mainz Germany
Feb 23rd, 2005

1193.   My six years as governor of Texas have been invaluable to me as I carry out my duties as the presidency.

Washington DC
Feb 27th, 2005

1194.   Congresswoman Melissa Hart, thank you for being here. ...Melissa happens to be a board of this community college system.

Pittsburgh Pennsylvania
Mar 7th, 2005

At least he didn't call her a "broad"

479

1195.   I'm lookin' forward to meeting these uhh -- very brave souls. They've, uhh, committed themselves to a peaceful solution, and hopefully, their loved one'd will not have died in vain. I mean, out of this -- hopefully, some good will come out of the evil perpetuated on this family.

Washington DC
Mar 16th, 2005

> I mean, I think, Iraqis, I think, feel that if we drove smaller cars, maybe we wouldn't have to kill them for their oil.
>
> - Bill Maher

1196.   WASHINGTON POST:
Will you talk to Senate Democrats about your privatization plan?

BUSH:
You mean, the personal savings accounts?

WASHINGTON POST:
Yes, exactly. Scott has been --

BUSH:
We don't want to be editorializing, at least
in the questions.

WASHINGTON POST:
You used partial privatization yourself last year, sir.

BUSH: Yes?

WASHINGTON POST:
Yes, three times in one sentence. We had to figure this out, because we're in an argument with the RNC [Republican National Committee] about how we should actually word this. [Post staff writer] Mike Allen, the industrious Mike Allen, found it.

480

BUSH:
Allen did what now?

WASHINGTON POST:
You used partial privatization.

BUSH:
I did, personally?

WASHINGTON POST: Right.

BUSH: When?

WASHINGTON POST:
To describe it.

BUSH:
When, when was it?

WASHINGTON POST:
Mike said it was right around the election.

BUSH:
Seriously?

WASHINGTON POST:
It was right around the election.
We'll send it over.

BUSH:
I'm surprised. Maybe I did. It's amazing what happens when you're tired.

Air Force One
Jan 14th, 2005

1197.   That's part of -- that's part of the advice my new National Economic Council head will be giving me as to whether or not we need to -- here is the plan, or here is an idea for a plan, or why don't you just fix it. I suspect given my nature, I'll want to be -- the White House will be very much involved with -- I have an obligation to lead on this issue -- I think this will be an administrative-driven idea -- to take it on. And therefore, that that be the case, I have the responsibility to provide the political cover necessary for members, I have the responsibility to make the case if there is a problem, and I have the responsibility to lay out potential solutions. Now, to the specificity of which, we'll find out -- you'll find out with time.

Wall Street Journal Interview
Jan 11th, 2005

Not a comprehensive sentence in the lot!

1198.   To address the cost of medical care, we need to apply 21st century information technology to the health care field. We need to have our medical records put on the IT.

Collinsville Illinois
Jan 5th, 2005

1199.   I'm also mindful that man should never try to put words in God's mouth. I mean, we should never ascribe natural disasters or anything else to God. We are in no way, shape, or form should a human being, play God.

Washington DC
Jan 14th, 2005

1200.   BUSH:
Mary is with us. Mary Morin. How are you, Mary?

MS. MORNIN:
I'm fine.

BUSH:
Good. Okay, Mary, tell us about yourself.

MS. MORNIN:
Okay, I'm a divorced, single mother with three grown, adult children. I have one child, Robbie, who is mentally challenged, and I have two daughters.

BUSH:
There's a certain comfort to know that the promises made will be kept by the government.

MS. MORNIN:
Yes.

BUSH:
And so thank you for asking that. You don't have to worry.

MS. MORNIN:
That's good, because I work three jobs and I feel like I contribute.

BUSH:
You work three jobs?

MS. MORNIN:
Three jobs, yes.

BUSH:
Uniquely American, isn't it? I mean, that is fantastic that you're doing that. Get any sleep?

Omaha Nebraska
Feb 4th, 2005

President Bush is taking his summer vacation. It's a five-week vacation. This is his fiftieth vacation in the last five years -- that's about the national average isn't it? During his five-week vacation, he will continue to receive national security briefings. He won't be reading them, but he will receive them.

-David Letterman

483

1201.　BUSH:
Andrew Biggs is with us. He is the Associate Commissioner for Retirement Policy of the Social Security Administration, Washington, D.C. In other words, he is an expert on the subject. Andrew, step forth. Let the people of Arkansas -- no, sit forth -- let the people of Arkansas --

DR. BIGGS:
Thanks very much.

BUSH:
Tell them whether or not we got a problem or not, from your perspective.

DR. BIGGS:
Put simply, we do, in fact, have a problem.

BUSH:
By the way, this guy -- PhD. See, I was a C student. He's a PhD, so he's probably got a little more credibility. I do think it's interesting and should be heartening for all C students out there, notice who's the President and who's the advisor. All right, Andrew, get going. Andrew's got a good sense of humor.

Little Rock Arkansas
Feb 4th, 2005

Self-deprecation is a good move, whether you're trying to get a date or run the country, because it's endearing and softens you and brings in the pity factor. But with Bush, you still have the feeling that he thinks he's the coolest guy in the frat.
　　　　　　　　　　　　　　—Humorist Michael Colton

484

1202.   That's how interest works. It compounds. It grows. Now, people say, what does that mean, a personal savings account? Can I take the money and go right down to the road where I was staying in this part of the world and put it in the slots?

Shreveport Louisville
Mar 11th, 2005

People say that....really? Apparently Straw Man
has a little gambling problem.

1203.   I repeat, personal accounts do not permanently fix the solution.

Washington D.C.
March 16th, 2005

1204.   In this job you've got a lot on your plate on a regular basis; you don't have much time to sit around and wander, lonely, in the Oval Office, kind of asking different portraits, 'How do you think my standing will be?'

Washington D.C.
March 16th, 2005

1205.   In terms of timetables, as quickly as possible—whatever that means.

Washington D.C.
March 16th, 2005

1206.   Like the idea of people running for office. There's a positive effect when you run for office. Maybe some will run for office and say, vote for me, I look forward to blowing up America. I don't know, I don't know if that will be their platform or not. But it's -- I don't think so. I think people who generally run for office say, vote for me, I'm looking forward to fixing your potholes, or making sure you got bread on the table.

Washington DC
Mar 16th, 2005

1207.   I think it's important for me to be thoughtful and sensitive to those who have got something to say. But I think it's also important for me to go on with my life, to keep a balanced life.

Qualifying his reason for not meeting with
protestor and grieving mother Cindy Sheehan
Crawford Texas
Aug. 13th, 2005

> It is not because the truth is too difficult to see that we make mistakes... we make mistakes because the easiest and most comfortable course for us is to seek insight where it accords with our emotions - especially selfish ones.
>
> - Alexander Solzhenitsyn

1208.   I want to thank you for the importance that you've shown for education and literacy.

Washington D.C.
April 13th, 2005

1209.   We look forward to analyzing and working with legislation that will make—it would hope—put a free press's mind at ease that you're not being denied information you shouldn't see.

Washington, D.C.
April 14th, 2005

Whenever the people are well informed, they can be trusted with their own government; that whenever things get so far wrong as to attract their notice, they may be relied on to set them to rights.
                                        - Thomas Jefferson

1210.   I understand there's a suspicion that we—we're too security-conscience.

Washington D.C.,
April 14th, 2005

1211.   I'm going to spend a lot of time on Social Security. I enjoy it. I enjoy taking on the issue. I guess, it's the Mother in me.

Washington D.C.
April 14th, 2005

1212.   Part of the facts is understanding we have a problem, and part of the facts is what you're going to do about it.

Kirtland Ohio,
April 15th, 2005

> A good way to threaten somebody is to light a stick of dynamite. Then you call the guy and hold the burning fuse up to the phone. "Hear that?" you say. "That's dynamite, baby.""
>
> - Jack Handy SNL

1213.   It's in our country's interests to find those who would do harm to us and get them out of harm's way.

White House
Apr. 28th, 2005

1214.   But you bet, when we find somebody who might do harm to the American people, we will detain them and ask others from their country of origin to detain them. It makes sense. The American people expect us to do that. We, we -- we still at war.

White House
Apr. 28th, 2005

1215.   One of the great sources of energy for the future is liquefied natural gas. There's a lot of gas reserves around the world. Gas is -- can only be transported by ship, though, when you liquefy it, when you put it in solid form.

White House
Apr. 28, 2005

Just one word....YALE

488

1216.   Faith-based is an important part of my life, individually, but I don't -- I don't ascribe a person's opposing my nominations to an issue of faith.

White House
Apr. 28th, 2005

It is in our lives and not our words that our religion must be read.

- Thomas Jefferson

1217.   But Iraq has—have got people there that are willing to kill, and they're hard-nosed killers. And we will work with the Iraqis to secure their future.

Washington D.C.
April 28th, 2005

1218.   Well, we've made the decision to defeat the terrorists abroad so we don't have to face them here at home. And when you engage the terrorists abroad, it causes activity and action.

Washington D.C.
April 28th, 2005

It's reasonably clear that the official reasons for the war cannot be taken seriously. The Bush Administration is carrying out a serious assault against the general population. They have to prevent people from paying attention, and the only way anyone has ever figured out how to do that is to terrify them with tales of monsters who are about to destroy us.

Noam Chomsky *The New Yorker*
March 31, 2003,

1219. We expect the states to show us whether or not we're achieving simple objectives—like literacy, literacy in math, the ability to read and write.

Washington D.C.
April 28th, 2005

1220. It means your own money would grow better than that which the government can make it grow. And that's important.

Falls Church Virginia.
April 29th, 2005

1221. Haley [Barbour] married well, and so did I. I don't know about you, Haley, but my wife has become quite a one-liner, and she can deliver those one-liners.

Canton Mississippi
May 3rd, 2005

1222. I think younger workers—first of all, younger workers have been promised benefits the government—promises that have been promised, benefits that we can't keep. That's just the way it is.

Washington D.C.
May 4th, 2005

490

1223.   For my own country, the process of becoming a mature, multi-ethnic democracy was lengthy and violent. Our journey from national independence to equal injustice included the enslavement of millions, and a four-year civil war.

Riga Latvia
May 7ᵗʰ, 2005

At least the injustice is equal.

1224.   We got people working all their life at hard work, contributing by payroll taxes into a Social Security system."

Washington, D.C.
May 13ᵗʰ, 2005

1225.   We know that democracies do not forment terror or invade their neighbors.

Washington D.C.
May 18ᵗʰ, 2005

Maybe because they don't know
what "forment" means.

1226.   You know, I don't think a photo inspires murderers. I think they're inspired by an ideology that is so barbaric and backwards that it's hard for many in the Western world to comprehend how they think.

White House
May 20ᵗʰ, 2005

491

1227.   REPORTER:
What is your reaction to the news about the South Koreans on embryonic --

BUSH:
I'm -- first, I'm very concerned about cloning. I worry about a world in which cloning becomes acceptable. Secondly, I made my position very clear on embryonic stem cells. I'm a strong supporter of adult stem cell research, of course. But I made it very clear to the Congress that the use of federal money, taxpayers' money to promote science which destroys life in order to save life is -- I'm against that.

White House
May 20th, 2005

First, stem cell research uses biological material that would be destroyed anyway...that's my understanding.

Second, why is it OK to wage pre-emptive war and kill people "over there" because they might kill people "over here". Isn't that destroying life to preserve it? These Republican positions seem to directly contradict each other.

> Bush reiterated his stand to conservatives opposing his decision on stem cell research. He said today he believes life begins at conception and ends at execution.
>
> - Jay Leno

492

1228.	If you've retired, you don't have anything to worry about. The third time I've said that. I'll probably say it three more times, see, in my line of work you gotta keep repeating things over and over and over again for the truth to sink in, to kinda catapult the propaganda.

Greece New York
May 24th, 2005

Propaganda – noun -
Ideas, facts, or allegations spread deliberately to further one's cause or to damage an opposing cause.
Synonyms – misinformation, half-truths, party line.

> Over the last several weeks, several of TV's so-called armchair generals, of which there are many, along with many of the Army's so-called real generals, have been openly critical of the U.S. military planning. Donald Rumsfeld's frustration with these critics boiled over at a press conference earlier this week. Rumsfeld said the only way you're going to be able to get people to believe something is true is if you print it up two million times and drop it from airplanes."
>
> -Jon Stewart

> If you tell a lie big enough and keep repeating it, people will eventually come to believe it. The lie can be maintained only for such time as the State can shield the people from the political, economic and/or military consequences of the lie. It thus becomes vitally important for the State to use all of its powers to repress dissent, for the truth is the mortal enemy of the lie, and thus by extension, the truth is the greatest enemy of the State.
>
> - Joseph Goebbels
Nazi Propagandist

1229.   BUSH:
First thing is, is there any doubt in your mind that you're going to get your check?

MRS. CEGLINSKI:
I'm getting my check, and it's wonderful.

BUSH:
They're still coming.

MRS. CEGLINSKI:
It's still coming. And I'm planning on it for a while yet.

BUSH:
Well, you need to, yes. Heading toward 80.

MRS. CEGLINSKI:
That's right.

BUSH:
Right around the corner. You look great.

MRS. CEGLINSKI:
Thank you very much.
BUSH:
You look like 100 to me. That's where you're going to be.
Thirty more years?

Greece New York
May 24th, 2005

In Camden, N.J., an 80-year-old has been working as a
prostitute or, as people are calling it, the Bush Social
Security plan.

- Jay Leno

1230.   There is something healthy about people campaigning,
saying, this is what I'm for. [Palestinian] President [Abbas] ran
on a peace platform. You know, maybe somebody will run on
a war platform -- you know, vote for me, I promise violence. I
don't think they're going to get elected, because I think

494

Palestinian moms want their children to grow up in peace just like American moms want their children to grow up in peace. As a matter of fact, I think the people that campaign for peace will win.

White House
May 26th, 2005

Inspiring developments -- Democracy is on the march in the Middle East. Yesterday, hundreds of thousands of Palestinians hit the polls for the first time of parliamentary elections in ten years. Which democratically elected party walked away victorious? Oh, it's Hamas! Yes, Hamas the militant Islamic group that is very anti-American and calls for the destruction of Israel, and wants a theocracy in Palestine. Though, on the plus side, they have returned all the money given to them by Jack Abramoff.

-Jon Stewart

1231. In terms of, umm -- you know, the -- the detainees, we've had thousands of people detained. We've investigated every single complaint against the detainees. It seemed like to me they based some of their decisions on, on the word of, uhh -- and the allegations -- by people who were held in detention, people who hate America, people that had been trained in some instances to disassemble -- that means not tell the truth. And so it was an absurd report. It just is. And, uhh, you know -- yes, sir.

Commenting on Amnesty International's
Report on the Treatment of Detainees
at Guantanamo Bay
White House
May 31st, 2005

Disassemble – verb – something done to Ikea furniture

Dissemble – verb - To hide under a false appearance; to hide the truth or true nature of.

495

1232.   And the second way to defeat the terrorists is to spread freedom. You see, the best way to defeat a society that is -- doesn't have hope, a society where people become so angry they're willing to become suiciders, is to spread freedom, is to spread democracy.

Washington D.C.
Jun. 8th, 2005

Apparently you spread it with bombs

> The U.S. army confirmed that it gave a lucrative fire fighting contract in Iraq to the firm once run by the Vice President Dick Cheney without any competitive bidding. When asked if this could be conceived as Cheney's friends profiting from the war, the spokesman said 'Yes.'
>
> — Conan O'Brien

1233.   Do you realize we've got 250 million years of coal?

Washington D.C.
Jun. 8, 2005

> There are risks and costs to a program of action. But they are far less than the long-range risks and costs of comfortable inaction.
>
> — John F. Kennedy

1234.   One of the main jobs we have here in Washington is to protect our country. You see, not only did the attacks help accelerate a recession, the attacks reminded us that we are at war.

Washington D.C.
Jun. 8th, 2005

Hello? Red Flag???
Bush was at war in principlebefore 9/11?

1235.　As your President, it seems like to make sense to me to say, if we treat you this way, you treat us -- that's what fair trade is all about.

University Park Pennsylvania
Jun. 14th, 2005

President Bush left for Canada today to attend a trade summit. Reportedly, the trade summit got off to an awkward start when the president pulled out his baseball cards.

—Conan O'Brien

1236.　In terms of your Prime Minister, he's a -- interesting guy. He's a lot of fun to be around. He promotes, uhh, serious business in a, in a, in a way that, endears himself to people. And so, uhh, I think his presidency has been an important presidency for the EU during difficult times, and he's handled it well. And, umm, I was gonna say he's a piece of work, but that might not translate too well. Is that all right, if I call you a piece of work?

Press Conference with Jean-Claude Juncker,
Prime Minister of Luxonburg and President
of the European Union
White House
Jun. 20th, 2005

Remember last week when Jessica Simpson declined to meet President Bush? She now says they have plans to sit down together and talk face-to-face. President Bush talking to Jessica Simpson? That should be a real no-brainer.

-Jay Leno

1237.   The relations with, Europe are important relations, and
        they've, -- because, we do share values. And, they're
        universal values, they're not American values or, you know --
        European values, they're universal values. And those values -
        - uhh -- being universal, ought to be applied everywhere.

Press Conference with European
Union Delegates
White House
Jun. 20th, 2005

Incidentally those values are also hemispheric, solidly liquefied
and found lurching in our neighborhoods

1238.   REPORTER:
        Mr. President, we were told that you planned to sharpen your
        focus on Iraq. Why did this become necessary? And given
        the recent surge in violence, do you agree with Vice
        President Dick Cheney's assessment that the insurgency is in
        its last throes?

        BUSH:
        Adam, I think about Iraq every day -- every single day --
        because I understand we have troops in harm's way...
        [seconds later] And so, you know, I think about this every day
        -- every single day -- and will continue thinking about it,
        because I understand we've got kids in harm's way.

Washington D.C.
Jun. 20th, 2005

He keeps saying 'sacrifice' and the 'war on terror,' and
you turn around and he's in a field of poppies with
Lance Armstrong.

- Jon Stewart

498

1239. BUSH:
I appreciate the Secretary of Energy joining me today. He's a good man, he knows a lot about the subject, you'll be pleased to hear. I was teasing him -- he taught at MIT, and -- do you have a PhD?

SECRETARY OF ENERGY BODMAN:
Yes.

BUSH:
Yes, a PhD. Now I want you to pay careful attention to this -- he's the PhD, and I'm the C student, but notice who is the advisor and who is the President.

Lusby Maryland
Jun. 22nd, 2005

George W Bush surrounds himself with smart people like a hole surrounds itself with a donut.
- Dennis Miller

1240. I want to thank the President and the CEO of Constellation Energy, Mayo Shattuck. That's a pretty cool first name, isn't it, Mayo. Pass the Mayo. His wife, Molly, appreciated that.

Lusby Maryland
Jun. 22nd, 2005

1241. I'm looking forward to a good night's sleep on the soil of a friend.

Weird, Weird Comment on
Upcoming Denmark Visit
White House
Jun. 29th, 2005

Ewwwww!

With Iraq plunging into chaos and gas prices at record highs President Bush took time out this weekend for a ride on his bicycle, but unfortunately he fell off and sustained cuts to his face and hands. Apparently Bush was distracted by the enormous responsibilities of the presidency. I'm just kidding. He hit some gravel or something.

—Craig Kilborn

1242.　When you ride hard on a mountain bike, sometimes you fall. Otherwise you're not riding hard.

Auchterarder Scotland
Jul. 7th, 2005

Why does this comment remind me of sex?

1243.　The best place for the facts to be done is by somebody who's spending time investigating it

On the Probe into How CIA Agent
Valerie Plame's identity was leaked.
Washington D.C.
July 18th, 2005

The overall picture, as the boys say, is of a degraded community whose idealism even is largely fake. The pretentiousness, the bogus enthusiasm, the constant drinking, the incessant squabbling over money, the all-pervasive agent, the strutting of the big shots (and their usually utter incompetence to achieve anything they start out to do), the constant fear of losing all this fairy gold and being the nothing they have never ceased to be, the snide tricks, the whole damn mess is out of this world.

- Raymond Chandler

> Whether we and our politicians know it or not, Nature is party to all our deals and decisions, and she has more votes, a longer memory, and a sterner sense of justice than we do
>
> - Wendell Barry

1244.   REPORTER:
Did they misinform you when you said that no one anticipated the breach of the levees?

BUSH:
No, what I was referring to is this. When that storm came by, a lot of people said we dodged a bullet. When that storm came through at first, people said, whew. There was a sense of relaxation, and that's what I was referring to. And I, myself, thought we had dodged a bullet. You know why? Because I was listening to people, probably over the airways, say, the bullet has been dodged. And that was what I was referring to. Of course, there were plans in case the levee had been breached. There was a sense of relaxation in the moment, a critical moment. And thank you for giving me a chance to clarify that

New Orleans Louisiana
Sept. 12th, 2005

1245.   The good news is -- and it's hard for some to see it now -- that out of this chaos is going to come a fantastic Gulf Coast, like it was before. Out of the rubbles of Trent Lott's house -- he's lost his entire house -- there's going to be a fantastic house. And I'm looking forward to sitting on the porch.

Mobile Alabama
Sept. 2nd, 2005

I'm sure they are all relieved to here that

501

1246.   Here's what I believe. I believe that the great city of New
        Orleans will rise again and be a greater city of New Orleans. I
        believe the town where I used to come -- from Houston,
        Texas, to enjoy myself, occasionally too much -- will be that
        very same town, that it will be a better place to come to.

New Orleans Louisiana
Sept. 2nd, 2005

1247.   Right now, we need to get food and clothes and medicine to
        the people, and we'll do so. And one of the main delivery
        systems will be the armies of compassion.

Biloxi Mississippi
Sept. 2nd, 2005

Finally today convoys of troops and aid started to arrive
along the Gulf Coast. Five days after the hurricane hit.
Kind of makes you miss the innocent days when Bush
only sat on his ass for seven minutes. It only took him
four days to make a plan, but finally today he said he
had a plan. Unfortunately it's a faith-based plan that
involves getting two of every animal onto a big boat.
                                              - Bill Maher

1248.   It's totally wiped out. ... It's devastating, it's got to be doubly
        devastating on the ground.

Surveying Hurricane Katrina Flood Damage
Aboard Air Force One
Aug. 31st, 2005

Stupidity is an elemental force for which no earthquake
is a match
                                              - Karl Kraus

1249.   Steps we're taking will help address the problem of availability, but it's not going to solve it. Americans should be prudent in their use of energy during the course of the next few weeks. Don't buy gas if you don't need it.

Washington, D.C.
Sept. 1ˢᵗ, 2005

Good idea, no recreational petroleum purchases....now what will the kids do for kicks?

Some are weather-wise, some are otherwise.
                                                                    - Benjamin Franklin

1250.   I don't think anyone anticipated the breach of the levees.

Good Morning America
Sept. 1ˢᵗ, 2005

1251.   Well, there's a lot of food on its way. A lot of water on the way. And there's a lot of boats and choppers headed that way. Boats and choppers headed that way. It just takes a while to float 'em.

Good Morning America
Sept. 1ˢᵗ, 2005

As you know, FEMA stands for 'Fix Everything My Ass.'
                                                                    -Jay Leno

1252.   Brownie, you're doing a heck of a job.

Mobile, Alabama
Sept. 2ⁿᵈ, 2005

503

Thank you all very much. Thank you. I admit he's not very pretty to look at. But he's doing a heck of a job. I'm so proud of my friend -- It's become clear to all the hardworking FEMA employees that I didn't pick Joe Allbaugh because of his haircut.

To Brownie's predecessor at FEMA
Washington, D.C.
Oct. 1, 2001

This is inarguably a failure of leadership from the top of the federal government. Remember when Bill Clinton went out with Monica Lewinsky. That was inarguably a failure of judgment at the top. Democrats had to come out and risk losing credibility if they did not condemn Bill Clinton for his behavior. I believe Republicans are in the same position right now. And I will say this: Hurricane Katrina is George Bush's Monica Lewinsky. The only difference is that tens of thousands of people weren't stranded in Monica Lewinsky's vagina.

-Jon Stewart

1253.   My thoughts are, we're going to get somebody who knows what they're talking about when it comes to rebuilding cities

Biloxi Mississippi.
Sept. 2nd, 2005

Revolutionary idea...makes more sense than appointing someone who knows about say, Arabian Horses or the ancient Japanese paper-folding art of Origami... (nothing against Origami).

504

1254.   I believe the town where I used to come – from Houston, Texas, to enjoy myself, occasionally too much – will be that very same town, that it will be a better place to come to.

New Orleans Airport
Sept. 2nd, 2005

Ha ha ha ha...Oh that president is just like us...
one of the guys...ha ha ha...funny too...
.can someone feed us now?

1255.   What didn't go right?'

Bush to Nancy Pelosi (D-CA), after she requested
he fire FEMA Director Michael Brown "because of all that
went wrong after Hurricane Katrina "

> How many folks have been watching the mini-series on HBO called 'Rome?' Amazingly, exciting episode this week -- Rome is burning while Nero refuses to cut his vacation short. And don't miss next week's episode when FEMA shows up a week late at Pompeii.
>
> -David Letterman

1256.   I can't wait to join you in the joy of welcoming neighbors back into neighborhoods, and small businesses up and running, and cutting those ribbons that somebody is creating new jobs

Poplarville, Mississippi
Sept. 5, 200

> The president said much of the aid is going towards job training. And when they heard that, the people of New Orleans rose as one and said, 'Can we start with you?'
>
> -Bill Maher

1257.   Bureaucracy is not going to stand in the way of getting the job done for the people.

On Katrina Recovery Efforts
Press Conference
Sept. 6, 2005

1258.   If you want to grow something, you shouldn't tax it. If you want to encourage small business growth, we ought to incent it to grow in that part of the world. Somebody said the other day, well, that's a tax break. That region is going to have zero income anyway.

Washington, D.C.
Sep. 21st, 2005

506

1259.   We'll get the debris removed, get the water up and running
         and get the bridges rebuilt. But what you need to do is
         develop a blueprint for your own future. We look forward to
         hearing your vision so we can more better do our job.

Gulfport Mississippi
Sept. 20th, 2005

President Bush was on the ground all day today, you
saw him there hugging the starving and touring the
devastated area. His quote was 'New Orleans is more
devastated than New York on 9/11.' Then he grabbed a
bullhorn and vowed that we would get Mother Nature
dead or alive.

-Bill Maher

Politics is supposed to be the second oldest profession. I
have come to realize that it bears a very close
resemblance to the first.

- Ronald Reagan

507

Chapter Twelve

Paging Dr Freud

Fehlleistung & Parapraxis

A slip-of-the-tongue that appears trivial, bizarre or even nonsensical, but shows some deeper significance or insight into the speaker's unconscious beliefs or intentions.

Be Afraid...Be Very Afraid!

All of the following quotes are from this book and have been reduced to their most revealing nugget of relevance and rearranged to illustrate my point. What's my point? That George W Bush isn't just a dumbass...he's scary too.

Consider it Freudian Existential Poetry

**I will never apologize
for the United States of America
- I don't care what the facts are.**

I'm doing what I think what's wrong.

**We live in a culture of moral indifference,
where movies and videos
glamorize violence
and tolerance is touted
as a great virtue.**

**Well, I think
if you say you're going to do something
and don't do it,
that's
trustworthiness.**

511

If you're sick and tired
of the politics
of cynicism
and polls
and
principles,
come and join
this campaign.

I do not believe we've put a guilty
... I mean innocent person to death
in the state of Texas.

The woman who knew
that I had dyslexia
—I never interviewed her.

I would strongly reject
that assumption
—that John Ashcroft
is a open-minded,
inclusive person.

we understand how
unfair the death penalty is
... er ..
. the death tax is.

... we would not accept a treaty
that would not have been ratified,
nor a treaty that
I thought
made sense
for the country.

... our neighborhoods will
be ultimately safer
for crime.

We will not have
an all-volunteer army.
And yet,
this week
---- we will have
an all-volunteer army!

We will use our technology
to enhance
uncertainty
abroad..

...when I put my hand on the Bible,
I will swear
to not
-- to uphold the laws of the land.

If this were a dictatorship,
it'd be a heck of a lot easier,
just so long as

I'm the dictator.

There ought to be limits
to freedom.

All we ask
is that you use
the same amounta effort
the United States will
to win this war
against
freedom...

... the Guard protected the early colonists
and
helped win the War on
Independence.

We will stand up for terror.

Our journey from
national independence
to equal
injustice

I think the job of a
problem
is to confront
problems

We're making the right decisions
to bring the solution
to an end.

The truth of the matter is,

if you listen carefully,
Saddam would still be in power
if he [John Kerry] were the
President of the United States,
and the world
would be
a lot better off.

... and they want us to leave.
That's what they want us to do.
And I think
the world would be better off
if we did leave.

....the vast majority of Iraqis
want to live
in a peaceful,
free world.
And we will find these people
and we will
bring them
to justice.

We're on an international manhunt
for those who would do harm
to America,
or
for anybody else
who loves freedom.

... a free Iraq
will be
a major defeat
in the cause
of
freedom.

... this country
cannot
achieve any objective
we put our mind to.

And we will not relent
to any terrorist
who think they can
take our freedom
or the freedom
from anybody else
in the world
away from
us.

I've
not made up our mind
about
military action.

... there needs to be a focused,
coalition effort
in the region
against
peace ...

We share a vision of two states,
Israel and Palestine,
living side by side
in peace
and insecurity.

... uhh,
you know,
it'll take time to
restore chaos,
and order,
but we

-- but we will.

It's not a dictatorship
in Washington, but
I tried to
make it one ....

We resolved to
arm
the terrorist enemy.

It's in our country's interests
to find those who would
do harm to us and
get them
out of harm's way.

And there's
no doubt in my mind,
not one doubt
in my mind,
that we will
fail.

The second pillar of peace
and security in our world
is the willingness
of free nations,
when the last resort arrives,
to retain
aggression
and
evil
by
force.

By the way,
to whom much has been given,

much is owed.

The Traitor
Marcus Tullius Cicero

A nation can survive its fools,
and even the ambitious.

But it cannot survive treason from within.

An enemy at the gates is less formidable,
for he is known and carries his banner openly.

But the traitor moves amongst those within the gate freely,
his sly whispers rustling through all the alleys,
heard in the very halls of government itself.

For the traitor appears not a traitor;
he speaks in accents familiar to his victims,
and he wears their face and their arguments,
he appeals to the baseness that lies deep in the
hearts of all men.

He rots the soul of a nation,
he works secretly and unknown in the night
to undermine the pillars of the city,
he infects the body politic
so that it can no longer resist.

A murderer is less to fear.

The traitor is the plague.

518

An Open Letter to the President
Bill Maher - Real Time with Bill Maher - HBO

This transcript is used without permission, though not for lack of trying. Nobody at HBO has responded to my emails. They are probably acting on the same premise that I do...no one is going to buy my book and it's not worth worrying about. So, I'm printing it.. It's beautiful. Bill Maher is fabulous.. Please enjoy it, watch his show on HBO and remember to send me cookies in jail. (chocolate chip, hermit cookies, homemade ginger snaps and any cookie involving jam)

Mr. President, this job can't be fun for you any more.

There's no more money to spend--you used up all of that. You can't start another war because
you used up the army. And now, darn the luck, the rest of your term has become the Bush family nightmare: helping poor people.

Listen to your Mom. The cupboard's bare, the credit cards maxed out. No one's speaking to you. Mission accomplished.

Now it's time to do what you've always done best: lose interest and walk away. Like you did with your military service and the oil company and the baseball team. It's time. Time to move on and try the next fantasy job. How about cowboy or

519

space man? Now I know what you're saying: there's so many other things that you as President could involve yourself in.

Please don't.

I know, I know. There's a lot left to do. There's a war with Venezuela. Eliminating the sales tax on yachts,. turning the space program over to the church and Social Security to Fannie Mae.. Giving embryos the vote.

But, Sir, none of that is going to happen now. Why? Because you govern like Billy Joel drives. You've performed so poorly I'm surprised that you haven't given yourself a medal. You're a catastrophe that walks like a man.

Herbert Hoover was a shitty president, but even he never conceded an entire city to rising water and snakes.

On your watch, we've lost almost all of our allies, the surplus, four airliners, two trade centers, a piece of the Pentagon and the City of New Orleans.

Maybe you're just not lucky. I'm not saying you don't love this country. I'm just wondering how much worse it could be if you were on the other side.

So, yes, God does speak to you. What he is saying is: "Take a hint."

Stephen Colbert Addressing the White House Correspondent's Dinner
April 29, 2006

This transcript is taken from the internet and used entirely without permission. It's brilliant, brave and hysterically funny. I figure that it's worth the risk of a lawsuit to share it with you here. Enjoy!

Wow, what an honor. The White House Correspondents' Dinner. To actually sit here, at the same table with my hero, George W. Bush, to be this close to the man. I feel like I'm dreaming. Somebody pinch me. You know what? I'm a pretty sound sleeper -- that may not be enough. Somebody shoot me in the face.

Is he really not here tonight? Dammit. The one guy who could have helped.

By the way, before I get started, if anybody needs anything else at their tables, just speak slowly and clearly into your table numbers. Somebody from the NSA will be right over with a cocktail.

Mark Smith, ladies and gentlemen of the press corps, Madame First Lady, Mr. President, my name is Stephen Colbert and tonight it's my privilege to celebrate this president. We're not so different, he and I. We get it. We're not brainiacs on the nerd patrol. We're not members of the factinista. We go straight from the gut, right sir? That's where the truth lies, right down here in the gut. Do you know you have more nerve endings in your gut than you have in your head? You can look it up.

I know some of you are going to say "I did look it up, and that's not true." That's 'cause you looked it up in a book. Next time, look it up in your gut. I did. My gut tells me that's how our nervous system works. Every night on my show, the Colbert Report, I speak straight from the gut, OK? I give people the truth, unfiltered by rational argument. I call it the "No Fact Zone." Fox News, I hold a copyright on that term.

I'm a simple man with a simple mind. I hold a simple set of beliefs that I live by. Number one, I believe in America. I believe it exists. My gut tells me I live there. I feel that it extends from the Atlantic to the Pacific, and I strongly believe it has 50 states. And I cannot wait to see how the Washington Post spins that one tomorrow.

Ambassador Zhou Wenzhong, welcome. Your great country makes our Happy Meals possible. I said it's a celebration. I believe the government that governs best is the government that governs least. And by these standards, we have set up a fabulous government in Iraq.

I believe in pulling yourself up by your own bootstraps. I believe it is possible -- I saw this guy do it once in Cirque du Soleil. It was magical. And though I am a committed Christian, I believe that everyone has the right to their own religion, be you Hindu, Jewish or Muslim. I believe there are infinite paths to accepting Jesus Christ as your personal savior.

Ladies and gentlemen, I believe it's yogurt. But I refuse to believe it's not butter. Most of all, I believe in this president.

Now, I know there are some polls out there saying this man has a 32% approval rating. But guys like us, we don't pay attention to the polls. We know that polls are just a collection of statistics that reflect what people are thinking in "reality." And reality has a well-known liberal bias.

522

So, Mr. President, please, pay no attention to the people that say the glass is half full. Sir, pay no attention to the people who say the glass is half empty, because 32% means it's 2/3 empty. There's still some liquid in that glass is my point, but I wouldn't drink it. The last third is usually backwash.

Okay, look, folks, my point is that I don't believe this is a low point in this presidency. I believe it is just a lull before a comeback. I mean, it's like the movie "Rocky." All right. The president in this case is Rocky Balboa and Apollo Creed is -- everything else in the world. It's the tenth round. He's bloodied. His corner man, Mick, who in this case I guess would be the vice president, he's yelling, "Cut me, Dick, cut me!," and every time he falls everyone says, "Stay down! Stay down!" Does he stay down? No. Like Rocky, he gets back up, and in the end he -- actually, he loses in the first movie.

OK. Doesn't matter. The point is it is the heart-warming story of a man who was repeatedly punched in the face. So don't pay attention to the approval ratings that say 68% of Americans disapprove of the job this man is doing. I ask you this, does that not also logically mean that 68% approve of the job he's not doing? Think about it. I haven't.

I stand by this man. I stand by this man because he stands for things. Not only for things, he stands on things. Things like aircraft carriers and rubble and recently flooded city squares. And that sends a strong message, that no matter what happens to America, she will always rebound -- with the most powerfully staged photo ops in the world.

Now, there may be an energy crisis. This president has a very forward-thinking energy policy. Why do you think he's down on the ranch cutting that brush all the time? He's trying to create an alternative energy source. By 2008 we will have a mesquite-powered car!

And I just like the guy. He's a good Joe. Obviously loves his wife, calls her his better half. And polls show America agrees. She's a true lady and a wonderful woman. But I just have one beef, ma'am. I'm sorry, but this reading initiative. I'm sorry, I've never been a fan of books. I don't trust them. They're all fact, no heart. I mean, they're elitist, telling us what is or isn't true, or what did or didn't happen. Who's Britannica to tell me the Panama Canal was built in 1914? If I want to say it was built in 1941, that's my right as an American! I'm with the president, let history decide what did

or did not happen.

The greatest thing about this man is he's steady. You know where he stands. He believes the same thing Wednesday that he believed on Monday, no matter what happened Tuesday. Events can change; this man's beliefs never will.

As excited as I am to be here with the president, I am appalled to be surrounded by the liberal media that is destroying America, with the exception of Fox News. Fox News gives you both sides of every story: the president's side, and the vice president's side.

But the rest of you, what are you thinking, reporting on NSA wiretapping or secret prisons in eastern Europe? Those things are secret for a very important reason: they're super-depressing. And if that's your goal, well, misery accomplished.

Over the last five years you people were so good -- over tax cuts, WMD intelligence, the effect of global warming. We Americans didn't want to know, and you had the courtesy not to try to find out. Those were good times, as far as we knew.

But, listen, let's review the rules. Here's how it works: the president makes decisions. He's the Decider. The press secretary announces those decisions, and you people of the press type those decisions down. Make, announce, type. Just put 'em through a spell check and go home. Get to know your family again. Make love to your wife. Write that novel you got kicking around in your head. You know, the one about the intrepid Washington reporter with the courage to stand up to the administration. You know - fiction!

Because really, what incentive do these people have to answer your questions, after all? I mean, nothing satisfies you. Everybody asks for personnel changes. So the White House has personnel changes. Then you write, "Oh, they're just rearranging the deck chairs on the Titanic." First of all, that is a terrible metaphor. This administration is not sinking. This administration is soaring. If anything, they are rearranging the deck chairs on the Hindenburg!

Now, it's not all bad guys out there. Some are heroes: Christopher Buckley, Jeff Sacks, Ken Burns, Bob Schieffer. They've all been on my show. By the way, Mr. President, thank you for agreeing to be on my show. I was just as shocked as everyone here is, I promise you. How's Tuesday for you? I've got Frank Rich, but we can bump him. And I mean bump him. I know a guy. Say the word.

See who we've got here tonight. General Moseley, Air Force Chief of Staff. General Peter Pace, Chairman of the Joint Chiefs of Staff. They still support Rumsfeld. Right, you guys aren't retired yet, right? Right, they still support Rumsfeld.

Look, by the way, I've got a theory about how to handle these retired generals causing all this trouble: don't let them retire! Come on, we've got a stop-loss program; let's use it on these guys. I've seen Zinni and that crowd on Wolf Blitzer. If you're strong enough to go on one of those pundit shows, you can stand on a bank of computers and order men into battle. Come on.

Jesse Jackson is here, the Reverend. Haven't heard from the Reverend in a little while. I had him on the show. Very interesting and challenging interview. You can ask him anything, but he's going to say what he wants, at the pace that he wants. It's like boxing a glacier. Enjoy that metaphor, by the way, because your grandchildren will have no idea what a glacier is.

John McCain is here. John McCain, John McCain, what a maverick! Somebody find out what fork he used on his salad, because I guarantee you it wasn't a salad fork. This guy could have used a spoon! There's no predicting him. By the way, Senator McCain, it's so wonderful to see you coming back into the Republican fold. I have a summer house in South Carolina; look me up when you go to speak at Bob Jones University. So glad you've seen the light, sir.
Mayor Nagin! Mayor Nagin is here from New Orleans, the chocolate city! Yeah, give it up. Mayor Nagin, I'd like to welcome you to Washington, D.C., the chocolate city with a marshmallow center. And a graham cracker crust of corruption. It's a Mallomar, I guess is what I'm describing.

Joe Wilson is here, Joe Wilson right down here in front, the most famous husband since Desi Arnaz. And of course he brought along his lovely wife Valerie Plame. Oh, my god! Oh, what have I said? [looks horrified] I am sorry, Mr. President, I meant to say he brought along "Joe Wilson's wife. "Patrick Fitzgerald is not here tonight? OK. Dodged a bullet.

And, of course, we can't forget the man of the hour, new press secretary, Tony Snow. Secret Service name, "Snow Job." Toughest job. What a hero! Took the second toughest job in government, next to, of course, the ambassador to Iraq.

Got some big shoes to fill, Tony. Big shoes to fill. Scott McClellan could say nothing like nobody else.

Afterword

Love Your Neighbor As Yourself.

When I was growing up, that statement was always closely followed by, "Do unto others as you would have them do unto you." Bush is fond of the former, yet conspicuously silent on the latter.

It's to be expected I guess. When your daily bread is served up alongside a litany of unspeakable crimes against humanity like torture, murder, lying and stupidity, the last thing you want to do is invite reciprocation in-kind.

The democratic system's checks and balances have been revealed, most graphically under this administration, to be deeply flawed and utterly worthless. Power is bought, not earned. The truth is whatever they say it is and subject to change without notice.

The once great systems of American democracy and justice have long been perverted and corrupted beyond all recognition. Perhaps it's time to wonder if this system you call "democracy", is in fact democratic at all. It leans a little closer to plutocracy and/or theocracy from where I sit.

The Constitution and the Bill of Rights are simply the lipstick and pretty dress America throws on when it wants to look beautiful. America's once noble quest to spread democracy throughout the world has lost any and all credibility.

We don't wake up one day and discover we have cancer. It's a chronic disease that grows silently one mutant cell at a time until the symptoms can no longer be ignored. The tumors are suddenly clearly visible and the body we thought was healthy just weeks before is suddenly ravaged by seemingly unstoppable forces. It's insidious and incredibly lethal, but it's not instant. It happens right under our own skin. While we are blissfully oblivious. We may have experienced symptoms, but it's easier to believe that what we know is happening…isn't really happening. Truth can be terrifying.

Although it's frightfully simple to blame Bush for most of what's wrong in the world, he is merely the most visible tumor. The conditions that enabled his rise to power were years in the making. He is simply the manifestation of widespread systemic breakdown. It is the viral proliferation of self-interest over good governance fueled by constituents comfortable in their ignorance and easily distracted by shiny, polished rhetoric.

As much as we would like to excise Bush's toxic influence from the White House, it represents nothing more than a cosmetic procedure. The pathology that bred him remains deeply rooted and it will continue to propagate malignant leaders until it's radically addressed.   .

Blind and dumb loyalty to ideology over reality will be the death of us all. Ignorance is a luxury that we can no longer afford, (a lot like oil.)

America's virtue wasn't stolen from her. It was freely and enthusiastically surrendered. She's always been a slut to power, spreading for any smooth-talking jerk who tells her what she wants to hear. Like infants, people submit to whatever is most immediately gratifying. It feels good right now, I'll let someone else worry about the consequences tomorrow.

Now, America has been knocked-up with democracy's mutant love child. She has finally borne the demonic spawn of greed,

528

narcissism and civilian indifference. (Congrats on a second term Mr Bush)

It was an accident of course.

It was dark. She was drunk.

Looking back, did you honestly think that President George W Smirk would still respect you in the morning?

Somewhere deep down, between the political rohypnol and apple martinis, you knew you were being fucked and it just didn't matter.

Now, before you trot off spreading American "democracy" throughout the world, you need to take a long hard look at what has happened to your own government and the retarded, illegitimate offspring it's produced.

Do you still feel qualified to tell everyone else what to do and how to do it?

Take some advice from your bible…

Physician Heal Thyself.

Do Unto Others As You Would Have Them Do Unto You

Love Your Neighbor As Yourself

Hey is that a log in your eye…or are you just happy to see me?. …wait….that's not right….

And to President Bush,

We aren't laughing *at* you…

We're laug….

OK, we're laughing at you…

About the Author

Jules Carlysle lives in Northwestern Ontario Canada.

For more information visit her site at
www.julescarlysle.com

Mankind must put an end to war, or war will put an end to mankind... War will exist until that distant day when the conscientious objector enjoys the same reputation and prestige that the warrior does today.

John F Kennedy

Printed in the United States
61267LVS00005B/7-51